ROUSSEAU'S POLITICAL PHILOSOPHY

Rousseau's Political Philosophy

An Exposition and Interpretation

RAMON M. LEMOS

The University of Georgia Press

ATHENS

Library of Congress Catalog Card Number: 74–18584
International Standard Book Number: 0–8203–0376–3

The University of Georgia Press, Athens 30602

Copyright © 1977 by the University of Georgia Press
Set in 10 on 12 point Janson type
Printed in the United States of America

TO

MAMIE LOU

Thou shalt love the Lord thy God with all
thy heart, and with all thy soul, and with
all thy mind. This is the first and great
commandment. And the second is like unto
it, Thou shalt love thy neighbour as thyself.

Matt. 22:37–39

If a man say, I love God, and hateth his
brother, he is a liar: for he that loveth not
his brother whom he hath seen, how can he
love God whom he hath not seen?

I John 4:20

CONTENTS

PREFACE

The actual writing of this book was begun in August of 1968. My initial intention was to do a detailed study of the political philosophy not only of Rousseau, but also of Hobbes and Locke, taking them as the three classic expositors of a natural right, natural law, social contract approach to political philosophy. But the work grew to such great length that it has seemed advisable to divide it into two books, the present one and another on Hobbes and Locke which is also being published by the University of Georgia Press. Neither of these books, however, presupposes the other; each is independent of the other, in the sense that each is intelligible independent of any knowledge of the other. But though independent of one another, they are nonetheless complementary. In these two books taken together I have attempted to present a systematic exposition, interpretation, development, and assessment of the political philosophy of these three classic representatives of the natural law, natural right, social contract approach to political philosophy.

I have limited my discussion of Rousseau in three ways. First, I have considered only those works in which he presents his political philosophy most fully and systematically. These are his *Discourse on the Origin and Foundation of Inequality among Men*, his *Discourse on Political Economy*, and *The Social Contract*. Although Rousseau discusses various aspects of his political thought in a number of different works, the essentials of his political philosophy are contained in the three works mentioned. The aspects of his political thought touched upon in his other writings are for the most part only variations upon the fundamental themes presented in these three works, so that if we understand these we understand the essentials of his political philosophy. Second, although there are a number of excellent books and essays dealing with various aspects of Rousseau's political thought, I have not discussed any of them. The literature on his political philosophy is so vast that were I to attempt to deal at all adequately with it I should undoubtedly become so mired in digression that I should be prevented from presenting systematically my own interpretation and assessment of his position. Readers familiar with this literature will find it an easy matter to relate what I have to say to what others have had to say and to see to what extent I concur in and differ with their interpretations and assessments. Third, I have limited myself to a purely philosophical treatment of his position and have not concerned myself with historical questions having to do with such matters as which of his predecessors and contemporaries may have influenced him in one way or another and how what he says on some topic may have been due to some purely contingent historical circumstance or situation. I have been concerned throughout, not with such historical matters, but rather with what we may with some propriety refer to as the timeless philosophical significance of his position and arguments.

But although I have limited my discussion in these three ways, I have endeavored throughout to present Rousseau's position in as much detail as is necessary to provide anyone not familiar with it an account sufficiently detailed to enable him to evaluate my treatment of it. At the same time, my aim has also been to present interpretations, developments, and assessments of his position that will be of some slight interest at least to those thoroughly familiar with it. And though I have been concerned primarily with the spirit rather than the letter of the writings I have examined, I have also striven never to violate the letter, on the theory that the spirit of a work cannot well be captured if the letter is violated. This, however, does not mean that I have limited myself to an exposition of the letter of his position. On the contrary, as for example throughout much of sections xiii–xx and xxv–xxvii, I have embarked on somewhat speculative excursions designed either to render more intelligible what Rousseau says explicitly or else to develop more fully than he himself did certain of the implications of what he explicitly says. Rousseau is frequently a very cryptic, even enigmatic, writer who does not trouble to expatiate in detail either upon what his meaning is or upon the implications of what he explicitly says, and this terseness both requires and justifies one in transcending at times the express letter of his writing in order to render explicit its meaning and implications.

Finally, I have not presented Rousseau and his writings as antiquarian relics to be looked down upon condescendingly, as though we have attained heights of insight and wisdom greater than any he ever attained, but rather as a great political philosopher whose thought is still significant and from whom we can still learn much. If political philosophers since Rousseau have in fact succeeded in attaining heights greater than those he attained, this is due in no small measure to the fact that they have stood upon his shoulders. And if they have stood upon his shoulders they ought also to be willing to sit at his feet, with an attitude not of condescension but of gratitude.

There are various persons and groups to whom I am grateful for various kinds of assistance: to the Sabbatical Leave Committee of the University of Miami for approving my application for sabbatical leave during the fall semester of 1968, to the Research Council of the University of Miami for a summer humanities research grant in the summer of 1969, and to Dr. Gerrit Schipper, then the Chairman of the Department of Philosophy at the University of Miami, for giving me reduced teaching loads during the spring and fall semesters of 1970. It was during this period from August of 1968 to December of 1970 that I completed the first draft, not only of the present study, but also of the one on Hobbes and Locke mentioned earlier. My gratitude extends too to Professor Schipper for reading the manuscript of this book and making many helpful suggestions. I am grateful also to the students, both graduate and undergraduate, in the various classes and seminars in social and political philosophy which I have taught at the University of Miami since 1956. Their questions, arguments, and criticisms have compelled me, I hope, to think more carefully and to speak and write more clearly. They certainly have enabled me to see certain things which otherwise I should not have seen. Although it is perhaps a mistake to let them know it, I am confident that I have learned much more from them than they have from me. But most of all I am grateful to my wife, to whom this book is dedicated. What I could say here could not possibly convey an adequate idea of the debt I owe her.

RAMON M. LEMOS

Coral Gables, Florida

I. Morality and Civilization

Rousseau's moral, social, and political philosophy is given its most systematic and comprehensive statement in a series of three works, an understanding of each of which is essential to an understanding of these aspects of his philosophy. These are his *Discourse on the Origin and Foundations of Inequality among Men*, finished in 1754, his *Discourse on Political Economy*, published in 1758, and *The Social Contract*, published in 1762. The latter work was extracted from a larger work on political institutions (on which he had worked on and off for twenty years). Deciding that he could not complete the larger work, he destroyed the draft of everything in it with the exception of the parts that he developed into *The Social Contract*. Each of these works can be adequately understood only if taken in connection with the other two. We shall therefore be concerned with a detailed examination of each of the three.

There is, however, another work of Rousseau's of which some mention must be made here. This is his *Discourse on the Arts and Sciences*. This work was submitted in competition for the prize offered by the Academy of Dijon in 1750 for the best essay on the subject of whether the restoration of the arts and sciences had tended to purify morals. His *Discourse on the Origin and Foundations of Inequality among Men* was also submitted to the same academy in 1755, in competition for a prize offered for the best essay on the question of what the origin of inequality among men is and whether it is authorized by natural law. The first discourse won the prize; the second did not. If we consider only the intrinsic merit of each of these discourses in abstraction from such factors as the possible prejudices or preferences of the contest judges and the fact that Rousseau had already won a prize from the same academy when he submitted the second discourse, it is difficult, even impossible, to comprehend how the first but not the second could win the prize. If we consider only the literary merits of the two, the second is at least the equal of the first and, in my opinion, is superior to it. But though the first discourse doubtlessly has some literary merit, as philosophy it is unquestionably inferior to the second. The second discourse, the *Discourse on Political Economy*, and *The Social Contract* are all reasoned statements of a philosophical position elaborated, as we shall see, with considerable logic and consistency. In contrast, the first discourse is an impassioned explosion, a *cri de coeur*. It is true that all Rousseau's philosophical writing constitutes a kind of *cri de coeur*; but that of the second and third discourses and *The Social Contract* is a reasoned *cri de coeur*, whereas that of the first discourse contains more passion and heat than reason and light.

This, however, means neither that the position presented in the first discourse is irrelevant to that developed in the second and third discourses and *The Social Contract* nor that it is incompatible with it. Although Rousseau doubtlessly exaggerates when he claims that all his ideas are consistent, there is nonetheless a fundamental consistency of outlook from the first discourse through the second and third to *The Social Contract*. There are, of course, certain shifts of emphasis and changes of opinion and attitude as he progresses from the first discourse through the second and the third to *The Social Contract*. But this is only to be expected as a philosopher develops his position over a period of years and in a series of works written and published at different times. These shifts and changes, however, are minor compared with the constancy of basic outlook and position from the first discourse to *The Social Contract*.

The impassioned explosion of the first discourse can be at least partly accounted for in terms of Rousseau's reaction to the intellectual atmosphere of mid-eighteenth–century France. It was fashionable among French intellectuals of the time to look upon the development of civilization since the Renaissance as ushering in an epoch that might properly be referred to as the age of reason or enlightenment, particularly in eighteenth-century France. It will be recalled that the subject of the contest conducted by the Academy of Dijon in 1750 was the question: has the restoration of the arts and sciences tended to purify morals? "The restoration of the arts and sciences" refers particularly to the development of European civilization since the Renaissance, and especially to the development of the arts and sciences in eighteenth-century France. The philosophers of the Age of Reason generally assumed that the restoration of the arts and sciences had had a purifying effect upon morals, whereas Rousseau argues in the first discourse that it had had precisely the opposite effect—that it had corrupted rather than purified morals. Indeed, Rousseau argues for the more general thesis that the development of the arts and sciences in every age, and not merely since their restoration beginning with the Renaissance, has a corrupting effect upon morals. His thesis, in short, in both the first and the second discourses, is that the development of civilization has been achieved only at the cost of corrupting morals.

This thesis may be stated briefly as follows. Man is by nature good, or at least innocent. He is corrupt only as a consequence of living in a corrupt society. Almost every society throughout history has been corrupt to some degree, and in consequence the human beings living in these societies have been corrupted by them. What applies to society applies also to civilization, even more so, and particularly to the society and civilization of eighteenth-century France. Given the corruption of society and civilization and the consequent corruption of man, only two solutions are possible. One is to abandon society and civilization altogether and return to the state of nature. Rousseau considers this solution in the second discourse without proposing it. The other solution is to replace corrupt societies with just societies, which Rousseau proposes in *The Social Contract*, the primary purpose of which is to delineate the conditions that must be satisfied if a society is to be just.

Throughout the first, second, and the third discourses to *The Social Contract*, Rousseau is primarily a moralist. Indeed, no philosopher has ever been more of a moralist. In all his political writing his fundamental position is that the claims of morality are superior to the claims of culture or civilization, so that if the satisfaction of the claims of morality is incompatible with the existence of culture or civilization, it is the latter that must be sacrificed for the sake of the former, not the reverse. He was convinced that the development of the arts and sciences and of culture and civilization in every age, and particularly in eighteenth-century France, had been achieved only at the cost of sacrificing the claims of morality, and therefore that every civilization, especially that of eighteenth-century France, had been more or less morally corrupt. The first discourse was an attempt to show this. In this discourse he is unclear as to whether morality and civilization are necessarily incompatible, regardless of the form a civilization takes, but it can reasonably be interpreted as arguing that they are essentially incompatible. In the second discourse, however, he has come to believe that moral salvation may be possible without abandoning society and civilization, and in the third discourse, and especially in *The Social Contract*, he seeks to show how such salvation can be attained while retaining society and civilization. But, as we shall see, he argues in *The Social Contract* that its attainment coupled with the retention of society is possible only through a radical re-constitution of existing society. But regardless of how radical the change of existing societies must be in order that the claims of morality be satisfied, the primacy of these claims requires and justifies the change.

It will therefore become evident, at least by the time we complete our examination of Rousseau—if, indeed, it is not apparent from what has already been said—that there is at least one sense in which Rousseau is a Christian thinker. Notice, dear reader, that I said "Christian thinker," not "Christian man." Because of his remarkably candid autobiographical *Confessions* we know much more about the intimate details of his life and about his sins, neuroses, mistakes, peccadilloes, *amours*, difficulties, and failures than we do about those of most philosophers. But his personal life is one thing, the philosophy expressed in his philosophical writings another, and we should be just as guilty of *ad hominem* reasoning if we permitted our knowledge and opinion of his personal life to influence our philosophical interpretation and assessment of his philosophical writings as we should be in the case of any philosopher. His philosophical writing, like that of any other philosopher, stands on its own philosophical feet and can be properly interpreted and assessed philosophically only by bringing to bear upon it philosophical standards and considerations of the same sort used in the philosophical assessment of other philosophers. We are, in short, interested here only in Rousseau the philosopher, not Rousseau the man, and Rousseau the philosopher can and ought to be approached philosophically in abstraction from Rousseau the man fully as much as any other philosopher. To fail to do so in his case would vitiate our philosophical interpretation and assessment of his philosophy just as much as a failure to do so would in the case of any other philosopher.

In saying, then, that there is at least one sense in which Rousseau is a profoundly Christian thinker, I am saying nothing at all about whether he was a Christian man. Whether he was a Christian man is not the business of the philosopher, if, indeed, it is the business of any man. And should someone be so bold as to decide this question, he could decide it as a Christian only by tempering his judgment with charity toward Rousseau. Nor am I claiming, in saying that there is a sense in which Rousseau is a Christian thinker, that he is within the Christian natural law tradition represented by such thinkers as Aquinas. Instead, what I am claiming is that his position that morality and justice are more important than culture or civilization is the position of Christianity. This does not mean that the Christian, any more than Rousseau, need maintain that the two are incompatible. On the contrary, all he need maintain is that the former is more important than the latter, regardless of whether or not the two are compatible. This is the position ascribed to Jesus in the Gospels and the position to be found in the epistles of St. Paul and St. John, in the writings of Church Fathers such as St. Augustine, and in the lives of saints such as St. Francis of Assisi. It is summed up succinctly in these words from St. Paul. "Though I speak with the tongues of men and of angels, and have not charity, I am become as sounding brass or a tinkling cymbal."[1] It is summed up also in these words from Kant, Rousseau's disciple in moral, social, and political philosophy. "Nothing in the world—indeed nothing even beyond the world—can possibly be conceived which could be called good without qualification except a *good will*."[2] We do not, then, do excessive violence to Rousseau's position if we interpret him, not only in his first discourse but also in the second and third discourses and in *The Social Contract*, as addressing the words of St. Paul not only to *les philosophes* of the Age of Reason, but also to intellectuals of every age. Regardless of how beautifully, how elegantly, how eloquently they may speak, they are only sounding brass and tinkling cymbals if they lack charity. And regardless of how magnificent the achievements of a culture or a civilization may be, they cannot be commended unconditionally with a clear conscience if they are made possible only at the cost of a corrupt and unjust society and the consequent corruption of the men in that society.

Rousseau's position that morality and justice are more important than culture or civilization does not in itself mean that he is anti-intellectual, any more than its espousal by previous Christian thinkers and by Kant means that they are anti-intellectual. Someone, however, whose knowledge of Rousseau is limited to what can be gleaned from reading only the first discourse might understandably convict him of a kind of anti-intellectual romanticism. But as I have said, the first discourse can be adequately understood only when taken in connection with the second and the third and *The Social Contract*. It is to be understood as a prelude to these later works, and as a hyperbolic expression of his indignation at those who praise the achievements in the arts and sciences of various cultures or civilizations while overlooking the moral corruption and injustices of the societies that produced these achievements. In this work he is interested only in drawing the attention of his readers to what he conceives to be their moral blindness and corruption, and not in seriously proposing a solution, perhaps on the assumption that they must first be shocked into recognizing that there is a problem before they will attend seriously to any solution he may propose. This, I think, accounts for, even if it does not excuse, the rhetorical excesses of the work. Although, then, there is a serious philosophical purpose behind the first discourse, the work itself is more a piece of rhetoric than a piece of philosophy. For a philosophical exposition of his moral, social, and political philosophy we must turn to the second and third discourses and to *The Social Contract*.

II. The Historicity of the State of Nature

The primary purpose of *The Social Contract* is to specify the conditions that must be satisfied if, taking men as they are and laws as they might be, a just society is to be possible, in which the interests of each member of the society are promoted. Rousseau makes this clear in the very first sentence of Book I. "I mean to inquire if, in the civil order, there can be any sure and legitimate rule of administration, men being taken as they are and laws as they might be. In this inquiry I shall endeavour always to unite what right sanctions with what is prescribed by interest, in order that justice and utility may in no case be divided." Rousseau thus makes it clear that it is laws, and not men, that need to be changed if justice is to be possible, or, to be more precise, that it is only through changing laws that we can effect whatever changes in man are necessary for justice to be possible. He assumes that the nature of man is more constant and less plastic than laws are, and thus that the effectuation of changes in laws is more directly subject to our control than is the effectuation of changes in men. This, however, means only that human nature is relatively more constant than a system of laws. It does not mean that it is not plastic in any sense at all or to any extent at all, but only that laws can be changed more easily than human nature, and that such changes in human nature as we can effect can be brought about most effectively by working indirectly, through first changing the laws that affect men. Indeed, one of the primary purposes of the second discourse is to show that human nature is plastic—that the natural man is distinct from the social man, and that the nature man assumes in society varies from one to another, depending upon the nature of the society. As I have said, Rousseau maintains that man is naturally good, or at least naturally innocent, and becomes corrupt only through living in a corrupt society. If, then, he is to be rescued from his corruption, the corruption of the society in which he lives must be eliminated. Hence the primary purpose of *The Social Contract* is to show how man can be rescued from his corruption and how his goodness can be restored through eliminating the corruption in society and establishing a just society.

In the second discourse Rousseau seeks to uncover the nature of the natural man, as distinct from the nature of man in society, through an extended discussion of the state of nature, a discussion much more extended and detailed than that of either Hobbes or Locke. His purpose in discussing the state of nature is therefore somewhat different from that of Hobbes and Locke. Hobbes' purpose had been to show that life in the state of nature would be so miserable and dangerous that any form of political association providing an escape from its misery and danger would be preferable to a return to it, whereas Locke's purpose had been to delineate the rights and obligations men have by nature, as distinct from civil rights and obligations, and to show how political societies may legitimately be instituted. But Rousseau's purpose is different. It is to get at the nature of the natural man as distinct from social man by prescinding

from all the characteristics that man acquires only in society, since for him
the natural man is what remains after all the influences of any form of
society have been eliminated. Thus for Rousseau the state of nature is the
complete absence of all forms of human society and settled or permanent
associations. This accounts for his view that previous philosophers who
had felt the necessity of going back to the state of nature had never in fact
gotten there.

The philosophers, who have inquired into the foundations of society, have all felt
the necessity of going back to a state of nature; but not one of them has got there.
Some of them [such as Locke?] have not hesitated to ascribe to man, in such a state,
the idea of just and unjust, without troubling themselves to show that he must be
possessed of such an idea, or that it could be of any use to him. Others [again, such
as Locke?] have spoken of the natural right of every man to keep what belongs to
him, without explaining what they meant by 'belongs.' Others again [presumably
Hobbes?] beginning by giving the strong authority over the weak, proceeded
directly to the birth of government, without regard to the time that must have
elapsed before the meaning of the words 'authority' and 'government' could have
existed among men. Every one of them, in short, . . . has transferred to the state of
nature ideas which were acquired in society: so that, in speaking of the savage,
they described the social man.[1]

Rousseau's account of his predecessors' version of the state of nature is
not entirely accurate, for Locke explains in some detail what he means by
"property." Nor is he correct in saying that "It has not even entered into
the heads of most of our writers to doubt whether the state of nature ever
existed," if by this he means that neither Hobbes nor Locke ever raise any
question as to its historicity. For both do raise this question. Hobbes raises
and answers it in the following words.

It may peradventure be thought, there was never such a time, nor condition of
warre as this; and I believe it was never generally so, over all the world: but there
are many places, where they live so now. For the savage people in many places of
America, except the government of small Families, the concord whereof dependeth
on naturall lust, have no government at all; and live at this day in that brutish
manner.[2]

Locke also asserts the historicity of the state of nature.[3] But neither
Hobbes nor Locke, in discussing the state of nature, is interested primarily in asserting its historicity. Instead, for each the concept of the state of
nature is essentially a methodological device. Rousseau, however, is more
explicit than either Hobbes or Locke had been in asserting that he uses this
concept as such a device and does not intend to assert the existence of a
state of nature as actual historical fact.

It is clear from the Holy Scriptures that the first man, having received his under-standing and commandments immediately from God, was not himself in such a state; and that, if we give such credit to the writings of Moses as every Christian philosopher ought to give, we must deny that... men were ever in the pure state of nature ....

Let us begin then by laying facts aside, as they do not affect the question. The investigations we may enter into, in treating this subject, must not be considered as historical truths, but only as mere conditional and hypothetical reasonings, rather calculated to explain the nature of things, than to ascertain their actual origin; just like the hypotheses which our physicists daily form respecting the formation of the world. Religion... does not forbid us to form conjectures based solely on the nature of man, and the beings around him, concerning what might have become of the human race, if it had been left to itself.[4]

Although Rousseau thus makes it clear in the second discourse that he is using the concept of the state of nature as a methodological device and does not intend to assert the historicity of that state, there are nevertheless passages in *The Social Contract* that can be interpreted to mean that there he is asserting its historicity. For there he writes as follows:

The most ancient of all societies, and the only one that is natural, is the family: and even so the children remain attached to the father only so long as they need him for their preservation. As soon as this need ceases, the natural bond is dissolved. The children, released from the obedience they owed to the father, and the father, released from the care he owed his children, return equally to independence. If they remain united, they continue so no longer naturally, but voluntarily; and the family itself is then maintained only by convention.[5]

Here Rousseau clearly seems to be saying both that the family is the only natural society and also that it antedates political society. But the attempt to determine the precise meaning of his words must be postponed for a time. Later on in *The Social Contract* he again clearly seems to assert the historicity of the state of nature.

I suppose men to have reached the point at which the obstacles in the way of their preservation in the state of nature show their power of resistance to be greater than the resources at the disposal of each individual for his maintenance in that state. That primitive condition can then subsist no longer; and the human race would perish unless it changed its manner of existence.[6]

Still later on, in discussing the changes that occur in man as a consequence of leaving the state of nature to enter civil society, he also writes in such a way as to imply the historicity of the state of nature. This passage is of supreme importance for understanding Rousseau's conception of the difference between natural man, i.e., man in the state of nature, and what social man, i.e., man in civil society, can become.

The passage from the state of nature to the civil state produces a very remarkable change in man, by substituting justice for instinct in his conduct, and giving his actions the morality they had formerly lacked. Then only, when the voice of duty takes the place of physical impulses and right of appetite, does man, who so far had considered only himself, find that he is forced to act on different principles, and to consult his reason before listening to his inclinations. Although, in this state, he deprives himself of some advantages which he got from nature, he gains in return others so great, his faculties are so stimulated and developed, his ideas so extended, his feelings so ennobled, and his whole soul so uplifted, that, did not the abuses of this new condition often degrade him below that which he left, he would be bound to bless continually the happy moment which took him from it for ever, and, instead of a stupid and unimaginative animal, made him an intelligent being and a man.[7]

Although, then, in the second discourse Rousseau makes it clear that he is not asserting the historicity of the state of nature, but, instead, is using the concept of such a state only as a methodological device, in *The Social Contract* there are passages in which he seems to assert, or at least to imply, its historicity. This, however, does not mean that *The Social Contract* contradicts the second discourse on this point, nor even that Rousseau has changed his mind on it. For although he does not assert the historicity of the state of nature in the second discourse, neither does he deny it. It is true that he says that no Christian philsopher can maintain that "men were ever in the pure state of nature." This is because a philosopher, to be a Christian thinker, must accept the account of the creation of man given in *Genesis*. According to this account, the first man "received his understanding and commandments immediately from God." This means that according to *Genesis* the understanding of the first man was as fully developed as is the understanding of man in society, and also that according to *Genesis* the first man, in receiving commandments immediately from God, was fully a moral agent, conscious of a moral law that he was obligated to obey, and free either to obey or disobey it. But as we shall see more fully as we proceed, and as is already evident from the passages quoted from Rousseau, his conception of the state of nature, both in the second discourse and also in *The Social Contract*, is such that anyone who accepts his account of it and asserts its historicity must also reject these two inferences from *Genesis*. For Rousseau denies that man's understanding in the state of nature would be as fully developed as it is in society; indeed, he argues, it would be only a little above that of brutes, and in fact would resemble that of brutes more than that of man in society. From this it follows, according to Rousseau, that man in the state of nature could not be a moral agent, at least not in the developed sense in which such agency is possible in society. For moral agency presupposes the possibility of conceiving a law or rule which the agent believes to be obligatory and which he is free either to obey or disobey, whereas the possibility of conceiving such a law would not exist in the state of nature, since the natural man would not have a sufficiently developed understanding.

Rousseau's view of the conditions that must be satisfied if moral agency is to be possible is anticipatory of Kant's position and seems sound as far as it goes. But whether his reading of *Genesis* is satisfactory is another matter. If we read it as Rousseau does, then I think we must agree that he shows that a Christian philosopher cannot assert the historicity of the state of nature. This, however, does not mean that his reading is the only possible or acceptable one. What he does is to interpret *Genesis* somewhat literally, as asserting the factuality or historicity of the account given there of the creation of man, the Garden of Eden, and the fall of man. Anyone who thus interprets it literally or historically cannot also assert the historicity of the state of nature as conceived by Rousseau. But there is another interpretation that may reasonably be applied to *Genesis*. This is that its account of the creation of man and of the nature of the first man is not to be taken literally or factually, but symbolically or allegorically, or perhaps as a methodological device, analogous to Rousseau's use in the second discourse of the concept of a state of nature, which the author of *Genesis* uses to reveal what he believes to be certain truths about the nature of man and his relationship to God. Someone who interprets it in this way would perhaps then be free to assert the historicity of the state of nature as conceived by Rousseau while remaining a Christian philosopher. Whether the author of *Genesis* believed his account of the creation of man, of the Garden of Eden, and of the fall of man to be factually or historically true or, instead, intended it only as an allegory or myth we shall perhaps never know. But we do him more honor if we suppose him to have intended it allegorically, for to suppose him to have believed his account to be literally true is to ascribe to him such an excessive simpleness of mind as to treat him in an insultingly irreverent way. Rousseau, however, is right in insisting that you cannot have it both ways. You cannot both interpret *Genesis* literally and also assert the historicity of the state of nature as Rousseau conceives it. He seems to go wrong only in appearing to assume a literal interpretation of *Genesis*.

But not only does Rousseau assert, at least implicitly, the historicity of the state of nature in *The Social Contract*, while declining to do so in the second discourse—he also appears to modify his view of it in the later work. For there, as we have seen, he speaks of the family as "the most ancient of societies" and as the only natural society, whereas in the second discourse the state of nature is conceived as the total absence of any form of society at all, except for that of mother and child. In thus supposing the family to be a natural society he approaches the view of Hobbes[8] and Locke,[9] both of whom supposed the family to exist in the state of nature. But in the second discourse he accuses those who suppose the family to have existed in the state of nature of importing "ideas gathered in a state of society" into their view of the state of nature.

Thus they constantly consider families as living together under one roof, and the individuals of each as observing among themselves a union as intimate and permanent as that which exists among us, where so many common interests unite them; whereas, in this primitive state, men had neither houses, nor huts, nor any kind of property whatever; every one lived where he could, seldom for more than a single night; the sexes united without design, as accident, opportunity, or inclination brought them together, nor had they any great need of words to communicate their designs to each other; and they parted with the same indifference. The mother gave suck to her children at first for her own sake; and afterwards, when habit had made them dear, for theirs: but as soon as they were strong enough to go in search of their own food, they forsook her of their own accord; and, as they had hardly any other method of not losing one another than that of remaining continually within sight, they soon became quite incapable of recognizing one another when they happened to meet again.[10]

The discrepancy between the second discourse and *The Social Contract* on the question of whether the family would exist in the state of nature can, however, perhaps be accounted for. In the second discourse Rousseau's primary concern, as we have seen, is to distinguish between the social man, i.e., man as affected by and molded through living in society, and the purely natural man, i.e., what would remain as characteristic of man if everything that society contributes to the formation of his nature were removed. Thus in the second discourse he is attempting to describe what he sometimes refers to as "the pure state of nature."[11] This is a state in which there are absolutely no forms of society whatever, except, of course, for the society of mother and child that exists only until the child is old enough to fend for itself and leaves its mother. Indeed, Rousseau ought to have argued that not even this simple form of society would exist in an absolutely pure state of nature, for the society of mother and child would have some effect on both. Perhaps his reason for admitting it into his pure state of nature is that he saw that it is the one form of society that is necessary if the child is to survive at all. But given the necessity of the simple society of mother and child, a pure state of nature would exist only if the child leaves its mother as soon as it is able to do so, and Rousseau accordingly supposes that it does. Here it is especially important to remember that Rousseau's account of the pure state of nature is purely hypothetical or conditional, and is not intended as a factual account. He is not supposing that, given the society of mother and child, the child would in fact leave its mother as soon as it can, but, instead, is postulating that it does so because he could not otherwise give as complete an account of the hypothetical pure state of nature.

As contrasted with the pure state of nature that Rousseau seeks to describe in the second discourse, the expression "state of nature" may also be used to refer simply to the condition in which men would live if there were no civil society. This would be an intermediate state between the pure state of nature on the one hand and civil society on the other. Although there would be no civil society in it, there would exist some form of society, such as that of the family. Thus the expression "state of nature" may be used both in an extended sense to refer to the absence of all forms of society whatsoever and in a more limited sense to refer simply to the absence of civil society. Locke uses the expression only in the latter sense. Hobbes, on the other hand, is not always consistent in his use of it, for sometimes he uses it in the more limited sense, as when he supposes that the family exists in the state of nature,[12] whereas at other times, e.g., when he writes that the life of man would be "solitary, poor, nasty, brutish, and short," he supposes that in the state of nature each man would lead a solitary existence. Rousseau, of course, uses it in the extended sense in the second discourse. But in *The Social Contract* he uses it in both senses. He uses it in the more limited sense when he supposes the family to be "the most ancient of all societies, and the only one that is natural," but also in the more extended sense, both when he supposes that men form political associations when the obstacles to their preservation in the state of nature are too great for them to overcome singly,[13] and also when he speaks of the transition from the state of nature into civil society as effecting a remarkable transformation in man, changing him from "a stupid and unimaginative animal" into "an intelligent being and a man."[14]

Thus Rousseau's complaint that none of the philosophers who had "felt the necessity of going back to a state of nature" had in fact gotten there is true if the expression "state of nature" is used in the extended sense, but not if it is used in the more limited sense. It therefore does not apply to Locke at all, for he never felt the necessity of going back to a state of nature in the extended sense. Thus when Locke says that men in the state of nature would have some idea of just and unjust, he is not saying that they would have such an idea if they existed totally isolated from all forms of society, for by "the state of nature" he does not intend such complete isolation. Rousseau's criticism therefore misses its mark here. And although Hobbes sometimes uses the expression in the extended sense, he need not have done so, for his interest in describing the state of nature is merely to contrast the condition of life in civil society with what it would be in the absence of such society, and to do this it is not necessary to assume that there would be no form of society at all in the absence of civil society. Rousseau's criticism is therefore misdirected if he intended it to apply, as he undoubtedly did, to Hobbes and Locke. They cannot properly be criticized for transferring "to the state of nature ideas which were acquired only in society; so that, in speaking of the savage, they described the social man." For they were not purporting to speak of the savage that Rousseau seeks to describe.

Moreover, the distinction between an extended and a limited sense of the expression "state of nature" serves to establish the reasonableness of the positions all three thinkers take concerning the question of the historicity of the state of nature. As we have seen, Rousseau is careful not to commit himself as to the historicity of the state of nature in the extended sense of the expression, but treats the concept of such a state of nature purely as a methodological device. On the other hand, Locke and Hobbes, insofar as they assert or imply the historicity of the state of nature, are careful to use the expression in the limited sense. This is obvious in the case of Locke, for he never uses it in the extended sense. It is also obvious in the case of Hobbes, for when he asserts that "the savage people in many places of *America* . . . live at this day" in the "brutish manner" of the state of nature, he is also careful to note that they live in small families. And although Rousseau in *The Social Contract* sometimes writes as though he were asserting the historicity of a state of nature approximating that described in the second discourse, he also quite clearly asserts that the family precedes the state in time, for he writes that it is "the most ancient of all societies." The positions of all three philosophers are reasonable because, although it would be unreasonable to assert the historicity of the state of nature in the extended sense, none of them asserts its historicity in this sense, and also because it does seem reasonable, or at least not unreasonable, to assert its historicity in the weak sense.

III. Nature, Reason, and Freedom

We turn now to examine more fully the account Rousseau gives in the second discourse of the state of nature and the natural man, stripped of all the accretions he acquires through life in society. Stripped of these accretions he is reduced to a savage—indeed, as we have seen, to little more than a brute. To some slight extent both Hobbes and Locke anticipate

Rousseau on this point. For although Locke discusses and asserts the historicity of the state of nature only in the limited sense of the term, he nevertheless maintains that the art of letters is acquired only after men enter political society,[1] and it may not be wholly unjustifiable to read him as implying also that the existence of civil society is a necessary condition of the possibility not only of the art of letters but of civilization itself. And Hobbes, as we have seen, describes the state of nature as brutish. Yet Rousseau is right in claiming that previous philosophers had not gotten to the state of nature in the extended sense of the term. Certainly neither Locke nor Hobbes got there. For both Hobbes and Locke ascribe reason to man in the state of nature. For Locke it is by means of reason that man in the state of nature has some notion of natural law, of right and wrong, of just and unjust. And for Hobbes also it is by means of reason that men in the state of nature apprehend the fundamental command of reason to preserve themselves and discover that to do so they must abandon the state of nature for civil society.

For Rousseau, on the other hand, the primitive man of the pure state of nature would be incapable of the reason that Hobbes and Locke ascribe to man in the state of nature, and therefore could have no consciousness of natural law, right and wrong, just and unjust nor deduce an obligation to enter civil society by reasoning from abstract principles of natural law. The definitions of natural law presented by learned men, "all differing in everything else, agree only in this, that it is impossible to comprehend the law of nature, and consequently to obey it, without being a very subtle casuist and a profound metaphysician."[2] Thus if men had to apprehend the principles and conclusions of natural law before they could leave the state of nature they would have had to exercise "in the establishment of society, a capacity which is acquired only with great difficulty, and by very few persons, even in a state of society."[3] The apprehension of the abstract principles and conclusions of natural law, then, is not necessary if men are to leave the state of nature. If it were, men could never have done so, for they acquire the reason which would enable them to do so only after they have entered society. Nor is reason necessary for self-preservation. "Although it might belong to Socrates and other minds of the like craft to acquire virtue by reason, the human race would long since have ceased to be, had its preservation depended only on the reasonings of the individuals composing it."[4]

The reason Rousseau denies reason to the primitive man is that "men need speech to learn to think,"[5] and speech is possible only in society. The kind of reasoning and thinking of which Rousseau is speaking is only the kind that requires language. But this is precisely the kind that is necessary if abstract principles and conclusions of natural law and morality are to be apprehended. For the apprehension of such principles and conclusions involves the employment of general ideas and abstract concepts. But "general ideas cannot be introduced into the mind without the assistance of words,"[6] and purely abstract concepts "are only conceivable by the help of language."[7] Rousseau does not deny, however, that the primitive man would be capable of a kind of rudimentary thinking and reasoning closely tied to sensation and imagination, and in fact even ascribes this kind of thinking and reasoning to brutes. "Every animal has ideas, since it has senses; it even combines those ideas in a certain degree; and it is only in degree that man differs, in this respect, from the brute."[8] In saying here that in this respect man differs only in degree from the brute, he is speaking only of primitive man, not of man in society. For man in society possesses language, and thus is capable of a kind of thinking that differs in kind from that of which brutes are capable.

What Rousseau seems to be maintaining is that the primitive man of the pure state of nature, considered merely in terms of what he would be in actuality and not in terms of what he would have the potentiality of becoming in society, would be merely a natural or animal creature, like any other animal, not a rational or moral agent. More than anything else, what would distinguish him in actuality from all other animals would be his bodily form. But even in respect to bodily form there might be some difficulty in distinguishing sharply between what we should be willing to count as a human being and what not, for Rousseau clearly anticipates the theory of the evolutionary development of the present human form out of earlier bodily forms, and a problem would therefore arise as to when the bodily form of our prehistoric ancestors was sufficiently similar to our own to count as that of a human being. Though Rousseau does thus anticipate evolutionary theory, he refuses to speculate on the character of these earlier bodily forms.

I shall not follow his [man's] organization through its successive developments, nor shall I stay to inquire what his animal system must have been at the beginning, in order to become at length what it actually is... On this subject I could form none but vague and almost imaginary conjectures. Comparative anatomy has as yet made too little progress, and the observations of naturalists are too uncertain, to afford an adequate basis for any solid reasoning. So that, without having recourse to the supernatural information given us on this head, or paying any regard to the changes which must have taken place in the internal, as well as the external, conformation of man, as he applied his limbs to new uses, and fed himself on new kinds of food, I shall suppose his conformation to have been at all times what it appears to us at this day; that he always walked on two legs, made use of his hands as we do, directed his looks over all nature, and measured with his eyes the vast expanse of Heaven.[9]

Although, Rousseau is saying here, the present bodily form of man may have evolved out of earlier and different forms, he will suppose the primitive man of the pure state of nature to have had the same form as we have today. This supposition is reasonable, for a reason Rousseau does not mention, which is that we should refuse to count some species of animal as human unless it did have much the same form as human beings have today. Although we might hesitate to count some prehistoric progenitor of the present human species as itself human, this hesitation would arise from a difficulty in deciding whether its form is sufficiently like that of man as we know him today.

On this point Rousseau appears to have come close to hitting upon a fundamental truth—the importance of the human bodily form. This is a truth that we all recognize, at least implicitly, in our conception of the necessary and sufficient conditions that must be satisfied for something to count as a human being. For it is not necessary that something be capable of rational or moral agency to be a human being. If it were, then we should refuse to recognize as human those animals possessing the human form, yet who lack the capacity for rational agency and sometimes lack even the intelligence displayed by certain brutes, and whom we accordingly label "idiots." The fact that we persist in regarding idiots as human beings, even though they be completely incapable of rational agency, would seem to indicate that in practice we regard the possession of the human form as a sufficient condition of the possession of humanity, even though in theory we may continue to claim that the possession of the capacity for rational agency is also necessary. Nor is it sufficient that a being have this capacity if it is to count as a human being. For even though there should be beings on another planet or disembodied intelligences or angels who possess the capacity for rational agency, we should nevertheless refuse to recognize them as human beings simply because they lack the human form. It seems clear, then, that Rousseau is right in implying that the possession of rationality is neither a necessary nor a sufficient condition of humanity, and that the possession of the human form is both necessary and sufficient.

For Rousseau, then, the primitive man of the pure state of nature, if considered only in terms of what he would then actually be, and thus in abstraction from what he has the potentiality of becoming, would be only one animal among others. In actuality he would be merely a natural being, like any other animal, not a rational or moral agent, and would differ from other animals essentially only in virtue of his possession of a distinctive bodily form. Like other animals, his behavior would be determined by instinct and the kind of rudimentary thinking of which other animals are also capable.[10] But whereas in actuality he would be a purely natural creature in the same sense other animals are, he would nevertheless possess one potentiality that no other animal possesses, that of becoming a rational or moral agent. In this connection Rousseau sharply distinguishes, in a manner anticipatory of Kant, between purely natural creatures on the one hand and rational or moral agents on the other. Kant distinguishes between the two as follows. "Everything in nature works according to laws. Only a rational being has the capacity of acting according to the conception of laws, i.e. according to principles."[11] Whereas a natural being acts or behaves in accordance with laws of nature that are imposed upon it from without (or which describe its nature and action or behavior) and of which it therefore need not be conscious, a rational or moral agent acts in accordance with laws of reason which it freely imposes upon itself and of which it must therefore be conscious.

This means that "natural law" has two distinct senses, which, according to Rousseau, the Roman jurists failed to distinguish. Accordingly, they "subjected man and the other animals indiscriminately to the same natural law, because they considered, under that name, rather the law which nature imposes on herself than that which she prescribes to others."[12] On the other hand, "The moderns, understanding by the term 'law' merely a rule prescribed to a moral being, that is to say intelligent, free, and considered in his relations to other beings, consequently confine the jurisdiction of natural law to man, as the only animal endowed with reason."[13] Thus animals, though subject to natural law in the sense that they are subject to laws imposed upon them from without and of which they therefore need not be conscious, are not subject to natural law in the sense that they have a natural obligation to impose it upon themselves, for, "being destitute of intelligence and liberty, they cannot recognize that law."[14] But though they cannot be subject to natural law in this sense, they may be said "to partake of natural right." This is because of "the sensibility with which they are endowed." Since they as well as men can suffer pain, "mankind is subjected to a kind of obligation even toward the brutes." Indeed, if men have an obligation to do no injury to their fellow-creatures, "this is less because they are rational than because they are sentient beings: and this quality, being common both to men and beasts, ought to entitle the latter at least to the privilege of not being wantonly ill-treated by the former."[15]

But although Rousseau rejects the Cartesian denial of consciousness, sentience, and rudimentary forms of thinking to brutes, he accepts the Cartesian contention that in principle the behavior of beasts can be understood in terms of mechanistic principles. "I see nothing in any animal but an ingenious machine, to which nature hath given senses to wind itself up, and to guard itself, to a certain degree, against anything that might tend to disorder or destroy it."[16] Rousseau's reference here to animals as ingenious machines does not, of course, mean that he denies that they are sentient and capable of rudimentary forms of reasoning, for we have just seen that he asserts the latter. What it means, instead, is that the behavior, sentience, and reasoning of animals is explicable in mechanistic terms, that is, that animals are purely natural creatures, in the sense that they act in accordance with natural laws imposed upon them from without. Thus "in the operations of the brute, nature is the sole agent . . . the brute cannot deviate from the rule prescribed to it, even when it would be advantageous for it to do so . . . Nature lays her commands on every animal, and the brute obeys her voice."[17] The same thing is true of the human body, at least so far as it operates independently of distinctively human reasoning and choice. Considered in abstraction from such reasoning and choice, it too is merely a natural organism, operating in accordance with laws of nature imposed upon it from without. It is no more conscious of the laws governing or describing its operations than is any brute or anything else in nature, and thus is free neither to accept nor to reject these laws. Its nature and its operations, like those of everything else in nature, are determined from without, in accordance with laws of which it has no consciousness, independent of any choices or acts of will on its part.[18]

This, however, applies to the human body only as considered in abstraction from the influences which human reasoning and choice have upon it. It does not apply to the total human person, which consists of intellect and will as well as sentience and the body. The operations of the human will are free and cannot be accounted for in purely naturalistic or mechanistic terms. "Man has some share in his own operations, in his character as a free agent." Whereas the brute "chooses and refuses by instinct," man does so "from an act of free will . . . ."[19] This means that man is a spiritual being, not merely a natural or mechanical creature.

It is particularly in his consciousness of this liberty that the spirituality of his soul is displayed. For physics may explain, in some measure, the mechanism of the senses and the formation of ideas; but in the power of willing or rather of choosing, and in the feeling of this power, nothing is to be found but acts which are purely spiritual and wholly inexplicable by the laws of mechanism.[20]

Accordingly, Rousseau maintains that "it is not . . . so much the understanding that constitutes the specific difference between the man and the brute, as the human quality of free agency."[21] Whereas man is subject to more or less the same natural impulses as brutes are, he alone is free and knows himself to be free, either to acquiesce in or to resist these impulses. The brutes are simply subject to them.[22]

In saying, however, that it is not so much man's understanding as his freedom and his consciousness of his freedom that distinguish him from the brutes, Rousseau is not to be interpreted as meaning that man's understanding is of no importance with regard to the distinction between man and brute. We have already seen that he maintains that man, in virtue of his possession of language, is capable of a kind of abstract understanding of which no other animal is capable. Moreover, one might argue, it is only in virtue of the development of a level of understanding or consciousness that brutes seem incapable of attaining that man is capable of the kind of freedom Rousseau ascribes to him. For whereas a brute is not conscious of itself and does not distinguish itself from the natural impulses that assail it and determine its behavior, it is necessary that man distinguish himself from the impulses impinging upon him, and thus that he be conscious of himself as something distinct from these impulses, if he is to be free either to acquiesce in or to resist them. Certainly self-consciousness is necessary if the kind of moral freedom which consists in the imposition of a law upon oneself is to be possible, for unless one is conscious of oneself as something upon which the law can be imposed, it is impossible for it to be self-imposed. Given these considerations, it may not be wholly unreasonable to interpret Rousseau's assertion that it is not so much man's understanding as his freedom and his consciousness of his freedom that distinguish him from the animals as meaning that although the possession of abstract understanding and self-consciousness is in itself sufficient to distinguish man from the brutes, and although such understanding and self-consciousness are necessary if man is to be morally free, it is nevertheless his moral freedom that is most important in separating him from other animals. This would be compatible with his rejection of naturalism, as it would amount to saying that the thing that essentially distinguishes man from all brutes and from everything else in nature is that the latter, as mere natural beings, can act only in accordance with laws imposed upon them from without of which they have no consciousness and which, therefore, they are free neither to accept nor reject, whereas man, as a spiritual being, has the capacity of acting from a consciousness of laws that are not imposed upon him from without, and that he is therefore free either to reject or impose upon himself.

But, Rousseau goes on, even if it be denied that there is any sense in which man, as distinguished from brutes, is free, there is nevertheless another metaphysical or moral distinction between them which admits of no dispute. This is man's perfectibility or faculty of self-improvement. It is this faculty "which, by the help of circumstances, gradually develops all the rest of our faculties, and is inherent in the species as in the individual: whereas a brute is, at the end of a few months, all he will ever be during his whole life, and his species, at the end of a thousand years, exactly what it was the first year of that thousand."[23] Here, however, Rousseau is not as clear as one would wish. He speaks of this faculty of self-improvement as developing, with the help of circumstances, all our other faculties, as though it were itself a faculty distinct from them, yet he does not tell us what it is. It would seem, in fact, to be not a distinct faculty at all, but, instead, simply man's capacity for language, abstract thought, and acting from a consciousness of law. It is in virtue of these capacities that man is capable of self-improvement, and not because of a faculty of self-improvement, unless, of course, one takes the latter expression merely as an abbreviated way of referring to the other more specific capacities. Rousseau may, however, be read simply as asserting that regardless of whether man is free in some sense in which brutes are not, it is undeniable that man is capable of self-improvement in a sense in which brutes are not, and may therefore be distinguished from them by being labelled simply "the perfectible animal." The only changes and developments that occur among beasts, leaving aside those brought about as a consequence of human action, are natural changes occurring as a consequence of the operation of natural laws. Thus whereas brutes have a natural history, they have no cultural or spiritual history, and, again prescinding from the effects of human action, the life and activity of a cow or a dog is precisely the same today as it was three thousand years ago. But man, unlike the brutes, has, in virtue of his perfectibility, a cultural or spiritual history, and the life of a civilized man today is considerably different from that of a savage and that of a civilized man living three thousand or even three hundred or a hundred years ago.

But though man is the perfectible animal, the capacity for self-improvement would remain wholly unactualized so long as he remains in the pure state of nature. In that state he would be perfectible only in the sense that his capacity for self-improvement could be exercised if his circumstances were different and he were transferred from the pure state of nature to society. So long as he remained in this state his capacity for self-improvement would lie dormant, and his perfectibility would be only implicit. With regard to the actual development of any of his capacities, he would be distinguishable from other animals primarily in terms of his physical differences from them, such as his bodily form and upright posture, and not in terms of the metaphysical or moral differences mentioned above. He would be "left by nature solely to the direction of instinct," his desires would "never go beyond his physical wants," the only goods he would recognize are "food, a female, and sleep," and the only evils he would fear are "pain and hunger." He would not, however, fear death, "for no animal can know what it is to die; the knowledge of death and its terrors being one of the first acquisitions made by man in departing from an animal state."[24] Moreover, in the pure state of nature man, like the brutes, would have only a natural history—he would make no cultural or spiritual progress whatever and would thus have no cultural or spiritual history.

If by accident he made any discovery, he was the less able to communicate it to others, as he did not know even his own children. Every art would necessarily perish with its inventor, where there was no kind of education among men, and generations succeeded generations without the least advance; when, all setting out from the same point, centuries must have elapsed in the barbarism of the first ages: when the race was already old, and man remained a child.[25]

Primitive man, therefore, in the pure state of nature, though containing within himself the germ of perfectibility and of the capacity for self-improvement, and in this respect potentially different metaphysically or morally from other animals, would nevertheless remain in actuality a merely natural creature as distinct from a rational or moral agent, devoid of any cultural or spiritual history, and hence a savage, little more than a brute.

IV. Self-love and Natural Compassion

But though man in the pure state of nature would be a savage, he would be a savage of such a sort that we may properly refer to him as a "noble savage," even though this expression is to be found neither in *The Social Contract* nor in any of the three discourses. His nobility would issue primarily from two sources—from his independence and from his natural compassion. Of his independence I have already spoken, to some extent, in speaking of the pure state of nature, for this is a state of independence. In it there are no settled or permanent relations or associations among men. Such associations exist only in society, and bring with them the dependence of one man upon another, with the attendant evils of which we shall speak later. But in the pure state of nature no man is dependent upon any other man, and every man is therefore free from the evils attendant upon such dependence. Instead, each is independent of every other and therefore self-dependent. Each man depends upon himself alone for his preservation and well-being and thus attains a kind of nobility inaccessible to the dependent person. But this is only the natural nobility of the independent savage, not the rational and moral nobility attainable by man in society. Rousseau makes it clear that the two kinds of nobility cannot be completely possessed by the same person. Natural nobility is possible only for the independent savage, rational or moral nobility only for man in society. But man's entrance into society not only terminates his natural independence—it also dulls, and in some instances destroys, his natural compassion. It therefore contaminates both sources of his natural nobility.

According to Rousseau, there are two principles operating naturally within the human soul, prior to or independent of reason, "one of them deeply interesting us in our own welfare and preservation, and the other exciting a natural repugnance at seeing any other sensible being, and particularly any of our own species, suffer pain or death."[1] The first of these principles is self-love. This "is a natural feeling which leads every animal to look to its own preservation, and which, guided in man by reason and modified by compassion, creates humanity and virtue."[2] Self-love is to be distinguished from egoism. The former, as has just been seen, is a natural sentiment present in every animal and therefore in man, both in the pure state of nature and in society. Egoism, on the other hand, "is a purely relative and factitious feeling, which arises in the state of society, leads each individual to make more of himself than of any other, causes all the mutual damage men inflict one on another, and is the real source of the 'sense of honour.'"[3] Accordingly,

in our primitive condition, in the true state of nature, egoism did not exist; for as each man regarded himself as the only observer of his actions, the only being in the universe who took any interest in him, and the sole judge of his deserts, no feeling arising from comparisons he could not be led to make could take root in his soul; and for the same reason, he could know neither hatred nor the desire for revenge, since these passions can spring only from a sense of injury: and as it is the contempt or the intention to hurt, and not the harm done, which constitutes the injury, men who neither valued nor compared themselves could do one another much violence, when it suited them, without feeling any sense of injury. In a word, each man, regarding his fellows almost as he regarded animals of different species, might seize the prey of a weaker or yield up his own to a stronger, and yet consider these acts of violence as mere natural occurrences, without the slightest emotion of insolence or despite, or any other feeling than the joy or grief of success or failure.[4]

Although self-love, along with natural compassion, is one of the two fundamental principles operating naturally, i.e., independent of reason, in the soul of man, regardless of whether he be the primitive man of the pure state of nature or man in society, egoism is not. Instead, egoism presupposes the operation of the kind of reason of which man is capable only in

SELF-LOVE AND NATURAL COMPASSION

society, and therefore it is possible only in society. Egoism is therefore not natural to man, at least not in the way in which self-love and natural compassion are. Accordingly, Hobbes, in ascribing egoism to man in the state of nature, is guilty of attributing to the natural man a characteristic that is acquired only in society. He is therefore mistaken in supposing that glory, along with competition and diffidence, would be one of the three main causes of quarrel in the nature of man in the state of nature as well as in civil society. For glory leads men to quarrel for the sake of reputation or honor,[5] and in the pure state of nature there would be no reputation and no honor. Instead, the desire for glory is a vice possible only in society. Thus all its attendant evils, such as hatred, contempt, flattery, hypocrisy, revenge, and so on, along with its silencing of the voice of natural compassion, are also possible only in society. The absence of vainglory in the state of nature does not, however, mean that in that state there would be a total absence of quarreling and fighting and of the wounding and killing of man by man, for competition and diffidence are natural to man. But their effects would be moderated by the absence of vanity. For in the state of nature men

maintained no kind of intercourse with one another, and were consequently strangers to vanity, deference, esteem, and contempt; they had not the least idea of *meum* and *tuum*, and no true conception of justice; they looked upon every violence to which they were subjected, rather as an injury that might easily be repaired than as a crime that ought to be punished; and they never thought of taking revenge, unless perhaps mechanically and on the spot, as a dog will sometimes bite the stone which is thrown at him. Their quarrels would therefore seldom have very bloody consequences; for the subject of them would be merely the question of subsistence.[6]

But not only would the quarrels of the state of nature be minimized and their effects lessened by the absence of vanity—the operation of natural compassion would have the same result.

Natural compassion is pre-reflective, and is "so natural, that the very brutes themselves sometimes give evident proofs of it."[7] But not only is it pre-reflective, it is also more fundamental than morality, which, as presupposing reason, is reflective. For "in spite of all their morality, men would have never been better than monsters, had not nature bestowed on them a sense of compassion, to aid their reason."[8] Here Rousseau seems to be saying that moral principles must ultimately be grounded in compassion rather than reason, that no one could seek to act in accordance with the principles of a non-egoistic ethic, independent of considerations of self-love or of egoistic considerations, unless he were moved by natural compassion. Reason alone is cold, whereas compassion is warm, and unless reason is warmed by compassion the engine of moral agency will not move.

To this the rationalist in ethics may object that if morality must ultimately be grounded in natural compassion, then the consequence is a kind of pernicious relativism or subjectivism. For it would then be impossible rationally to convince those lacking in compassion to act in accordance with non-egoistic moral principles, except insofar as they can be convinced that to do so is compatible with the promotion of their own good. But if they lack compassion and cannot be convinced that action in accordance with non-egoistic principles is compatible with the promotion of their own good, then the only way in which they can be induced to act in accordance with such principles is to convince them of the intrinsic rationality of these principles. This, however, is easier said than done. For the ethical egoist can also insist that his ultimate egoistic principles are intrinsically rational. In this case we should have a situation in which two persons hold ultimately conflicting moral principles, yet claim that their ultimate principles are intrinsically rational. If so, there would seem to be no rational way to resolve the conflict between them, except through showing either that one of the two positions, egoism or non-egoism, is internally incoherent, or else that one of them is incompatible with some still more fundamental rational principle acceptable to both. It is doubtful that this could be done, however. Unpleasant as it may be for the ethical rationalist, the fact of the matter seems simply to be that genuinely ultimate ethical disagreements cannot be resolved by means of reason. The rationalist is therefore no better off in combatting relativism or subjectivism than he who makes his ultimate appeal to compassion. The rationalist therefore has no greater justification for claiming that attempts to ground morality in compassion lead to a pernicious relativism or subjectivism than he who makes such attempts would have for claiming that appeals to reason would lead to such a result. Indeed, the person who appeals to compassion is perhaps in a better position than the rationalist. For by not claiming to establish rationally his fundamental ethical principles, he does not disappoint those to whom the rationalist makes this claim by failing to make good on it. The rationalist, on the other hand, in failing to make good his claim, runs the risk of having those to whom he makes it regard not only him but also reason with a certain contempt.

For Rousseau, then, morality must ultimately be grounded in prereflective natural compassion, and the principles of morality are effective in guiding conduct only if and insofar as men are animated by such compassion. This compassion is ultimately "the only natural virtue."[9]

Other virtues, such as generosity, clemency, humanity, benevolence, and friendship, are simply specific developments of compassion. Generosity is compassion applied to the weak, clemency is compassion applied to the guilty, and humanity is compassion applied to mankind in general.[10] Compassion occupies much the same place in the thought of Rousseau as charity does in that of St. Paul, so that Rousseau might well paraphrase the apostle: "Though I speak with the tongues of men and of angels, and have not compassion, I am become as sounding brass, or a tinkling cymbal."

But for Rousseau compassion would be much stronger in a state of nature than in a state of reason. For it is stronger "the more the animal beholding any kind of distress identifies himself with the animal that suffers," and such identification would be "much more perfect in a state of nature than it is in a state of reason." For "it is reason which turns man's mind back upon itself, and divides him from everything that could disturb or afflict him. It is philosophy that isolates him, and bids him say, at sight of the misfortunes of others: 'Perish if you will, I am secure.'" Uncivilized man, on the other hand, "for want of reason and wisdom, is always foolishly ready to obey the first promptings of humanity."[11] In other words, it is by means of reason that man becomes conscious of himself as an individual distinct from other individuals. Man in the pure state of nature is not thus self-conscious and therefore does not sharply demarcate himself as an individual distinct from other individuals. Whereas the civilized man—the philosopher—in virtue of his self-consciousness and his consciousness of his distinctness from others, can separate himself from the sufferings of others, and even take comfort in the fact that it is they and not he who suffer, the primitive man, devoid of reason and therefore of self-consciousness, and thus unable to draw precise, exquisite, and comforting distinctions between himself and others, simply identifies or confuses himself with his fellow creatures, takes joy in their joy and suffers from their suffering in a spontaneous, natural, and wholly unreflective and un-self-conscious way. The civilized man, conscious of himself and his distinctness, confronted with the suffering of another, can simply turn away and gaze upon himself and his own good fortune, whereas the primitive man, lacking this sophistication, is fixated by the suffering of another, which, like a fire, consumes his soul as well as that of the unhappy creature upon whom his gaze is fixed. Thus should a murder be committed under the philosopher's window, "he has only to put his hands to his ears and argue a little with himself, to prevent nature, which is shocked within him, from identifying itself with the unfortunate sufferer." The primitive man lacks "this admirable talent."[12]

Though he undoubtedly exaggerates, Rousseau is pointing to an important truth. For even though the primitive man may not necessarily be
more compassionate than the civilized man, it seems fairly certain that an
increase in intellectual sophistication and virtuosity within civilization is
by no means invariably accompanied by a concomitant increase in compassion. Socrates, Rousseau claims, is mistaken. Virtue is not knowledge,
nor does it rest ultimately upon knowledge. On the contrary, virtue is
compassion to the extent that it stems ultimately from and is impossible
without compassion. The rationalist or intellectualist in ethics might reply
that just as percepts without concepts are blind, so also is compassion
without reason. Rousseau, however, says nothing to deny this. He does
not deny that the use of reason is necessary, especially in society, if the
purposes posited by compassion are to be fulfilled. But though reason is
necessary if compassionate ends are to be attained, it, alone, is not
sufficient to make moral action possible. Indeed, just as concepts without
percepts are empty, so is reason without compassion. Just as neither concepts nor percepts are sufficient without the other to afford knowledge of
the world, neither is reason nor compassion sufficient by itself to effect
moral action. Instead, each is necessary—compassion to get the engine of
moral agency to move and reason to guide it once it is made to move. It is
the importance of compassion, however, that Rousseau emphasizes. His
point is that a man may be the most exquisite of reasoners and, if he lacks
compassion, still be morally corrupt or egoistic.

We have seen, however, that in the pure state of nature no one would be
an exquisite reasoner. Yet neither would anyone be either morally corrupt
or a convinced egoist. Instead, the natural feeling of compassion

in a state of nature supplies the place of laws, morals, and virtues, with the
advantage that none are tempted to disobey its gentle voice: it is this which will
always prevent a sturdy savage from robbing a weak child or a feeble old man of
the sustenance they may have with pain and difficulty acquired, if he sees a
possibility of providing for himself by other means: it is this which, instead of
inculcating that sublime maxim of rational justice, *Do to others as you would have them
do unto you*, inspires all men with that other maxim of natural goodness, much less
perfect indeed, but perhaps more useful: *Do good to yourself with as little evil as
possible to others*. In a word, it is rather in this natural feeling than in any subtle
arguments that we must look for the cause of that repugnance, which every man
would experience in doing evil, even independently of the maxims of education.[13]

There are at least three points in these words that require comment.

The first is that compassion, though natural to man, is not quite as
fundamental as self-love. Although the presence of natural compassion
within the primitive man would mean that egoism could not properly be

ascribed to him, the natural man would still seek his own good first. But his self-love would be moderated by his natural compassion, and he would naturally seek his own good through attempting to do as little harm as possible to others.

The second point is that although the maxim of natural goodness, "Do good to yourself with as little evil as possible to others," would be more useful in the pure state of nature than the maxim of rational goodness, "Do to others as you would have them do unto you," it is less perfect. As we shall see more fully later, this means that Rousseau distinguishes sharply between the order of nature on the one hand and the order of reason and morality on the other. This brings us to the third point.

This is that the natural maxim of the state of nature is natural, not rational. This means that in the state of nature man would naturally act in accordance with this maxim, without necessarily being conscious either of the maxim or that he is acting in accordance with it. This in turn means that this maxim would not, properly speaking, be a maxim. For a maxim is a rule one imposes upon oneself, and of which one must therefore be conscious; it is also, therefore, a rational precept, in the sense that it is a rule that only a rational agent can impose upon himself. Thus Rousseau's maxim of natural goodness would be a kind of natural law describing rather than prescribing the behavior of the natural man. Just as unsupported bodies fall and hungry beasts seek food without any consciousness of a law ordaining that they do so or without even being aware of the fact that they do so, so also the natural man naturally seeks to do good to himself with as little evil as possible to others from a necessity of his nature, independent of any consciousness of a law prescribing that he do so and that he freely imposes upon himself.

V. Perfectibility and Corruptibility

It is clear, then, that for Rousseau the primitive man of the pure state of nature would be a thoroughly natural creature, not a rational or moral agent. He would, in other words, be a complete savage. But he would be a noble savage, his nobility issuing from his independence and his natural compassion. Given, however, his nature as a purely natural creature, his nobility would also issue from his innocence. Since he would behave merely in accordance with natural laws imposed upon him from without and would have no consciousness of laws that he is free either to impose upon himself or to reject, he would be innocent of, because incapable of, immorality or sin. Rousseau concurs with Hobbes that "The Desires, and other Passions of man, are in themselves no Sin. No more are the Actions, that proceed from those Passions, till they know a law that forbids them."[1] For Rousseau both morality and immorality or sin presuppose the possibility of moral agency, which in turn presupposes the possibility of rational agency—that is, consciousness of a law that one is free either to accept or reject. The natural man acquires such consciousness and becomes a rational and a moral agent only within society, and therefore is capable of acting either morally or immorally only as a member of society.

We have also seen that Rousseau maintains that man, even in the pure state of nature, is the perfectible animal. Although his capacity for rationality and moral agency can be exercised only in society, it is nevertheless present within him as implicit, nascent, or dormant even in the state of nature. To say, however, that man is the perfectible animal is also to say that he is the corruptible animal. Just as no other animal is perfectible in the way in which man is, so also is no other animal corruptible in the way in which man is. Just as his capacity for moral action is present, though dormant, within him in the state of nature, so also is his capacity for immoral action present within him in the state of nature. Indeed, this capacity is even more profoundly present within him in that state than is his capacity for moral action. This is the case for two reasons.

The first is that self-love is naturally more fundamental or powerful than natural compassion. Although, as we have seen, natural compassion would naturally moderate self-love in the state of nature, it would not replace it, and each man would naturally seek his own good first, moderating his quest for his own good with compassion for others only insofar as he believes, un-self-consciously, that such moderation is compatible with the promotion of his own good. That self-love is more fundamental or powerful than natural compassion is also supported by the fact that the latter is more easily destroyed than the former—by the fact, that is, that natural compassion is more easily muted by a morally corrupt society than self-love is moderated by a morally good one.

This brings us to the second reason man's capacity for immorality is more profoundly imbedded in his being than is his capacity for morality: the moral order is precisely the reverse of the natural order. The good the moral law commands us to seek is always the general or the common good, not our exclusive private good, whereas the good we naturally seek first is precisely our exclusive private good. Even in states with the best constitution and laws, in which there is a union of the general good and the private good, so that the individual promotes his private good through acting compatibly with the promotion of the general good, there is a tension between the moral order and the natural order, and the individual naturally tends to seek his exclusive private good at the expense of the common good.[2] The moral object of legislation is to reverse the natural order and, so far as possible, to replace the natural order with the moral order, by placing the general good first and one's exclusive private good second. Indeed, so powerful is the natural order and the impulse of self-love that the natural order can be reversed only through establishing a political order in which the private good of the individual is incorporated into the general good in such a way that the individual can promote his private good only by acting compatibly with the promotion of the common good. But Rousseau is not so optimistic as to suppose that such a political order can perfectly and permanently be established. Regardless of how perfect a political order may be, the natural pull of self-love and private interest inevitably exerts its force against the moral order, and every political order "begins to die as soon as it is born, and carries in itself the causes of its destruction."[3] These causes, we have just seen, are natural, not moral— every political order, because it contains a natural component, eventually dies a natural death. Therefore, "If we would set up a long-lived form of government, let us not even dream of making it eternal. If we are to succeed, we must not attempt the impossible, or flatter ourselves that we are endowing the work of man with a stability of which human conditions do not permit.[4]

Man, then, is not only the perfectible animal—he is also the corruptible animal. The seed of corruptibility as well as the seed of perfectibility are implanted within man at conception, and the extent to which each seed will develop, flower, and bear fruit depends upon the soil in which the man himself has his roots and the nourishment he receives. Should he be left to live in the barren soil of the pure state of nature, devoid of the nourishment that society alone can give, neither seed can develop. To expect either to develop under such conditions would be like expecting an acorn imbedded in a barren desert devoid of nourishment to develop into an oak. But though Rousseau emphasizes the importance of environmental conditions in influencing the extent to which the double seeds within man are developed, it is also important to recognize that he never says or implies that environmental conditions are everything. Although environmental circumstances play a fundamental role in influencing the development of man's potentialities, these potentialities must be present within him from the beginning, even in the pure state of nature. It is man alone among the animals who is at once perfectible and corruptible, and thus man alone who is capable of having a spiritual or cultural history as well as a natural history. Brutes are neither perfectible nor corruptible, regardless of the circumstances in which they are placed, and are thus capable only of a natural history, not a cultural or spiritual history. To expect a brute to develop into what a man can become by placing it in the most favorable of circumstances would be like expecting a pebble to develop into a tree by planting it in the most fertile soil and faithfully watering it daily. Just as there is something in the nature of an acorn, and not a pebble, that permits it to develop into a tree, so also there is something in the nature of man, but not in the brute, that permits him either perfectibility or corruption.

A potentiality both for moral good and for moral evil is inherent, then, in the nature of man, even in the pure state of nature. This potentiality, however, is actualized in either direction only as man becomes a rational and moral agent by living in society. In the pure state of nature he would be a completely natural creature, incapable of rational and moral agency, and thus incapable of moral good and evil. The pure state of nature is thus a state of innocence. Just as brutes and small children, through an inability to act as moral agents, are innocent of either moral good or moral evil, so man in the state of nature remains a child. But just as small children, according to traditional Christian theology, are born in a state of original sin, so also Rousseau's primitive man may be said to be in such a state, provided that "original sin" be interpreted as referring to an innate predisposition to prefer oneself before others, which in action is morally culpable and sinful when one comes to a consciousness of a law that forbids such action. For we have seen that for Rousseau self-love, though moderated by natural compassion, especially in the case of the primitive man, is nevertheless more powerful than compassion, even in the case of the primitive man. We have also seen that self-love, as part of the natural order, is opposed to the moral order, since it pulls us in a direction opposite to that commanded by the moral law. In the moral order the general good takes precedence over the exclusive private good of the individual, whereas in the natural order the exclusive private good of the individual takes precedence over the common good. Since each man's original nature predisposes him thus to prefer himself, his original nature is such as to make him sinful by nature. But this original or natural sin is only potential sin—it is only an original or natural predisposition to sin, and becomes actualized only after one has become a rational or moral agent, conscious of a general good distinct from one's private exclusive good, and pursues the latter at the expense of the former. Since small children eventually become rational agents, yet by nature continue to prefer their private good at the expense of the common good, they are in a state of original, natural, or potential sin from the moment of birth. The same applies to the primitive man of the state of nature, since he too has the potentiality of becoming a rational agent. But it does not apply to brutes, since they totally lack this potentiality.

Although, then, the natural man is naturally good, this does not mean that he is morally good. He is naturally good in the same sense in which the Christian is bound to regard every purely natural creature as naturally good, as something created and sustained by God. Though he is naturally good in the sense in which any purely natural creature is, the seeds of sin are nevertheless implanted within his original nature, and require only the transformation by society of the natural man into a rational and moral agent in order to develop into the fruit of actual sin. For the author of *Genesis*, of course, man's fall into sin came originally through his disobeying the divine command, and on this point Rousseau therefore seems to be in disagreement. It must be kept in mind, however, that Rousseau, in his account of the natural man, is prescinding from revelation as well as from the influences of society on man. He makes it clear in the second discourse that he is speaking philosophically and is no more theologizing than he is reciting history.[5] The author of *Genesis* had no more described the primitive man of the pure state of nature than had Hobbes or Locke, since he ascribes to the original man sufficient rationality to be conscious of the divine command and sufficient moral agency to be free either to obey or disobey it. This means that for the author of *Genesis*, as well as for Hobbes and Locke, the characteristic which essentially distinguishes man from the brutes is his rationality, whereas for Rousseau it is the human form. The primitive man of the pure state of nature would still be a man and not a brute in virtue of his body, even though he be a purely natural creature incapable of rational or moral agency.

This, however, does not mean that Rousseau is implying that man is nothing more than a body of a certain sort, for, as we have seen, he also recognizes that man alone among the animals is perfectible and corruptible. Whereas previous thinkers had tended to emphasize man's metaphysical and moral differences from the brutes and to neglect the physical differences, Rousseau recognizes that the physical differences are also important. But they are still not as important as the metaphysical and moral differences. For although man differs from the brutes in virtue of his human form, this difference is not as important as the fact that man, in virtue of his capacity for rational and moral agency, is at once both the perfectible and the corruptible animal, whereas no brute is, and the development of this capacity leads to greater and more significant differences between man and brute than any that consist only in physical differences between them.

VI. The Transition to Pre-civil Society

It is time now to turn to Rousseau's account of the transition from the state of nature to society. This transition is of supreme metaphysical and moral importance, as it is crucial in the development of all the metaphysical and moral differences between man and brute. Rousseau's account of this transition is presented in some detail in the second discourse. He admits, however, that his account of it, like his account of the state of nature, is conjectural. But just as he presents his conjectures concerning the latter as reasonable ones, in the sense that it is reasonable to make them if our object is to arrive at some notion of what would remain of the nature of man and what the human condition would be if we abstracted completely from the effects of society upon man, he also claims that his conjectures concerning the transition from a state of nature to society "become reasons, when they are the most probable that can be drawn from the nature of things, and the only means of discovering the truth."[1]

But regardless of how conjectural his account may be, he denies that the consequences of the transition are conjectural. For these consequences are simply society as it exists and its effects on man. Conjecture is not necessary in order to discover the nature of actual society and the condition of man in it, as observation is possible and sufficient. Accordingly, he maintains that it would be impossible to form a reasonable theory as an alternative to his account "that would not furnish the same results, and from which . . . the same conclusions" could not be drawn.[2] Given, that is, the nature of actual society and the condition of man in it, any theory presented as an account of the transition from the state of nature to society, to be acceptable, would have to be compatible with the nature of actual society and of man in it as these are observed. But although Rousseau concedes that his conjectural account of the transition is not the only possible and reasonable one, he nonetheless leaves his reader with the distinct impression that he has more than a little confidence in the acceptability of his own account.

But, the question now arises, since Rousseau presents his account of the state of nature only as reasonable conjecture and does not assert its historicity, is it necessary that he present an account of the transition from the state of nature to society, and is there even any point in attempting to do so? Is there, that is, any point in presenting an account of the transition from a state whose existence is not categorically asserted, much less established empirically or historically, to the actual state of society and the condition of man in it? Indeed, if the existence of the original primitive state is not categorically asserted, then neither can the transition from it to actual society be categorically asserted.

This last, of course, must be admitted. But although Rousseau does not categorically assert the historicity of the state of nature, neither does he categorically deny its historicity. On the contrary, he tends to leave open the question of its historicity, as if to say that we do not know for certain

THE TRANSITION TO PRE-CIVIL SOCIETY

whether men ever lived in such a state or not. If we knew that they never did, then the problem of accounting for the transition from such a state to society simply would not arise. But if they once did, then this problem does arise. And since it is at least logically or abstractly possible that they once did, it is necessary that some account be presented of how the transition from such a state to society could occur. Such an account, however, because of the lack of our knowledge as to the historicity of the state of nature, must be conjectural. There are no historical facts or data to which we can appeal in settling the question of how the transition, if it did in fact occur, came about. The best we can hope to do is to form reasonable conjectures.

Such a transition cannot be accounted for by supposing that one man imposes his rule on others. This is the case because there would be an approximate equality of power in the state of nature. Although there would be some inequality among men in this state, it would hardly be felt, and its influence would be "next to nothing."[3] There would be differences among men in this state, but many of the differences which are alleged to be natural are in fact "the effect of . . . the different methods of life men adopt in society."[4] It is therefore "easy to conceive how much less the difference between man and man must be in a state of nature than in a state of society, and how greatly the natural inequality of mankind must be increased by the inequalities of social institutions."[5] Whereas in society the strong oppress the weak, in the state of nature there would be no dominion and no servitude. One man "might seize the fruits which another had gathered, the game he had killed, or the cave he had chosen for shelter," but he would be unable to exact permanent obedience, for there can be no ties of dependence among men without possessions.

If, for instance, I am driven from one tree, I can go to the next; if I am disturbed in one place, what hinders me from going to another? Again, should I happen to meet with a man so much stronger than myself, and at the same time so depraved, so indolent, and so barbarous, as to compel me to provide for his sustenance while he himself remains idle; he must take care not to have his eyes off me for a single moment; he must bind me fast before he goes to sleep, or I shall certainly either knock him on the head or make my escape. That is to say, he must in such a case voluntarily expose himself to much greater trouble than he seeks to avoid, or can give me. After all this, let him be off his guard ever so little; let him but turn his head aside at any sudden noise, and I shall be instantly twenty paces off, lost in the forest, and, my fetters burst asunder, he would never see me again.[6]

From the fact that no man in the state of nature would have sufficient power to establish dominion over any other man, it follows that no man would have sufficient power to enslave another. Slavery is possible only

within society, not in the state of nature. Aristotle was correct in claiming
that men are not equal by nature and that "some are born for slavery, and
others for dominion" only as this claim applies to men in society, not as it
applies to men in the state of nature. For although men in society are
sometimes born in slavery, no man in the state of nature would be born a
slave. "Nothing can be more certain than that every man born in slavery is
born for slavery. Slaves lose everything in their chains, even the desire of
escaping from them: they love their servitude."[7] Aristotle is guilty of
taking "the effect for the cause." If a man is born into slavery and treated as
a slave his entire life, he may well behave as a slave and even love his
slavery. This confused Aristotle and led him to believe that men can be
slaves by nature. But it is not nature that makes slaves, but society, and in
the state of nature there is no such thing as slavery.

As the bonds of servitude are formed merely by the mutual dependence of men on
one another and the reciprocal needs that unite them, it is impossible to make any
man a slave, unless he be first reduced to a situation in which he cannot do without
the help of others: and, since such a situation does not exist in a state of nature,
every one is there his own master, and the law of the strongest is of no effect.[8]

Although a life lived in slavery may so affect a man's nature as to lead
someone such as Aristotle to suppose that some are slaves by nature, this
supposition can be made only by someone who fails to distinguish between, on the one hand, the original nature of man and, on the other, his
nature as affected and either perfected or corrupted by society. "If then
there are slaves by nature, it is because there have been slaves against
nature. Force made the first slaves, and their cowardice perpetuated the
condition."[9] But such force would be possible only in society, not in the
state of nature. No man, regardless of how powerful he might be, would
be able by himself permanently to subjugate another, if for no other
reason than that in sleep the strongest is as defenseless as the weakest if
there is no one to protect him. Although a group of men may possess
sufficient power permanently to subjugate individuals and other groups,
no individual acting singly could possess such power.

    From this it follows that the first associations could be formed only
through the consent of the individuals who form them. The question
therefore arises of what in the state of nature would lead men to form
associations. Rousseau answers this question quite succinctly in *The Social
Contract*. Associations are formed when men in the state of nature "have
reached the point at which the obstacles in the way of their preservation in
the state of nature show their power of resistance to be greater than the
resources at the disposal of each individual for his maintenance in that

state. That primitive condition can then subsist no longer; and the human race would perish unless it changed its manner of existence."[10] This, however, does not mean that the presence of impediments to one's preservation too great to be overcome singly would lead immediately to the formation of permanent associations. Instead, the primitive man of the state of nature would

distinguish the few cases, in which mutual interest might justify him in relying upon the assistance of his fellows; and also the still fewer cases in which a conflict of interests might give cause to suspect them. In the former case, he joined in the same herd with them, or at most in some kind of loose association, that laid no restraint on its members, and lasted no longer than the transitory occasion that formed it. In the latter case, every one sought his own private advantage, either by open force, if he thought himself strong enough, or by address and cunning, if he felt himself the weaker.

In this manner, men may have insensibly acquired some gross ideas of the advantages of mutual undertakings, and of the advantages of fulfilling them.[11]

This means that temporary associations formed for the purpose of solving transitory problems probably preceded the formation of permanent associations. Associations of the latter sort came to be formed only when men "ceased to fall asleep under the first tree, or in the first cave that afforded them shelter," and began to make huts. "This was the epoch of a first revolution," for two reasons. One is that it led to the establishing and distinguishing of families; the other is that it led to the introduction of a kind of property.[12] As the first huts were probably made by the strongest, who felt able to defend them, they were imitated by the weaker, who found it less trouble to build their own huts than to attempt to dislodge those who had already built huts, as this attempt would lead to a desperate battle with the family occupying the hut they sought to take.

The construction of simple huts united families under a single roof, and led to "the first expansions of the human heart.... and to the finest feelings known to humanity, conjugal love and paternal affection. Every family became a little society, the more united because liberty and reciprocal attachment were the only bonds of its union."[13] With the coming of the family there came also a division of labor between the sexes, which hitherto had led the same kind of life, and "both sexes also began to lose something of their strength and ferocity: but, if individuals became to some extent less able to encounter wild beasts separately, they found it, on the other hand, easier to assemble and resist in common."[14] Although the formation of the family made possible "the finest feelings known to humanity," it was also attended with certain evils. It afforded men the leisure to acquire conveniences that heretofore they could not acquire. Their acquisition was "the first yoke" that man "inadvertently imposed on himself, and the first source of the evils he prepared for his descendants." For "these conveniences lost with use almost all their power to please, and even degenerated into real needs, till the want of them became far more disagreeable than the possession of them had been pleasant."[15]

The existence of the family led naturally to the formation of larger societies, for "permanent neighborhood could not fail to produce, in time, some connection between different families." Eventually a distinct nation arose "united in character and manners, not by regulations or laws, but by uniformity of life and food, and the common influence of climate." As societies wider than the family came into existence, each man "began to consider the rest, and to wish to be considered in turn; and thus a value came to be attached to public esteem." Those who excelled in some respect "came to be of most consideration; . . . this was the first step towards inequality, and at the same time towards vice." For those who excelled and received esteem became vain and contemptuous, and those who did not began to feel shame and envy, "and the fermentation caused by these new leavens ended by producing combinations fatal to innocence and happiness."[16] Every man began to demand consideration, "and it became impossible to refuse it to any with impunity." In this way "the first obligations of civility" arose; "and every intended injury became an affront; because, besides the hurt which might arise from it, the party injured was certain to find in it a contempt for his person, which was often more insupportable than the hurt itself."[17] This led men to seek revenge, which was "bloody and cruel." This, Rousseau says, is "the state reached by most of the savage nations known to us." These tribes, however, have already left the state of nature, and it is because writers have confused their way of life with the state of nature that they "have hastily concluded that man is naturally cruel, and requires civil institutions to make him more mild; whereas nothing is more gentle than man in his primitive state."[18]

From the preceding it is clear that Rousseau distinguishes between three stages: (1) the state of nature prior to the formation of temporary associations for the purpose of solving transitory problems; (2) the state of nature subsequent to the formation of such temporary associations; and (3) the existence of permanent pre-civil societies such as families, tribes, and even nations. In the third stage man is no longer the natural and innocent creature he was in the state of nature, and has already begun to be corrupted by society. But although in the third stage there is some diminution of his natural compassion, his corruption is still not as complete as it is in civil society. Indeed, it is it rather than the state of nature that Rousseau refers to as "the happiest and most stable of epochs" and as "altogether the very best man could experience," in which there is an "expansion of the human faculties, keeping a just mean between the indolence of the primitive state and the petulance of our egoism."[19] Although subsequent advances seem to be "so many steps towards the perfection of the individual," in reality they have been so many steps "towards the decrepitude of the species." Man could have departed from this third stage "only through some fatal accident, which, for the public good, should never have happened."[20] The question therefore is: what was this fatal accident?

VII. The Institution of Property

The answer, stated simply, is the introduction of private property in land. As Rousseau rhetorically puts it, "The first man who, having enclosed a piece of ground, bethought himself of saying 'This is mine,' and found people simple enough to believe him, was the real founder of civil society."[1] The private enclosure of land, however, is not something that could have suddenly occurred out of the blue. On the contrary, certain conditions had to exist before such enclosure could occur. These were the development of agriculture and metallurgy. So long as men subsisted solely by hunting and fishing and by gathering fruits and nuts and berries there was no need for such enclosure. But agriculture is impossible unless land is enclosed, either by a group or by an individual. The development of agriculture in turn presupposed the development of metallurgy, which was "necessary to compel mankind to apply themselves to agriculture." Rousseau's reason for the latter claim is as follows.

No sooner were artificers wanted to smelt and forge iron, than others were required to maintain them; the more hands that were employed in manufactures, the fewer were left to provide for the common subsistence, though the number of mouths to be furnished with food remained the same: and as some required commodities in exchange for their iron, the rest at length discovered the method of making iron serve for the multiplication of commodities. By this means the arts of husbandry and agriculture were established on the one hand, and the art of working metals and multiplying their uses on the other.[2]

The development of metallurgy made the development of agriculture necessary because those who devoted their time to making iron implements could not also devote their time to producing food. Here Rousseau seems to be supposing that by this time men had come to see that more food could be produced through turning to agriculture than through relying simply upon hunting, fishing, and gathering fruits and nuts. The workers supplied the farmers with tools, the farmers supplied the workers with food, and the labor of each gave him title to what he produced, the worker acquiring title through the use of the hammer and the farmer through the use of the sickle.

The development of metallurgy and agriculture destroyed the natural equality and independence still extant in pre-civil society and replaced them with a dependence of one man upon another and an inequality of property. Prior to the introduction of these two arts men supplied their needs for food and clothing by hunting, fishing, and gathering nuts and fruits, all of which could be accomplished by a single individual working alone and none of which led to significant inequalities of wealth. Moreover, so long as men

undertook only what a single person could accomplish, . . . they lived free, healthy, honest, and happy lives, so long as their nature allowed . . . . But from the moment one man began to stand in need of the help of another; from the moment it appeared advantageous to any one man to have enough provisions for two, equality disappeared, property was introduced, work became indispensable, and vast forests became smiling fields, which man had to water with the sweat of his brow, and where slavery and misery were soon seen to germinate and grow up with the crops.[3]

Even after the entry into pre-civil society centuries must have elapsed before metallurgy and agriculture began to be developed, for they both require a foresight foreign to the savage. This is particularly true of agriculture, in which it is necessary "to consent to immediate loss, in order to reap a future gain," and in which it is necessary to prevent others from robbing one of the fruit of one's labor.[4]

Agriculture necessarily brought about the distribution of land, and this in turn brought about "a new kind of right." This is "the right of property, which is different from the right deducible from the law of nature."[5] It is clear that here Rousseau is using "property" in a much narrower sense than Locke had done. Locke had used it in such a way that even in the state of nature the deer a man kills, the fish he catches, and the fruit and nuts he gathers are all his property, provided that his possession of them does not violate the rights of others. Rousseau, on the other hand, is using it in such a way that none of these would count as property, at least not in the state of nature. Instead, he is using it to refer only to the possession of land and its produce. This is connected with his denial that the right of property is deducible from the law of nature.

As we shall see more fully in our examination of *The Social Contract*, Rousseau admits as natural rights only two of the three fundamental natural rights Locke distinguishes. These are life and liberty. For Rousseau, as for Locke, each man has a natural right to life, and no man is subject by nature to the authority of any other man. But although Rousseau denies that the deer a man kills, the fish he catches, and the fruit and nuts he gathers in the state of nature are his property, or at least does not refer to them as such, he does not deny that he has a natural right to them. He does have such a right, for this right is comprehended in his natural right to life, inasmuch as his right to life can be sustained only in getting and eating food. The right to property in land, on the other hand, is not a natural right, for such property is not necessary for the preservation of one's life, either in the state of nature or in pre-civil society prior to the institution of property in land. Even if property in land should become necessary for one's preservation subsequent to its institution, it still would not be a natural right, as it would become necessary only as a consequence of human acts or conventions and not as a consequence of the operations of nature. This is to say that it could be a natural right only if it were necessary for one's preservation under all conditions of life, whether in the state of nature, in pre-civil society, or in civil society, independent of any human acts or conventions.

Rousseau therefore insists, at least as strongly as Locke had done, that the possession of a natural right depends neither upon its recognition by any human being nor upon any other human act or convention, but instead upon the nature of man. This is at least part of the reason he goes to such great length to attempt to establish the natural equality of all men, and to show that the great inequalities among men are the product of society and not nature. He is convinced that the claim that every man has a natural right to liberty, in the sense that no man is subject by nature to the authority of any other man, cannot be grounded unless it can be shown that there is a natural equality among men, regardless of how obscured it may be as a consequence of the inequalities produced by various social conditions. Indeed, Rousseau is, if anything, more insistent than Locke upon the independence of natural right of human recognition, for he maintains that each man has a natural right to life, to everything necessary by nature for life, and to liberty even in the state of nature, in which no one recognizes, at least not abstractly or explicitly, the existence of such rights. Indeed, such rights are not thus recognized even in pre-civil society, and are recognized abstractly or explicitly only by some men and not all even in civil society. This contrasts with Locke, who, though he never maintained that natural rights depend upon human recognition, did maintain that there is a kind of implicit or obscure recognition of them on the part of every man, even in the state of nature. Rousseau's insistence on the independence of natural right of human recognition is therefore connected with his denial that there is a natural right to property, for in his view, as we have seen, the right to property is dependent upon human recognition.

Rousseau, then, admits only two of Locke's three fundamental natural rights—life and liberty. This, however, is misleading unless we bear in mind that Rousseau, in refusing to admit a natural right to property, is using the term "property" more narrowly than Locke had done. If we use the term in the broad sense in which Locke used it, then there is also for Rousseau a natural right to at least those forms of property, in Locke's sense of the term, which are necessary for the maintenance of life, whether in the state of nature, in pre-civil society, or in civil society. But this right, as we have seen, is for Rousseau simply part of the right to life. For Rousseau as for Hobbes, each man has a natural right to whatever is necessary to preserve his life, and since food is thus necessary, he has a natural right to food. But he does not have such a right concerning enclosure of land. As Rousseau puts it, "the fruits of the earth belong to us all, and the earth itself to nobody."[6] Each man, that is, has a natural right to appropriate as much of the fruit of the earth as he needs to preserve himself, but no man has by nature a right to enclose part of the earth in such a way as to exclude others from its use. Part of the reason for this, as we have seen, is that such enclosure is not absolutely necessary for survival in the way in which food is.

But part of Rousseau's reason for denying a natural right to enclose land also seems to be a belief that such enclosure eventually proves to be incompatible with the natural right to liberty. He appears, that is, to be assuming that nothing can be a natural right if it is incompatible with some more fundamental natural right. As the right to liberty is a fundamental natural right, and as the enclosure of land eventually proves to be incompatible with the protection of each man's natural right to liberty, there can be no natural right to enclose land. Therefore, the right to enclose land can only be a conventional right, arising from agreements made by those who are already in society. In the state of nature, there could be no such agreements. They are possible only after men have entered society. They do not, however, presuppose the existence of civil society; in fact, they antedate civil society and lead to its development, as one of the primary causes of the development of civil society is the eventual recognition, on the part of those who have enclosed land, of the desirability of positive laws regulating holdings in land and guaranteeing a positive title to such holdings.

But although Rousseau rejects Locke's position that there is a natural right to property he agrees with Locke that labor alone can give a man title to property. Although property is possible only when pre-civil society has reached a level of sophistication at which men can agree with one another to respect the claims of each to the land they enclose, a man's enclosure of land, even though it be acknowledged by others, is justifiable only if he labors to make the land he encloses productive. Indeed, Rousseau is, if anything, even more insistent on this point than Locke had been, and insists that the labor must be manual labor.

It is impossible to conceive how property can come from anything but manual labour: for what else can a man add to things which he does not originally create, so as to make them his own property? It is the husbandman's labour alone that, giving him a title to the produce of the ground he has tilled, gives him a claim also to the land itself, at least till harvest; and so, from year to year, a constant possession which is easily transformed into property.[7]

There are thus two conditions that must be satisfied if property is to be possible, one of which may be said to be the factual condition, the other the moral condition. The factual condition is that a level of sophistication must be attained at which men can claim property and recognize the claims of others. Since this level can be attained only after pre-civil society has reached a certain stage of development, there can be no property in the state of nature. The moral condition is that both the claim to property and the recognition of the claim by others are justifiable only if those who make and are granted the claim by others labor either for or upon that which they claim as their property.

Thus although for Rousseau there is no natural right to property, and the existence and possession of property depend upon agreements entered into by the members of a society, there is nevertheless a certain natural or non-conventional condition that must be satisfied if claims to property, the recognition of such claims, and conventions adopted for granting such recognition are to be morally justified. In other words, there is a natural law limitation to the justifiability of claims to property, their recognition by others, and the conventions adopted by a society for granting such recognition. Indeed, it may not be too extreme to say that there is a sense in which Rousseau comes close to conceding that, given the attainment by a society of the level of sophistication that is necessary if its members are to make and concede claims to property, each man has a natural right to that upon which he labors and to that which he produces by means of his labor.

But however close Rousseau comes to saying this, he does not in fact say it. For there is a difference between saying, on the one hand, that, given the satisfaction of the other conditions that must be satisfied if property is to be possible, labor alone gives a title to property, and, on the other hand, that, given the satisfaction of these conditions, each man has a natural right to the produce of his labor. Moreover, in his discussion in *The Social Contract* of the right of the first occupier of land, he says that although "the right of the first occupier" is "more real than the right of the strongest," there being, as we shall see, no right of the strongest, it nevertheless "becomes a real right only when the right of property has already been established."[8]

This passage is somewhat puzzling. This is partly because he uses the term "real" as though there could be degrees of reality, at least as far as rights are concerned. The right of the first occupier, though more real than the right of the strongest, is nevertheless not necessarily a real right unless the right of property has already been established. It would there-fore seem to be a right that is neither entirely real nor entirely unreal, but something between the two. Such language may well lead to the rejoinder that although it is possible to understand what is meant by saying that something is real and something is unreal, it is difficult to understand what could be meant by saying that something is neither wholly real nor wholly unreal. Yet Rousseau's use of this language is, I think, intelligible. First, there is no right of the strongest. This, as I said, we shall see more fully later. Second, in saying that "the right of the first occupier . . . becomes a real right only when the right of property has already been established," Rousseau seems to be using the expression "real right" or "true right" to mean positive right. For there can be no positive right to property until the right to property is established within a society. Moreover, in the sentence following the one from which the preceding quotation is taken, he refers to "the positive act" that makes a man the owner of something. Thus in the state of nature and in pre-civil society prior to the establishment of positive rights of property there is no real, that is no positive, right of the first occupier. At the same time, however, the right of the first occupier is more real than that of the strongest, even prior to its establishment as a positive right. This, I think, can only mean that, in contrast to the right of the strongest, there is some sense in which the right of the first occupier is real. The question is: in what sense is it real?

The answer is something like the following. Whereas the fact that one man is stronger or more powerful than another does not constitute a justifiable claim on his part to any right that the weaker or less powerful man cannot also claim, this is not so in the case of the first occupier of a piece of land. Occupancy of a previously unoccupied piece of land by some person does justify, to some extent, his claim to continued occu-pancy of it. But it does not amount to a natural right to continued occu-pancy of it. Although "every man has naturally a right to everything he needs,"[9] continued occupancy of a given piece of land could be claimed as a natural right only if it were necessary in order to enable the first occupier to preserve his life or his liberty, to both of which he does have a natural right. But, as we shall see more fully when we examine *The Social Contract* in more detail, when the first occupier of a piece of land becomes a party to the social contract, he places himself and all his possessions under the direction of the general will of the community which comes into being as a consequence of the contract. The terms of the contract are such that he will be treated as an indivisible member of this community, the general good of which will include his good as much as that of any other member of the association. Moreover, in thus placing himself and all his possessions under the direction of the general will, his possessions are transformed into his property, through the granting of a positive title to them by the community. Prior to his membership in the community his possessions were not his property, since he had no positive right to them and had a natural right to them only insofar as his possession of them was necessary for the maintenance of either his life or his liberty.

But it is also worth mentioning that the general will of the community may also revoke any positive titles to property if, in the judgment of the community, to do so would be conducive to the promotion of the common good. This is to say that the terms of the social contract are such that each party to the contract grants the community a kind of eminent domain over all his possessions. Thus the community, not the individual, may be said to acquire an ultimate or permanent title to his possessions. "The right which each individual has to his own estate is always subordinate to the right which the community has over all; without this, there would be neither stability in the social tie, nor real force in the exercise of sovereignty."[10]

But though the right of the first occupier is, in itself, neither a natural nor a positive right, Rousseau specifies conditions remarkably similar to those Locke specifies for acquiring property in land. "First, the land must not yet be inhabited; secondly, a man must occupy only the amount he needs for his subsistence; and, in the third place, possession must be taken, not by an empty ceremony, but by labour and cultivation, the only sign of proprietorship that should be respected by others, in default of a legal title."[11] Unless these conditions are satisfied, a man or a people, regardless of how powerful he or they may be, who seize land and claim it as their own so as to exclude others, are guilty of a punishable usurpation, "since all others are being robbed, by such an act, of the place of habitation and the means of subsistence which nature gave them in common."[12] Thus "when Nuñez Balboa, standing on the seashore, took possession of the South Seas and the whole of South America in the name of the crown of Castille," his act was not "enough to dispossess all their actual inhabitants, and to shut out from them all the princes of the world." If it were, then such "ceremonies are idly multiplied, and the Catholic King need only take possession all at once, from his apartment, of the whole universe, merely making a subsequent reservation about what was already in the possession of other princes."[13] Thus although Rousseau refuses to assert forthrightly, as Locke had done, that there is a natural right to property, he does assert, no less than Locke, that ultimately it is labor alone that justifies the granting of a title to property.

If anything at all emerges from this involved discussion, it is that Rousseau's conception of the status of the right to property is at once both more complex and more sophisticated than that of Locke. Locke states forthrightly that each man has a natural right to property, including a natural right to enclose land, whereas Rousseau denies that there is such a right. Although each man has a natural right to whatever is necessary to enable him to maintain his life and liberty, no man has a natural right to enclose land. Second, whereas Rousseau recognizes explicitly that the enclosure of land presupposes a social situation in which the pure state of nature has been abandoned, Locke does not. Part of the reason for this is that Locke never envisages a pure state of nature devoid of all forms of human society, whereas Rousseau does. Because Locke supposed that men have always lived in some form of society, though not always in civil society, the question of whether property in land would exist in a pure state of nature was not as likely to occur to him as to Rousseau. But since it does occur to Rousseau, it is he rather than Locke who states explicitly that property in land is essentially social in nature. Finally, Rousseau is more explicit than Locke in his discussion of the effects of the institution of property upon the equality of men. This also is connected with the presence of a discussion of the pure state of nature in Rousseau and the absence of such a discussion in Locke. For it is easier to see how the natural equality of the pure state of nature is eventually destroyed through the enclosure of land if one considers what the nature of human life would be in the pure state of nature. This is to say that the effects upon equality of property in land can more easily be grasped if one contrasts a situation in which land is enclosed with at least a hypothetical situation in which it is not. This fact alone constitutes a justification for Rousseau's conjectural examination of the pure state of nature.

Rousseau's discussion of what must be done, given the institution of property, if the possession and distribution of property are to be just must be postponed until we examine the *Discourse on Political Economy* and *The Social Contract* in more detail, for it is in these two works rather than in the second discourse that he discusses this question. In the latter work he is concerned primarily with the original institution of property in pre-civil society and its effect upon the nature of man once it is instituted. Its actual historical effect, he is convinced, has been so baneful that man would have been better off had others refused to recognize the claim of the first man who staked out a plot of ground and called it his. He expresses this rhetorically in these words: "From how many crimes, wars, and murders, from how many horrors and misfortunes might not any one have saved mankind, by pulling up the stakes, or filling up the ditch, and crying to his fellows: 'Beware of listening to this impostor.' "[14] At the same time, however, he admits that by the time the first man enclosed land "there is great probability that things had then already come to such a pitch, that they could no longer continue as they were."[15] This suggests that Rousseau's true position is not that some individual rather unaccountably and arbitrarily took it into his head to stake out some plot of ground as his own, but, instead, that the enclosure of land was a social rather than an individual act. This is implicit in his view of the social nature of property— with his view that property in land depends upon the recognition by others of a claim by an individual to a plot of ground. As to precisely what the conditions were that led to such recognition Rousseau is not clear. It is true, as we have seen, that he maintains that the development of metallurgy required the development of agriculture. But whatever the actual reason, it was probably that in some way men came to see that more food could be produced through turning to agriculture than through continuing to rely solely upon hunting, fishing, and the gathering of fruits and nuts.

But regardless of how the enclosure of land first came about, the natural equality of the state of nature begins to disappear as soon as property in land and a division of labor are instituted, and an inequality of wealth to take its place. As was mentioned above, significant inequalities of wealth could not arise so long as men relied solely upon hunting, fishing, and the gathering of fruits and nuts to satisfy their need for food and clothing. But given property in land and a division of labor, inequalities arise from a variety of accompanying factors. One is that certain natural inequalities are now able to manifest themselves in a way that was previously impossible. The strong tend to amass more wealth than the weak by being able to do more work, as do the skillful through making their labor more productive than the unskillful. In addition, some occupations are more remunerative than others, and, finally, differences in inheritance increase the dif-

ferences in wealth arising from other causes. Differences in wealth in turn
led to differences in rank, and this in turn led men to attempt "to appear
what they really were not. To be and to seem became two totally different
things; and from this distinction sprang insolent pomp and cheating trick-
ery, with all the numerous vices that go in their train."[16]

The introduction of property and a division of labor led also to a loss of
the independence of the state of nature and made men dependent both
upon one another and upon the things they had come to learn to want and
to need as a consequence of the introduction of property. This loss of
independence is common to men of all conditions—to the rich, to the
poor, and to those who are neither rich nor poor. Each man "became in
some degree a slave even in becoming the master of other men: if rich,
they stood in need of the services of others; if poor, of their assistance; and
even a middle condition did not enable them to do without one another."[17]
Thus man became "sly and artful in his behavior to some, and imperious
and cruel to others; being under a kind of necessity to ill-use the persons of
whom he stood in need, when he could not frighten them into compliance,
and did not judge it his interest to be useful to them."[18] But not only were
men interested in promoting their own good, an interest they had also had
in the state of nature and in pre-civil society prior to the introduction of
property—they also became afflicted with jealousy and an insatiable ambition to surpass others. They could not have suffered from these afflictions
prior to the appearance of property, for these vices arise not so much from
a concern for one's own good as from the comparison of one's own condition with that of others. These twin vices increase rivalry and competition, cause conflicting interests where there were none, and lead to a desire
to profit at the expense of others.[19]

The introduction of property, we have just seen, leads to a loss of
independence on the part of rich and poor alike. But it also affects these
two classes differently. The poor become obliged either to receive their
subsistence from the rich or to steal it from them. The first leads to the
dominion of the rich and the enslavement of the poor, the second to
violence. In this way the poor come to regard their misery, and the rich
their power, as a right to the possessions of others.

Usurpations by the rich, robbery by the poor, and the unbridled passions of both,
suppressed the cries of natural compassion and the still feeble voice of justice, and
filled men with avarice, ambition, and vice. Between the title of the strongest and
that of the first occupier, there arose perpetual conflicts, which never ended but in
battles and bloodshed. The new-born state of society thus gave rise to a horrible
state of war; men thus harrassed and depraved were no longer capable of retracing
their steps or renouncing the fatal acquisitions they had made, but, labouring by

the abuse of the faculties which do them honour, merely to their own confusion, brought themselves to the brink of ruin.[20]

Hobbes regards the state of nature as a state of war caused by competition, diffidence, and glory, whereas Rousseau denies that competition and diffidence would have the effects Hobbes ascribes to them, either in the state of nature or in pre-civil society prior to the introduction of private property in land, and denies that men would be afflicted by vainglory in either of these states. But once private property in land is introduced competition and diffidence do begin to have the effects ascribed to them by Hobbes, and vainglory also makes its appearance, so that pre-civil society subsequent to the introduction of private property approximates the state of war of Hobbes' state of nature. Thus although Hobbes is mistaken in his description of the state of nature, his description of it does have some truth if applied instead to pre-civil society subsequent to the appearance of private property in land.

In the preceding section we distinguished only between the state of nature prior to the formation of temporary associations for the purpose of solving transitory problems, the state of nature subsequent to the formation of such associations, and the existence of pre-civil societies such as families and tribes. We have now distinguished between pre-civil society prior to the introduction of private property in land and pre-civil society subsequent to the introduction of such property. For Rousseau, as we have seen, it is the first stage of pre-civil society rather than the state of nature that is "altogether the very best man could experience," for in it man has risen above certain of the inconveniences of the state of nature without losing the innocence, equality, and independence of that state. But in the second stage of pre-civil society man has fallen and lost his innocence, his equality, and his independence. The second stage is succeeded by civil society.

Just as there are two stages of pre-civil society, the second of which is corrupt whereas the first is not, so also there are two stages of civil society, as civil society also may be either morally good and just or morally corrupt and unjust. There are thus altogether six possible stages in man's development according to Rousseau—two stages in the state of nature, two in pre-civil society, and two in civil society. Of these six stages Rousseau categorically asserts the existence of only three—the two stages of pre-civil society and the corrupt stage of civil society. For, as we have seen, he does not categorically assert the historicity of either stage of the state of nature, and the just stage of civil society can be actualized only if the terms of the social contract are observed. We have examined in some detail his conception of the state of nature and of pre-civil society. We turn now to examine his account of the transition from the second stage of pre-civil society to the corrupt stage of civil society.

VIII. The Transition to Civil Society

It was impossible, Rousseau maintains, that men should not eventually come to reflect upon their wretched condition in the second stage of pre-civil society. This is especially true of the rich, who bore the expenses of a constant state of war, and who risked losing their property as well as their lives, whereas the poor risked only their lives. In addition, they knew, regardless of how they might attempt to disguise it, that their usurpations were acquired by force and might be lost to others by force. Indeed, Rousseau goes so far as to claim that even those who had enriched themselves by their own industry "could hardly base their proprietorship on better claims," and hyperbolically exclaims that they "ought to have had the express and universal consent of mankind" before appropriating more than they required for their maintenance. But the rich man, able to destroy individuals but subject to destruction himself by bandits, was led to conceive "the profoundest plan that ever entered the mind of man." This was "to employ in his favour the forces of those who attacked him, to make allies of his adversaries, to inspire them with different maxims, and to give them other institutions as favourable to himself as the law of nature was unfavourable."[1] Accordingly, after reminding his neighbors of the horror and wretchedness of their condition, in which every man was armed against the rest and in which neither rich nor poor were safe, he addressed the following words to them.

Let us join ... to guard the weak from oppression, to restrain the ambitious, and secure to every man the possession of what belongs to him: let us institute rules of justice and peace, to which all without exception may be obliged to conform; rules that may in some measure make amends for the caprices of fortune, by subjecting equally the powerful and the weak to the observance of reciprocal obligations. Let us, in a word, instead of turning our forces against ourselves, collect them in a supreme power which may govern us by wise laws, protect and defend all the members of the association, repulse their common enemies, and maintain eternal harmony among men.[2]

Rousseau, of course, does not suppose that precisely these words were employed in proposing the formation of civil society, nor, for that matter, does he maintain that civil society was in fact formed in the way he suggests. He is aware that other thinkers have suggested that it was initially formed through conquest by the powerful or through association by the weak. Indeed, he maintains that it is irrelevant to his argument whether one accounts for its origin by means of his explanation or by means of some alternative explanation. Presumably this is because he is interested more in the effect of civil society upon man than in the precise way in which it was first formed. Indeed, one might well argue that because his interest is primarily in showing the pernicious effects of actual civil societies upon men, and not in explaining their origin, he might even suppose that men have always lived in some form of political society.

Even so, there is still some point in discussing what the nature of man would probably be in the state of nature and in pre-civil society, both prior to and subsequent to the introduction of property. This is the case because one cannot specify the effect of civil society upon the nature of man unless one has some theory about his nature taken in abstraction from the effects of civil society upon it. Regardless, however, of how plausible the supposition that man has always lived in some form of civil society may be—and it does have some plausibility if civil society is contrasted simply with a pure state of nature, understood as the absence of all forms of society—it loses some of its plausibility when civil society is contrasted, not simply with the pure state of nature, but also with pre-civil society. For although it may be unreasonable to suppose that men ever did in fact live in a pure state of nature, it is not unreasonable to suppose that although they have always lived in some form of society, they may once have lived in some form of pre-civil as opposed to civil society. All that one might reasonably urge is that perhaps the distinction between pre-civil society, especially after the introduction of property, and civil society is not quite so sharp as Rousseau seems to want to make it, that the difference between the two is one of degree rather than of kind, and that in pre-civil society there are rules and sources of authority more or less analogous to those of civil society.

But although Rousseau admits that civil society may have originally been formed in some way other than that he suggests, he also maintains that it "may well have been" initially formed as he suggests,[3] and argues that his explanation of its origin is more natural than the suppositions that it was formed through conquests by the powerful or through associations of the weak. He presents three arguments in support of his account.

First, since no man has a right to conquer any other man, there is no right of conquest, and therefore the right of conquest cannot be a right on which any other right can be based. Thus a conqueror and those he conquers remain in a state of war with respect to one another unless the vanquished voluntarily choose the conqueror as their ruler. "For till then, whatever capitulation may have been made being founded on violence, and therefore *ipso facto* void, there could not have been on this hypothesis either a real society or body politic, or any law other than that of the strongest."[4] Here Rousseau is simply echoing Locke. Like Locke, he is arguing that since each man has a natural right to liberty, legitimate government depends on the consent of the governed, and no man, regardless of how great his power may be, has a right to impose his rule on others. This argument, however, is not particularly strong, for all that it establishes is that no *legitimate* civil society can be established by means of conquest (and that even this is established rests upon the acceptability of the assumption that there is no right of conquest). But the question that Rousseau is attempting to answer is not the question of what the origin of a legitimate civil society is, but, instead, the question of what the origin of the earliest civil societies is, regardless of whether they were legitimate or not. This is shown by the fact that his own account of the origin of civil society, as a device originated by the rich primarily to enable them to protect their possessions, is an explanation, not of the origin of legitimate civil societies, but of the earliest actual civil societies, leaving aside the question of their legitimacy. His first argument is therefore an *ignoratio elenchi*.

It is true that on his explanation civil society would arise only with the consent of those who are to be subject to it, as he supposes that the rich rely on persuasion rather than violence in inducing the poor to agree to its institution. But the persuasive techniques employed by the rich are intended to deceive the poor, and the civil society established as a consequence of these techniques is illegitimate because of the pernicious effects it immediately begins to have upon its members, particularly the poor, whereas the effects of a society established by conquest may well be less pernicious, or at least may be no more so, than one established through the poor succumbing and consenting to the persuasive rhetoric of the rich. In addition, those vanquished by a conqueror may well come to consent to his rule, even though they are given no opportunity to express their consent, in the sense that they would express it if they were given the opportunity to do so. It is true that an ambitious man must have the consent of certain allies if he is to acquire sufficient power to impose his rule on those who do not voluntarily consent to it. This, however, is not to deny that once such a man has allies he may then proceed by force to impose his rule on others. It is not, that is, to deny the proposition that civil societies can be established and, once established, expanded by means of conquest, and it is this proposition that Rousseau unsuccessfully repudiates.

This brings us to his second argument in support of the contention that his explanation of the origin of civil society is more natural than alternative accounts. The first argument was directed against the view that civil society originally arose from conquests of the powerful; his second is directed against the view that it was first formed by the weak, who formed associations in order to protect themselves from the strong. It consists essentially in his maintaining that during the interval between the establishment of the right of property and the formation of civil society the meaning of the words "strong" and "weak" is best expressed by the words "rich" and "poor." This is the case because during this interval the only way men had of compelling others to submit to them was either through attacking their possessions or else through offering those who possessed nothing some of their own in return for their submission.[5] But, it may be objected, even if we agree that during the stage of propertied pre-civil society the strong are the rich and the weak are the poor, it is still more plausible to suppose that political societies were initially instituted by the poor in order to protect themselves from the rich than to suppose that they were first formed as Rousseau suggests. This brings us to his third argument, which is a presentation of his own position as well as a reply to this objection.

This is that the poor have less to lose by remaining in pre-civil society than the rich, since in that state they could lose only their lives and their liberty, whereas the rich run the risk of losing their property as well as their lives and liberty. As it is therefore easier to harm the rich than the poor in this state, it is more advantageous for the rich to leave it than it is for the poor to do so. Indeed, Rousseau goes to the extreme of maintaining that it would be more advantageous to the poor to remain in the state of pre-civil society, as they are not enriched by entering civil society, and even lose the liberty they enjoyed in pre-civil society. It is the rich, not the poor, who benefit from the formation of civil society, and "it is more reasonable to suppose a thing to have been invented by those to whom it would be of service, than by those whom it must have harmed."[6] This last, of course, depends upon the assumption that the rich would be sufficiently intelligent to see the advantages to them of civil society, and sufficiently clever to induce the poor to join in the formation of an association that will benefit them at the expense of the poor.

But regardless of whether one accepts Rousseau's account of the origin of civil society as more plausible than any alternative account, one could nonetheless agree that the conditions of actual civil societies benefit the rich at the expense of the poor, that the rich are clever enough to see this, and that they are also clever enough to frame the conditions of political

association in such a way as to make it appear to the poor that each
member of the association, the poor as well as the rich, will benefit equally
from membership in it. In this connection it is interesting to observe that
the terms of association that Rousseau represents the rich as suggesting to
the poor are almost, although not quite, identical with those that Rousseau
himself suggests in *The Social Contract* as the conditions of association that
must be observed if a just civil society is to be possible. Rousseau may be
read as suggesting that justice would be possible and the good of each
member of the association promoted if either the terms of association
suggested by the rich to the poor or those suggested by Rousseau himself
in *The Social Contract* were observed. But they are not observed in actual
civil societies, and the rich, in recommending their observance to the poor,
are only presenting a deceitful scheme whereby they can promote their
own good at the expense of the poor. The result is that the poor, in biting
the bait proffered by the rich, descend into even worse conditions in actual
civil society than they would have suffered under the corruption of the
second stage of pre-civil society. Thus the passage from the second stage
of pre-civil society to actual civil society is a transition from better to
worse.

Nevertheless, the poor bit the bait dangled before them by the rich, and
have been biting the bait of the rich ever since. It was easy for the rich to
seduce "men so barbarous and easily seduced" as those of pre-civil society,
and also, Rousseau may be read as intending, to continue to seduce their
descendants. It is important, however, to recognize that he does not absolve the seduced from responsibility for succumbing. The temptations
presented by the rich are only the occasional cause of the fall of the poor.
The actual fall itself presupposed a disposition or inclination, on the part
of those who fell, to succumb to the proffered temptation. Such a disposition was in fact present among men at the second stage of pre-civil society,
for "they had too many disputes among themselves to do without arbi-
trators, and too much ambition and avarice to go long without masters."[7]
Accordingly, "all ran headlong to their chains, in hopes of securing their
liberty; for they had just wit enough to perceive the advantages of political
institutions, without experience enough to enable them to foresee the
dangers."[8] Those who were "most capable of foreseeing the dangers were
the very persons who expected to benefit by them; and even the most
prudent judged it not inexpedient to sacrifice one part of their freedom to
ensure the rest."[9] Such, then, were the conditions, or well might have
been the conditions, which led to "the origin of society and law, which
bound new fetters on the poor, and gave new powers to the rich; which
irretrievably destroyed natural liberty, eternally fixed the law of property

and inequality, converted clever usurpation into unalterable right, and, for the advantage of a few ambitious individuals, subjected all mankind to perpetual labour, slavery, and wretchedness."[10]

Once one political society was formed it became necessary that others be formed in order to protect those outside the first from the combined power of its members. Accordingly, political associations "soon multiplied and spread over the face of the earth, till hardly a corner of the world was left in which a man could escape the yoke."[11] Civil law and civil right replaced the law of nature in governing the relationships of individuals within a political community. Although the law of nature continued to obtain among independent communities under the designation of the right of nations, it was modified by various tacit conventions for the sake of commerce and as a replacement for natural compassion. These conventions, however, could not prevent the state of nature in which independent states remain relative to one another from degenerating into states of war in which more violence, bloodshed, suffering, and death occur in a single day than had occurred "in the state of nature during whole ages over the whole earth." These were the first effects that "followed the division of mankind into different communities."[12]

At first political societies consisted only of "a few general conventions, which every member bound himself to observe; and for the performance of covenants the whole community went security to each individual."[13] This means that initially the laws or conventions of the community were devised by the entire community and also enforced by it. But the difficulties of enforcement by the entire community soon became so great that this task was eventually assigned by the people to magistrates. It is interesting to note here that according to Rousseau it is the *enforcement* of laws that becomes so difficult as to lead to the appointment of magistrates to enforce them, and not their *enactment* by the community. Rousseau is perhaps here writing with a view of the position he later adopts in *The Social Contract*, according to which a just society is possible only if all who are to be subject to the laws delegate only the authority to enforce them, and never the authority to enact them, to magistrates, but always retain this authority for themselves. At any rate, his view in the second discourse is that it is the enforcement of law by the community, not its enactment, that becomes so difficult that it is assigned by the community to magistrates.

Here Rousseau seems also to have in view Hobbes' position that a sovereign must be designated before laws can be enacted. Hobbes' position would be unobjectionable if it amounted only to the contention that some form of sovereignty must be assumed if law is to be enacted. For "law" and "sovereignty" may be defined in such a way that the possession of sovereignty is simply the possession of authority to enact law, and Hobbes' position, as he admits the possibility of the legitimacy of democracy, is compatible with the view that sovereignty may be retained by those who are to be subject to the laws. But whereas Rousseau in *The Social Contract* insists that sovereignty must be retained by those who are subject to law if a legitimate political association is to be possible, Hobbes admits the legitimacy of instituting either a monarchic or aristocratic sovereign, and in fact prefers monarchy to either aristocracy or democracy. Rousseau, however, argues that it would be absurd to suppose that a monarchic or aristocratic sovereign was established prior to the establishment of a political society or the enactment of laws: "to say that chiefs were chosen before the confederacy was formed, and that the administrators of the laws were there before the laws themselves, is too absurd a supposition to consider seriously."[14]

Rousseau continues his attack upon Hobbes by arguing that it would be equally absurd "to suppose that men first threw themselves irretrievably and unconditionally into the arms of an absolute master, and that the first expedient which proud and unsubdued men hit upon for their common security was to run headlong into slavery."[15] His argument in support of this attack is drawn partly from Locke, because, like Locke, he argues that men institute political superiors in order to defend themselves from oppression and to protect their lives, liberty, and property, and that the institution of an absolute monarch would be incompatible with the preservation of their liberty and would amount to exposing themselves to the oppression of the monarch, an oppression greater than any from which they could suffer in the state of nature.[16] But to this he adds an argument, not to be found in Locke, which is related to his charge that previous philosophers had failed to get back to the state of nature through ascribing to the natural man qualities that he could only have acquired in society. Thus, he argues, philosophers "judge, by what they see, of very different things, which they have not seen," and ascribe "to man a natural propensity to servitude, because the slaves within their observation are seen to bear the yoke with patience."[17] What they fail to observe is "that it is with liberty as with innocence and virtue; the value is known only to those who possess them, and the taste for them is forfeited when they are forfeited themselves."[18] Men who have been enslaved may become so accustomed to their slavery that they are content in it—so much so that their servility becomes second nature to them to such an extent as to lead Aristotle to suppose that some men are slaves by nature. But neither the savage of the state of nature nor the primitive man of pre-civil society would willingly accept enslavement by others, much less enslave himself. This is attested to by the fact that savages brave "hunger, fire, the sword, and death, to preserve nothing but their independence" against the attempts of civilized Europeans to enslave them, as well as by the fact that "free-born animals dash their brains out against the bars of their cage, from an innate impatience of captivity."[19]

These are factual arguments against the Hobbesian supposition that civil societies were originally instituted through men subjecting themselves to an absolute monarch. And if the Hobbesian supposition be taken as a factual supposition (and this is how Rousseau does treat it), then the only arguments one can legitimately oppose to it must themselves be factual. Moreover, the question Rousseau is treating here, i.e., the question of whether men originally formed civil societies by instituting absolute monarchs, is itself a factual question, even though it must be treated conjecturally or philosophically because of the absence of any historical or anthropological empirical evidence to which one could appeal to settle the question. Rousseau, that is, is not raising the question of whether liberty is good and slavery and absolute monarchy bad, but is arguing that, given that liberty is regarded as a good by savages and primitive men who have not become so accustomed to being enslaved that they are content in their slavery, then they would not willingly accept enslavement by others or voluntarily enslave themselves, and thus would not willingly subject themselves to an absolute monarch. But though Rousseau is dealing with a factual question, and presents factual considerations in his treatment of it, he nevertheless also shifts suddenly to an ethical question, without clearly indicating that he is doing so. This is the question of whether men have a right to alienate their liberty, regardless of whether in fact they once did or have done so.

IX. The Inalienability of Liberty

His answer is that they do not have such a right. Because "liberty is the noblest faculty of man," we degrade our nature, reduce "ourselves to the level of brutes, which are mere slaves of instinct," and affront "the Author of our being" if we "renounce without reserve the most precious of all His gifts" and consent to "committing all the crimes He has forbidden, merely to gratify a mad or a cruel master."[1] Life and liberty are "the essential gifts of nature," and "it would be an offense against both reason and nature to renounce them at any price whatsoever," because to renounce our liberty would be to "degrade our being" and to renounce our life would be to attempt to annul our being.[2]

Here Rousseau is arguing that the preservation of our liberty is as important as the preservation of our life, since to live without liberty is to live as a brute and to degrade our nature as men. This can perhaps be put by saying that it is not life alone, but free life, to which we have a natural right and which natural law commands us to preserve. It is true that life is more fundamental than and separable from liberty, in the sense that liberty presupposes life and is impossible without it, whereas life does not presuppose liberty and is possible without it. Thus one man can deprive another of his liberty without depriving him of his life, but cannot deprive another of his life without also depriving him of his liberty. But it is not true that the life proper to a man is separable from liberty, for such a life is impossible without liberty, and therefore presupposes liberty. This being the case, no man has any more of a right to alienate his liberty than he has to kill himself, and no more of a right to deprive another of his liberty than he has to kill another. Given that the rights to life and to liberty are equally fundamental, these two rights can be referred to as the right to free life. One fails to fulfill one's obligation to respect this right if one deprives either oneself or another of either life or liberty.

But not only does Rousseau argue that no one has a *right* to alienate his liberty—he also argues, at least implicitly, that no one *can* alienate his liberty. This emerges in his claim that one has a right to alienate his property, but not his liberty, by transferring it to another by means of contracts. This claim he expresses somewhat imprecisely by saying that "the property I alienate becomes quite foreign to me, nor can I suffer from its abuse," whereas it does concern "me that my liberty should not be abused, and I cannot without incurring the guilt of the crimes I may be compelled to commit, expose myself to become an instrument of crime."[3] This, of course, will not quite do as it stands. For, first, the person to whom I give or sell my property may use or abuse it in such a way that I suffer. And, second, he may use it criminally, and, if he does, I may be accountable for his criminal use of it if I could reasonably be expected to know that he would so use it. Indeed, I as well as he may be guilty of the crime he commits through its use, since I may transfer it to him while knowing full well that he will use it criminally, and may even transfer it in order to enable him to do so. On the other hand, he may also use it in such a way as neither to injure me nor to commit any crime through its use and, moreover, in such a way that I cannot reasonably be held accountable for his use of it. In this event I am totally alienated both from the property I transfer to him and from his use of it, and both it and his use of it become foreign to me.

But, Rousseau argues, the situation is totally different in the case of my liberty. I cannot transfer it to another in such a way as completely to alienate myself either from it or from his use of it. It is not a thing, as a piece of property is, from which I can separate myself. Thus even though I consent to obey unconditionally the commands of another, and in this way seek to alienate my liberty and transfer it to him, I am still responsible for any crimes I may commit at his command. The fact that he commands me to commit them does not absolve me of responsibility for their commission, nor does it mean that it is he and not I who commits them. For he acquires the authority to command me only if I give it to him, and in obeying his commands I continue the act I began in consenting to obey. In willing, that is, to submit myself unconditionally to his authority, I will to perform every act he commands, and if I am initially responsible for willing to obey him, then I continue to be responsible for each act I perform at his command. I cannot, then, alienate myself from my liberty as I can from a piece of property. What another does with a piece of property, which I alienate by transferring it to him, may be done in complete independence of my will. Once I transfer the property both it and what he does with it become completely foreign to me. But in willing to obey unconditionally the commands of another I do not thereby alienate my will, for in obeying his commands I only do what I willed to do in willing to obey him.

Rousseau, however, does not deny that situations such as the following can and do occur. You and I may be trying to decide what to do this evening, and the choice may be among doing A, B, or C. I may prefer one of these alternatives to the others, or I may have no preference. In either event, I may let you choose. In this case I choose to have you choose for me, or will to do what you will that I do. Thus your choice is a necessary condition of the specific determination of what I shall do this evening. But it is not a sufficient condition. Instead, it is also necessary that I will that you choose for me, and your choosing for me may be said to be an execution of my will. It is not, however, an execution of my will alone and not also of yours, for you do not choose for me unless you and I both will that you do. Your choosing for me is therefore an expression or execution of both your will and mine, or, if you prefer, of our joint or common will. As such, you and I are both responsible for what we do this evening—I for willing that you choose what we do and for doing what you choose, and you for consenting to choose and for making the specific choice that you make. Moreover, even if I will that you choose for me, I must continue to will to do what you choose after you make the choice. For should I cease to do so and will to do something else instead, then I shall not do what you choose (unless, of course, you or something or someone else compels me to do so).

Although, then, I can choose, prior to your choice, to let your choice serve as the specific determination of what I shall do, I must also continue to will, after you choose and make your choice known to me, to do what you choose. Thus even if I may be said to alienate my will or my liberty in choosing to let you choose for me, I cannot alienate them once you make your choice known to me, for once it is known I must still will to do what you choose if I am to do it. It therefore remains the case that ultimately I cannot alienate my will or my liberty if I am to act. Action necessarily presupposes the will to act on the part of the agent who acts, and thus one thing that an agent is not at liberty to do is to alienate himself from the will or the liberty to act, which ultimately must be his alone, if he is to act at all. Even the attempt not to act presupposes the will not to act, and the man who wills not to act is in fact willing in doing so, just as the man who chooses not to choose is in fact choosing. We may therefore conclude that Rousseau is correct in maintaining that a man's will and liberty are essentially inalienable. Man is inescapably free and responsible and cannot transform himself into a complete puppet even if he should try.

But even if we accept Rousseau's position on the inalienability of liberty, the question arises as to what its point is. We may agree that it establishes that liberty, unlike property, is essentially inalienable, and that a man cannot escape responsibility for what he does on the ground that he is only doing what another, whom he has authorized to choose for him and to command and rule him, has commanded him to do. But it does not, as we have seen, establish that a man cannot choose to have another choose for him, nor that a man cannot submit himself unconditionally to the rule of another. Indeed, Hobbes was particularly careful to argue that each subject of the sovereign is the author of the acts of the sovereign, in virtue of their authorizing him to act for them, and may therefore be said to be responsible for his acts. In fact, one may argue, the effect of Rousseau's argument may, to some extent, be the opposite of what he intends, for what it shows is not that a man puppetizes himself by subjecting himself unconditionally to the authority of another, but, quite the contrary, that no man can completely transform himself into a puppet. Nor, one may continue, does it show that a man debases himself by thus subjecting himself to the authority of another. Although Rousseau maintains that such subjection does debase a man, and although it may in fact do so, the argument that liberty, unlike property, is essentially inalienable does not establish that it does so. Nor does it establish that a man has no right thus to subject himself to the authority of another. All it seems to establish is that liberty, unlike property, is essentially inalienable, and that a man is still responsible for what he does in doing what another to whom he has promised unconditional obedience commands him to do. But perhaps it is a sufficient accomplishment to have established this.

Rousseau is, if anything, even more emphatic in *The Social Contract* in his denial that a people have a right to enslave themselves, i.e. to submit themselves, to the absolute rule of a monarch. There he distinguishes between an individual's enslaving himself to another and an entire people's enslaving themselves to a monarch. To alienate something, he says, is either to give it away or to sell it. When an individual alienates his liberty by enslaving himself to another he does not give himself to the other, but, instead, "sells himself, at the least for his subsistence." In this case there is a *quid pro quo:* the slave sells his labor and liberty to his master in return for his subsistence. But if a people should enslave themselves to a monarch there would be no *quid pro quo.* The monarch would receive from them their labor and their liberty, but he would be in no position to give them their subsistence in return. "A king is so far from furnishing his subjects with their subsistence that he gets his own only from them; and, according to Rabelais, kings do not live on nothing."[4] It may, however, be objected that the people receive from the king civil tranquility. Rousseau grants this, but replies that his wars may bring down upon them more misery than their dissensions would have done. Besides, their tranquility itself may be miserable, for tranquility may also be found in dungeons, yet does not therefore make dungeons desirable places in which to live.[5] Rousseau, though arguing here explicitly against Grotius, is also arguing by implication against Hobbes, and it is easy to supply the answer Hobbes would make: the tranquility afforded by an absolute monarch would not be the tranquility of a dungeon so long as the monarch is obeyed, and would be preferable to the state of nature, in which there is no tranquility. Thus, Hobbes would continue, a multitude who sell a monarch their obedience in return for the peace he provides do not give themselves to him for nothing. On the contrary, there is a distinct *quid pro quo.* Rousseau's point, however, may be interpreted as being that in effect there is no *quid pro quo,* and that the people who give themselves to a monarch in effect receive nothing in return, for the peace he provides is obtainable without their subjecting themselves to his absolute rule.

But though this interpretation may be placed upon Rousseau's words, he nevertheless makes it clear that he is also arguing that there is no *quid pro quo* in a convention that provides for absolute rule on the part of a

monarch and unlimited obedience on the part of his subjects. Such a
convention, he argues, would be "empty and contradictory", for since it
would give the monarch the right to exact anything and everything from
his subjects, he would be under no obligations to them. They would
therefore have no rights against him, for everything they have would be
transferred to him, including any rights they may have had against him. It
is absurd to say that a man gives himself to another gratuitously and
completely; "such an act is null and illegitimate, from the mere fact that he
who does it is out of his mind. To say the same of a whole people is to
suppose a people of madmen; and madness creates no right."[6] Moreover,
the man who completely renounces his liberty thereby also renounces his
status as a man and surrenders "the rights of humanity and even its
duties.... Such a renunciation is incompatible with man's nature; to remove all liberty from his will is to remove all morality from his acts."[7]

At first glance Rousseau's position here seems incompatible with his
contention in the second discourse that although a man can alienate his
property, he cannot alienate his liberty, and is always responsible for his
acts, even when they are performed at the command of someone to whom
he has promised unlimited obedience. But his point here is that someone
who makes such a promise has surrendered his will to another, even
though he must continue to will the fulfillment of his promise if he is
voluntarily to fulfill it, in the sense that he can fulfill his promise only by
constantly willing to do whatever the person to whom he makes the promise commands him to do. Although, that is, he must constantly will to
fulfill his promise if he is to do so, he has promised to do anything the
promisee commands him to do, and in this sense he has alienated his
liberty to choose what in particular he will do. Although he cannot and
does not alienate his liberty to will to do whatever the promisee commands
him to do, he does alienate his liberty to determine what in particular he
will do. In this sense he becomes something less than a free and responsible agent in the full sense of this expression, and thereby debases himself
as a man.

In *The Social Contract*, then, as well as in the second discourse, Rousseau
makes it clear that he regards the man who submits himself unconditionally to the absolute rule of another as debasing himself. And in both works
he goes on to argue, like Locke, that even if men do have a right to enslave
themselves they have no right to enslave their children; for "liberty, being
a gift which they hold from nature as being men, their parents have no
right whatever to deprive them of it."[8] The same point is made in *The
Social Contract:* "Even if each man could alienate himself, he could not

alienate his children: they are born men and free; their liberty belongs to them, and no one but they has the right to dispose of it."[9] Just as it is "necessary to do violence to nature" to establish slavery, so, in order to perpetuate it as a right it is necessary to change nature, i.e., to change men into brutes. Thus those "jurists who have gravely determined that the child of a slave comes into the world a slave, have decided . . . that a man shall come into the world not a man," but only as a certain kind of animal.[10] Hence even though a group of men at a certain time and place should agree to submit themselves unconditionally to the absolute rule of some monarch, they cannot thereby also obligate their descendants to accept this rule. "It would therefore be necessary, in order to legitimize an arbitrary government, that in every generation the people should be in a position to accept or reject it; but, were this so, the government would be no longer arbitrary."[11] Hereditary political authority, like hereditary enslavement, is incompatible with man's natural right to liberty.

Although, then, Rousseau regards it as certain that civil society did not originate through the granting of arbitrary power to anyone, he also argues that since the granting of such power to anyone is itself illegitimate, such a grant, even if it had been made when civil societies were initially instituted, could not serve as a ground for the justification of the laws of a society and of the inequality instituted by these laws.[12] His argument, therefore, against political absolutism is both factual and moral—factual in the sense that he regards it as unreasonable to suppose that government was in fact first formed through granting absolute rule to anyone, and moral in the sense that he argues that should such a grant of authority ever be made it would be illegitimate and therefore could not serve as a legitimate basis for either law, rights, or obligations.

X. Right and Power

But if men do not have a right to enslave either themselves or their posterity, neither do they have a right to enslave other men. An attempt might be made to base the right to enslave on the right of war, by arguing that since the victor has "the right of killing the vanquished, the latter can buy back his life at the price of his liberty," an arrangement which "is the more legitimate because it is to the advantage of both parties." This argument fails simply because the conqueror has no right to kill the vanquished once the latter lay down their arms and surrender.[1] Whether Rousseau intends here to deny Locke's contention that the victor in a just war has a right to enslave an unjust aggressor is not clear, for he does not mention Locke's distinction between a just and an unjust conqueror.[2] But it is clear that he is unequivocally denying that an innocent person may rightly be enslaved by a conqueror. For Rousseau there is no right of conquest at all, for this alleged right would have "no foundation other than the right of the strongest," and, as we shall see presently, he denies that there is any such right. But if no man has a right to enslave himself or his posterity or others, then there is no right of slavery at all.

But, Rousseau continues, even if a right to enslave others were admitted, there would still be "a great difference between subduing a multitude and ruling a society." We have already seen that it is impossible that one man would by himself be able to enslave others. But if we waive this impossibility and suppose that one man successively enslaves a large number of scattered individuals, there would still be, regardless of how numerous they might be, only "a master and his slaves, and certainly not a people and its ruler." There would be "an aggregation, but not an association." An aggregation is only a multitude, not a people—it is only an association that is a people. The essential difference between the two is that a corporate, common, or general will to pursue a corporate, common, or general good exists only in a people or an association, and not in a multitude or an aggregation. In the latter there is only a collection of individuals, each pursuing what he conceives to be his particular or private good. Thus should one man succeed in enslaving a multitude we should have only a collection of individuals, including the conqueror, each of whom seeks only to promote his own particular good. So long as the conqueror and each of the vanquished continues to seek only his private good, there exists only an aggregation or a multitude of private persons, not an association or a people. The conqueror, "even if he has enslaved half the world, is still only an individual; his interest, apart from that of the others, is still a purely private interest," and when he dies "his empire, after him, remains scattered and without unity, as an oak falls and dissolves into a heap of ashes when the fire has consumed it."[3]

Rousseau's point here is not only that no one man or group has a right to enslave others, but also that it is in fact impossible that a body politic should be formed through conquest or enslavement. It is impossible that a single individual should ever acquire sufficient power to enable him singly to subdue a multitude of others against their will, so that if the conquest and enslavement of a collection of individuals is to be possible there must be some uncoerced concerted action on the part of a multiplicity of individuals. This means, in effect, that there must be a common will among a

collection of individuals to conquer and enslave others if they are to succeed in doing so, and thus that the conquering collection must already, at
least to some extent, be transformed from a mere aggregation or multitude
of individuals, each with his own particular will, into an association with a
corporate or common will. But even though a common will to vanquish
and enslave a multitude of persons should exist among a group of conquerors, no political association could be formed merely through conquering and enslaving a multitude. For those who are vanquished can become
members of the same association with their conquerors only if they, along
with their conquerors, will in common the good of the entire association.
Until this is done the only association that exists is that consisting of the
association of conquerors, and the only common will is therefore that of
this association. The aggregation of the vanquished remains only a multitude of individuals, each with his own particular will.

To over simplify somewhat, there are only two ways in which the
multitude of the vanquished can be transformed into an association with a
common or corporate will, only one of which leads to the formation of an
association including both conquerors and vanquished. The first is
through the formation of a common will of the vanquished in opposition to
that of the conquerors. As each of the vanquished comes to feel his enslavement and rule by the conquerors oppressive, there may gradually
grow up among them a common will in opposition to the conquerors'
common will to continue to oppress them. As this happens there begin to
appear, so to speak, two associations, that of the conquerors and an incip-
ient association of the vanquished in opposition to that of the conquerors.
The opposition of the wills of these two associations may eventually erupt
into violence as the association of the vanquished grows in strength, and
the latter association may eventually acquire sufficient power to overthrow
its rulers. This is at least part of what Rousseau has in mind when he
writes that "The strongest is never strong enough to be always the master,
unless he transforms strength into right, and obedience into duty."[4] The
other way in which the aggregation of the vanquished can be transformed
into an association, and the only way in which it can be transformed into a
single association including both conquerors and vanquished, is through
the conquerors' ruling in such a way as to eliminate the distinction between conquerors and vanquished, through ruling in the common interest
of both. But, as we shall see, Rousseau's position is that this ultimately
involves the elimination, not only of the distinction between conquerors
and vanquished, but also of the distinction between rulers and ruled,
through the formation of a single comprehensive association in which each

person subject to its laws is granted the status of citizen, i.e., the status of a person who has a voice equal to that of every other person in the association in the determination of its laws. Until each member of an association is granted the status of citizen it is not an association in the full sense of the word, and its members do not constitute fully a people.

There is a closer approximation to the existence of such associations when men initially leave the second stage of pre-civil society to form civil societies than there is in the later history of most civil societies. This means that the acquisition of absolute power, rather than occurring when political societies were initially instituted, is something that occurs only later in the history of such societies. The possession of absolute power "is the depravation, the extreme term, of government, and brings it back, finally, to just the law of the strongest," a law which the institution of government "was originally designed to remedy."[5] This is to say that should any man or group within society acquire absolute power, their acquisition of such power would issue from an exercise of power, and thus could never be legitimate. The laws they enact would therefore be only the laws of the strongest, and hence would lack legitimacy. Accordingly, although it would be prudent for their subjects to obey so long as they lack the power to disobey with impunity, they would have no obligation to obey, and, indeed, would have the same right to overthrow their rulers, once they acquire the power to do so, that their rulers had in acquiring their power in the first place.

This last, however, does not mean that the subjects of an absolute ruler have no more right to overthrow him than he had to acquire absolute power over them. It could mean this only if "right" be equated in meaning with "power." But if such an equation were made, then "right," as signifying something distinct from power, would lose its meaning. Those who equate the meaning of the two terms are guilty of a kind of pernicious naturalism, for it is the meaning of "right" that is reduced to the meaning of "power" rather than the other way around. This is precisely what Hobbes does in his definition of "natural right".[6] Yet those who reduce right to power are not always as careful as Hobbes was to carry through the reduction consistently. Instead, they tend to fall back, when it suits their purposes, into supposing—with varying degrees of awareness that they are doing so—the distinction between right and power which they seek to suppress in their reduction of right to power. They halfway give back, that is, with one hand what they have sought to take away with the other. This they do by talking in such a way as to imply that their reduction of right to power means that the subjects of those with the power to rule have an obligation to obey their rulers, rather than to seek to acquire sufficient power themselves to disobey successfully and even to establish themselves as rulers. Although, that is, they ostensibly seek to reduce right to power, their real purpose, often, perhaps, even half-concealed from themselves, is to justify the reign of the powers that be—it is to argue that since right reduces to power, the powers that be ought to be obeyed by their subjects, since it is the powers that be, and not their subjects, that have the power, and therefore the right, to rule.

But, Rousseau argues, both the reduction of right to power and the use of this reduction to justify the rule and the acts of the powers that be are illicit. To say that a man has the right to do something and to say that he has the power to do it are to say two entirely different things. Moreover, if the only right a man has to rule consists in or depends upon his power to rule, then he retains this right only so long as he retains the power, and his subjects, contrary to having an obligation to obey him, have as much right as they have power to disobey and even to overthrow him. This brings out the incoherence of the reduction of right to power. For if the powers that be have a right to rule, then their subjects have an obligation to obey, regardless of whether they have the power to disobey safely or not. But if the right of the powers that be to rule issues from or depends upon their power to rule, then their subjects cease to have an obligation to obey as soon as they acquire the power to disobey with impunity. Thus if right reduces to power obligation as well as right disappears, except in the sense of prudence, so that to say that I am obligated to do something, such as to obey the powers that be, is to say that I lack the power not to do it, i.e., to disobey with impunity. The reduction of right to power is therefore ultimately the elimination of morality altogether and the substitution for it of a kind of calculation of self-interest, the result of which "is a mass of inexplicable nonsense."

Force is a physical power, and I fail to see what moral effect it can have. To yield to force is an act of necessity, not of will—at the most, an act of prudence. . . . For, if force creates right, the effect changes with the cause: every force that is greater than the first succeeds to its right. As soon as it is possible to disobey with impunity, disobedience is legitimate; and, the strongest being always in the right, the only thing that matters is to act so as to become the strongest. But what kind of right is that which perishes when force fails? If we must obey perforce, there is no need to obey because we ought; and if we are not forced to obey, we are under no obligation to do so. Clearly, the word 'right' adds nothing to force: in this connection, it means absolutely nothing.

Obey the powers that be. If this means yield to force, it is a good precept, but superfluous: I can answer for its never being violated. All power comes from God, I admit; but so does all sickness: does that mean that we are forbidden to call in the doctor? . . . Let us then admit that force does not create right, and that we are obliged to obey only legitimate powers.[7]

Rousseau, then, like Locke and unlike Hobbes, draws a sharp distinction between right and power, and denies that rights can be established by appealing to facts. Although "it would be possible to employ a more logical method" of reasoning than to attempt to establish rights by citing facts, "none could be more favourable to tyrants."[8] This, however, does not mean that there is no sense at all in which Rousseau would admit that a citation of facts is appropriate to a determination of rights. All it means is that the rights which men have merely in virtue of their humanity, i.e., their natural rights, which ought to be recognized and respected by all societies, regardless of whether or not they are so recognized and respected, cannot be determined by ascertaining what rights have been conceded men, either by custom or by positive law, in various societies at different times and places. It does not mean that there is no sense at all in which a citation of facts is appropriate to a determination of rights. Indeed, Rousseau's entire program of attempting to go back to the state of nature may be regarded as an attempt to determine rights by citing facts. For what he seeks to show by returning to the state of nature is that the pronounced inequalities among men within society are the product of society and not of nature, that men are at least approximately equal by nature and would be in fact or actuality if they lived in a state of nature, and, therefore, that a denial of an equality in the possession of natural rights cannot legitimately be based upon the fact that certain inequalities among men have been produced within actual societies. On the contrary, the inequalities produced by society, rather than demonstrating the invalidity of the claim that there is an equality of natural rights among men, stand themselves condemned by the natural equality among men.

Rousseau, then, may be interpreted to be arguing as follows. If the inequalities among men in society were natural rather than merely the effects of society, then there might be some ground for denying an equality of natural rights among men. But since they are not natural, they cannot legitimately be accepted as a ground for denying an equality of natural rights. One man or group can legitimately claim for itself or for some other man or group a certain right as a natural right, while refusing to concede that other men also have this right, only if it can be shown that there is some relevant factual difference between the one man or group and the others to justify the claim. In the absence of such relevant factual differences, no one can legitimately claim some right as a natural right for one person or group and refuse to concede that others possess precisely the same right. The purport of Rousseau's argument is to emphasize that the relevant factual difference must be a natural difference, and not one produced as a consequence of societal inequalities, and that to attempt to argue that societal inequalities show that there is no equality of natural rights among men is to attempt to justify an injustice, namely, a denial of an equality of natural rights, by appealing to the very injustice in question.

For Rousseau, then, there is a sense in which an appeal to facts is relevant to the determination of natural rights. Such an appeal must eventually be made by anyone who accepts the precept that equals ought to be treated equally and who wishes to justify the claim that there is an equality of natural rights among men. For one who accepts this precept, an unequal treatment of persons can be justified only by showing that there is some relevant factual difference between them in virtue of which they are unequal. But the facts to which Rousseau and anyone else who claims that there is an equality of natural rights must ultimately appeal may be said to be philosophical or metaphysical rather than historical or empirical. They can be uncovered only through a philosophical or metaphysical analysis of the nature of man, and not through a mere historical or empirical investigation into the effects upon man of the various systems of rights which have been established in different societies at various times and places. The investigation must be non-historical because the relevant facts are not subject to the shifting vicissitudes of history, but, on the contrary, are as constant as the fundamental nature of man. And the results of the investigation, rather than being established historically or empirically, must themselves be used as a standard to assess the legitimacy of the systems of rights historically established by various societies. This is to say that the relative goodness or badness of any historical system of established rights can be determined only by measuring the system against a philosophical or metaphysical standard, and that the validity of the standard cannot be determined by measuring it against some historical system. When actual historical systems are measured against such a philosophical standard they will be found to be either good or bad in varying degrees. Rousseau, as we know, finds most of them bad. In fact, he finds the actual course of history—beginning with the introduction of property and the transition from the first to the second stage of pre-civil society and continuing throughout the entire history of civil society—to be so lamentable that it would have been better had man remained at the first stage of pre-civil society and, accordingly, had there been no history at all.

XI. The Course of Corruption

But man did not remain at the first stage of pre-civil society, and he does have a history. This history, according to Rousseau, consists at once of the development of civilization and the moral corruption of man, the first having been attained only at the cost of the second. We turn now to consider Rousseau's account, in the second discourse, of the progressive corruption of government, society, and man involved in the unfolding of the history of actual civil societies.

We shall begin by considering Rousseau's account of the contract by means of which political societies were first instituted. This contract is to be distinguished from the social contract presupposed by all legitimate political associations. In the second discourse he does not enter in detail into the nature of the latter contract. He does not do this until *The Social Contract* itself, although intimations of the final position presented in this work are clearly present, at least by implication, in both the second and the third discourses.

In *The Social Contract* Rousseau denies emphatically that the act by which a people submits itself to a government is a contract between the people on the one hand and the officials of the government on the other. Instead, he maintains, "it is simply and solely a commission, an employ-ment," by means of which the people as sovereign grant certain powers to the officials of the government and authorize them to act for the people as sovereign. But sovereignty throughout is retained by the people, and the power it grants the officials of the government it has a right to "limit, modify, or recover at pleasure; for the alienation of such a right is incom-patible with the nature of the social body, and contrary to the end of association."[1] In the second discourse, on the other hand, he contents himself with adopting "the common opinion" that the institution of a political society is "a real contract between the people and the chiefs chosen by them: a contract by which both parties bind themselves to observe the laws therein expressed, which form the ties of their union."[2] By means of this contract the people concentrate all their wills into one will, and the various articles of the contract, "concerning which this will is explained, become so many fundamental laws, obligatory on all the mem-bers of the State without exception, and one of these articles regulates the choice and power of the magistrates appointed to watch over the execution of the rest."[3] The power granted the magistrates "extends to everything which may maintain the constitution, without going so far as to alter it." The magistrate, on the other hand, promises to use the power he is entrusted with "only in conformity with the intention of his constituents, to maintain them all in the peaceable possession of what belongs to them, and to prefer on every occasion the public interest to his own."[4]

Rousseau's description of this contract may easily lead one to believe that he is guilty of a kind of anachronism, and is supposing the kind of detailed document to have been drawn up at the dawn of civil society which in fact presupposes generations and even centuries of legal and political experience. Such, however, is not the case. Hobbes, Locke, and Rousseau were all aware that the possibility of drawing up formal, written, detailed, complex, and technical contracts does presuppose generations, even centuries, of legal and political experience and the development of some degree of literacy and civilization, and all three agree that the development of the level of literacy and civilization necessary for drawing up such sophisticated documents presupposes the existence of civil society. Thus Rousseau maintains that civil "society consisted at first merely of a few general conventions," that "government had, in its infancy, no regular and constant form," that "the want of experience and philosophy prevented men from seeing any but present inconveniences," and that "they thought of providing against others only as they presented themselves."[5] Hobbes, Locke, and Rousseau may be read as maintaining that the rudimentary notion of a contract—considered merely as an agreement involving an exchange of promises or rights and the consequent acquisition of obligations—is no more sophisticated, complex, or advanced than the notion of forming a political society, and may even be regarded as presupposed by the possibility of the formation of such a society.

This certainly seems to be a reasonable position, for how would any form of political society be possible unless its members had some notion of an exchange of promises and some elementary notion of an obligation to keep one's promises, regardless of what the source of this obligation may be taken to be? The position that civil societies were first formed by means of some kind of rudimentary contract also seems to be reasonable when compared with the alternative suppositions that they developed naturally, as the family may be supposed to have done, or arose from conquests. For the family itself may reasonably be supposed to have originated only as a consequence of agreements entered into by male and female, and the acquisition of sufficient power to conquer others rests upon certain agreements made, one with another, by the conquerors. It is therefore not necessary, in order to place some plausibility upon the suppositions of Hobbes, Locke, and Rousseau that civil societies were initially instituted by means of rudimentary contracts, to interpret them as using the concept of a social contract only as a methodological device to justify the ascription of certain legal or political rights and obligations to various classes of persons. On the contrary, their supposition of the existence of such elementary contracts may reasonably be interpreted as a factual supposition (though admittedly conjectural or philosophical rather than historical or empirical) as plausible as any other alternative that may be presented to account for the origin of political societies.

After maintaining that governments were initially instituted by means of rudimentary contracts, Rousseau proceeds in the second discourse to discuss the origin of different forms of government. His position in the second discourse is somewhat different from that of *The Social Contract*. In the latter work he maintains that "the first societies governed themselves aristocratically," that "the heads of families took counsel together on public affairs," and that "the young bowed without question to the authority of experience." Thus in *The Social Contract* the earliest form of government was not elective, but a gerontocracy. But as the natural inequality of age came to have less influence than the "artificial inequality produced by institutions . . . , riches or power were put before age, and aristocracy became elective." This, however, was eventually replaced with a hereditary form of government as patrician families came to be created through the transmission of the father's political power along with his wealth to his sons, and young men of twenty came to inherit the position of senator. Rousseau therefore distinguishes in *The Social Contract* between three kinds of aristocracy—gerontocracy or natural aristocracy, elective aristocracy, and hereditary aristocracy—and supposes that in the infancy of civil society they succeeded one another in this order. But in relation to merit their order is different. "The first is only for simple peoples; the third is the worst of all governments; the second is the best, and is aristocracy properly so called."[6]

In the second discourse, on the other hand, Rousseau asserts that "the different forms of government owe their origin to the differing degrees of inequality which existed between individuals at the time of their institution."[7] If one man happened to be

pre-eminent in power, virtue, riches, or personal influence, he became sole magistrate, and the state assumed the form of monarchy. If several, nearly equal in point of eminence, stood above the rest, they were elected jointly, and formed an aristocracy. Again, among a people who had deviated less from a state of nature, and between whose fortune or talents there was less disproportion, the supreme administration was retained in common, and a democracy was formed. It was discovered in process of time which of these forms suited men the best.[8]

This last does not mean that Rousseau is maintaining that only one of these forms of government is the best for all men at all places and times, for in *The Social Contract* he argues that different forms of government are suitable for different peoples, depending upon such factors as their size, their character, and their circumstances, so that each form "is in some cases the best, and in others the worst." In general, monarchy is best for large states, aristocracy for middle sized states, and democracy for small states.[9]

In the second discourse Rousseau is also supposing that when governments were first instituted their task, regardless of the form of the government, was only to administer the laws agreed upon by the people, not to enact them. He is therefore supposing that when governments were initially instituted their function was in fact what in *The Social Contract* he says it ought to be and must be if a just society is to be possible. So long as governments continued to fulfill their proper function of merely administering the laws enacted by the people, and did not attempt to usurp the right of enacting laws, the people subject to them remained citizens as well as subjects. But, of course, they did not always continue to do so. Instead, whereas "some peoples remained altogether subject to the laws," and in doing so remained citizens, "others soon came to obey their magistrates," and in doing so ceased to be citizens and became only subjects. Whereas the former "laboured to preserve their liberty," the latter, "irritated at seeing others enjoying a blessing they had lost, thought only of making slaves of their neighbours." And thus whereas "happiness and virtue" grew among the former, "riches and conquests" arose among the latter.[10]

At first, Rousseau maintains in the second discourse, all governmental offices, regardless of the form of the government, were elective. This, as we have seen, conflicts with the position taken in *The Social Contract*. It means, however, that in the second discourse Rousseau is supposing that the ideal advocated in *The Social Contract* was in fact realized when civil society was in its infancy. Even then, though, he supposes that wealth sometimes influenced elections. But "when the influence of wealth was out of the question, the preference was given to merit, which gives a natural ascendancy, and to age, which is experienced in business and deliberate in council."[11] Here Rousseau treats men of merit as constituting a kind of natural aristocracy, whereas in *The Social Contract* he speaks only of a gerontocracy as a natural aristocracy. But in the second discourse, as in *The Social Contract*, elective aristocracy degenerates into hereditary aristocracy, especially as elections come to be felt to be a nuisance, and "magistrates, having become hereditary, contracted the habit of considering their offices as a family estate, and themselves as proprietors of the communities of which they were at first only the officers, of regarding their fellow-citizens as their slaves, and numbering them, like cattle, among their belongings."[12] This constitutes the third and last main moment in the progress of inequality. The first was "the establishment of laws and of the right of property," the second the institution of government, and this, the third, "the conversion of legitimate into arbitrary power." The first moment authorized the distinction between rich and poor, the second the distinction between the powerful and the weak, and the third the distinction between master and slave. The third moment constitutes "the last degree of inequality, and the term at which all the rest remain, when they have got so far, till the government is either entirely dissolved by new revolutions, or brought back again to legitimacy."[13]

Although Rousseau here speaks of hereditary government as the last major stage of inequality, he later maintains that the terminal stage of inequality is despotism, and describes it in such a way that the despot (or despots) need not be hereditary.[14] In both places the terminal stage of inequality is described as one in which legitimate power is converted into arbitrary power and in which the relationship of magistrate and subject is transformed into that of master and slave. But his later account of the last stage of inequality differs from the earlier, not only in his implying in the later account that the despot need not be hereditary, but also, and more importantly, in his maintaining in the later account that all private persons subject to the despot return to the equality of the state of nature. This difference between the two accounts in turn is based upon another difference, consisting in the amount of power possessed by the rulers. In the first account Rousseau supposes that the magistrates do not have sufficient power to usurp illegitimate power without, so to speak, sharing the spoils. It is therefore necessary that they make certain concessions to certain individuals or groups in order to receive their support and also that they countenance certain inequalities among their subjects which already obtain. In the latter case their acquisition of power contributes to the continuation of certain already existent inequalities among their subjects, and in the former it adds to these inequalities by establishing additional inequalities. Thus in his first account of the terminal stage of inequality Rousseau is supposing that although legitimate power is transformed into artibrary power, the power the magistrate possesses is not sufficiently great to enable him to reduce all his subjects to a level of equality as his slaves. On the contrary, since he must countenance certain already existent inequalities among his subjects and consent to the establishment of certain other inequalities among them, his acquisition of arbitrary power, rather than eliminating the already existent inequalities among his subjects, increases them. This stage of inequality may therefore be said to be the terminal stage in the sense that within it there is a maximum of inequality among the subjects of the ruler (or rulers).

Rousseau's first account of the final stage of inequality may therefore be said to be an account of a different stage of inequality from that of which he speaks in his second account. In his first account he is speaking of a maximum of inequality among the subjects of a ruler, and not of a maximum of inequality between the ruler on the one hand and the totality of his subjects on the other. In the second account, on the other hand, he is speaking of the second kind of inequality. This is to say that in his second account he is speaking of a situation in which a despot (or despots) has acquired such great power that the totality of his subjects has become equally subject to his will, which has become law for them, and therefore equally his slaves. In this case there may be said to be a maximum of equality among his subjects, since all are equally his slaves and equally subject to his will, and a maximum of inequality between the despot on the one hand and his subjects on the other. Thus Rousseau, in presenting two accounts of the terminal stage of inequality, may be read as presenting accounts of two distinct kinds of extreme inequality. In the first, power, to some extent, is distributed among various subjects and classes of subjects of the magistrates, and not concentrated in the magistrates, whereas in the second power is relatively concentrated in the despot. The first represents the polar opposite of the state of nature, since it constitutes the extreme opposite of the equality of the state of nature, whereas the second represents an approximation to the equality of the state of nature, since there is an equality among the subjects of the despot with respect to their subjection to him. But this last, of course, does not mean that under absolute despotism there is simply a return to the state of nature, for the subjects of the despot, though equal in their enslavement to him, are nevertheless still slaves and not free, whereas in the state of nature there is no slavery and no despotism, and no man is subject to the power of another.

The two accounts of the terminal stage of inequality may also be contrasted with each other by means of an analogy, somewhat imperfect, taken from Hegel's philosophy of history. Hegel distinguishes between three great epochs of world history—the Oriental, the Greco-Roman, and the Germanic-Christian. In the Oriental epoch one man only, the oriental despot, is recognized as free—all others within the realm he governs are his slaves. In the Greco-Roman epoch more than one man is free, since there is a multiplicity of citizens, but not all are free, for there are still slaves. In the Germanic-Christian epoch it comes to be recognized in theory, and increasingly in practice, that all men are free, and that slavery is therefore wrong. Hegel's characterization of these three epochs constitutes a kind of idealized or simplified hyperbolic model, as does Rousseau's second account of the terminal stage of inequality. For it is not literally true that during the Oriental epoch only one man was free, nor has it been literally true that during the Germanic-Christian epoch all men have been free. Nor, in the case of Rousseau, is it true that one man ever has or ever could acquire such great power as to be able to reduce all others to an equality of slavery. Instead, as we saw earlier, and as Rousseau recognizes in his first account of the terminal stage of inequality, the acquisition of power depends upon the support of others, and thus involves making certain concessions to them. At the same time, however, there is some point to the exaggerated abstractions of Rousseau and Hegel, taken as expressing the extreme limit towards which a certain situation tends. Thus there was a closer approximation during the Oriental epoch than during the Greco-Roman to a situation in which only one man is free, and a closer approximation during the Germanic-Christian epoch than during the Greco-Roman to a situation in which all men are free. And Rousseau's second account of the terminal stage of inequality may be taken as a description of the extreme limit of the concentration of power in one man, a limit that may be approximated. Thus although only his first account of the terminal stage of inequality may literally apply to any actual historical situation, some historical situations may nevertheless satisfy more fully than others the description of this terminal stage as presented in his second account.

Rousseau's second account of the terminal stage of inequality corresponds roughly to Hegel's account of the Oriental epoch, and his first account to Hegel's view of the Greco-Roman epoch. Rousseau's own position falls within Hegel's Germanic-Christian tradition. But whereas Hegel maintains that there is a dialectical and historical development of the Germanic-Christian epoch out of the Greco-Roman and of the latter out of the Oriental, Rousseau does not assert that there is either a dialectical or a historical development of either of the terminal stages of inequality out of the other. Instead, he writes as though either stage may occur independently of the other and without leading to the other. The increase of inequality may terminate in the extreme of either of these terminal stages without passing through the other, and each may be overcome through the restoration of at least an approximation to equality without first passing through the other. Moreover, whereas Hegel's account of history is optimistic, in the sense that on the whole there is an inevitable progress in human freedom and the realization of human potentialities, despite the occurrence of retrogressive periods and much violence, bloodshed, suffering, and death, Rousseau's by comparison is profoundly pessimistic. Whereas for Hegel history on the whole is the development of human freedom, for Rousseau it is essentially a dismal spectacle of the loss of equality and freedom.

But though Rousseau is by no means optimistic concerning the future prospects of history, he nevertheless refuses to acquiesce in its injustices. We have seen that he denies that right can either be reduced to or based upon power. The fact that a man or group has the power to rule and exercises this power does not mean that he has the right to rule, and should he rule without right, those he rules have the right to resist and depose him: "the despot is master only so long as he remains the strongest; as soon as he can be expelled, he has no right to complain of violence. . . . As he was maintained by force alone, it is force alone that overthrows him."[15] But the force used to overthrow a despot and to establish equality and a legitimate government, unlike the force employed by the despot in usurping power and increasing inequality, is used with right.

But though Rousseau refuses to acquiesce in the injustices of history, he nevertheless maintains, in a passage anticipatory of the dialectical histories of Hegel, Marx, and Engels, that the degeneration into inequality is necessary, and that to understand it "we must consider not so much the motives for the establishment of the body politic, as the forms it assumes in actuality, and the faults that necessarily attend it: for the flaws which make social institutions necessary are the same as make the abuse of them unavoidable."[16] The flaws that make social institutions necessary are reducible ultimately to the growth of egoism and the weakening of natural compassion that begin almost as soon as man leaves the state of nature, and certainly by the time he has reached the second stage of pre-civil society. But the increase of egoism and the lessening of natural compassion not only make social institutions necessary—they also make the abuse of these institutions unavoidable. Given the departure from the state of nature and the entrance into society, the development of egoism and the decline of natural compassion are inevitable, and must be curbed through the establishment of social institutions. But the institutions that have been established historically have, on the whole, only succeeded in accelerating the growth of egoism and the lessening of natural compassion. Part of the reason for this is that, with only a few exceptions, the laws that have been enacted historically have sought only to restrain rather than alter the nature of men and their passions.

As this is the case, equality and a just society can be established only by enacting laws and establishing institutions that seek not merely to restrain the egoistic inclinations men have acquired through living in corrupt societies but to change human nature itself and the passions of men. For Rousseau this task is not so impossible as it may seem to some. We have seen that he views human nature as plastic—man is at once the corruptible and the perfectible animal, and just as he has been corrupted through living under corrupt institutions, so also at least an approach toward perfecting him can be made through establishing just institutions. Rousseau's conception of the conditions that must be satisfied if a just society is to be possible is presented, however, not in the first two discourses, but in the third, and above all in *The Social Contract*. The first two discourses are essentially a diagnosis of the sickness pervading mankind and human society. The first discourse is simply an impassioned *cri de coeur* declaring the presence of sickness, whereas the second, though still a *cri de coeur*, is a reasoned account of the origin and course of the sickness. Neither presents a remedy for it. It is only in the third discourse and *The Social Contract* that the prescription for a cure is to be found.

XII. On Returning to the State of Nature

It might seem, however, given that the growth of egoism and the decline of natural compassion come about through man's leaving the pure state of nature and living in corrupt societies, that there are two possible remedies. One is the establishment of a just society, the other an abandonment of society altogether in order to return to the state of nature. As has just been mentioned, the first remedy is considered in the third discourse and *The Social Contract*. The second is considered in the second discourse. There Rousseau makes it clear that the second remedy is not a real possibility— that the problems occasioned by the growth of corruption and egoism cannot be solved through returning to the state of nature. The following passage makes this clear: "What, then, is to be done? Must societies be totally abolished? Must *meum* and *tuum* be annihilated, and must we return again to the forests to live among bears? This is a deduction in the manner of my adversaries, which I would as soon anticipate as let them have the shame of drawing."[1] Immediately following this passage Rousseau addresses these words to certain men.

O you, who have never heard the voice of heaven, who think man destined only to live this little life and die in peace; you, who can resign in the midst of populous cities your fatal acquisitions, your restless spirits, your corrupt hearts and endless desires; resume, since it depends entirely on yourselves, your ancient and primitive innocence: retire to the woods, there to lose the sight and remembrance of the crimes of your contemporaries; and be not apprehensive of degrading your species, by renouncing its advances in order to renounce its vices.

But that there are any among those who read these words "who have never heard the voice of heaven" and who have the power to renounce their "corrupt hearts and endless desires" and return to the state of nature is very doubtful. If there are any, their number is insignificant when compared with those who cannot make the return, either because they have "heard the voice of heaven" or because they cannot renounce their "fatal acquisitions." Rousseau includes himself among the latter, "whose passions have destroyed their original simplicity, who can no longer subsist on plants or acorns, or live without laws and magistrates."[2] But even though one may have the power to make the return, he would be forbidden by "the voice of heaven" to do so. This is the case for the following reasons.

The fundamental reason is that "the Divine Being has called all mankind to be partakers in the happiness and perfection of celestial intelligences."[3] This, however, is a happiness and perfection unattainable within "this little life" we live on earth, regardless of whether we live it in the state of nature or in civil society, so that if there is no life beyond the life we live on earth the happiness and perfection to which God calls mankind cannot be attained. It is therefore attainable only in a life beyond the life we live on earth. But it can be attained only through meriting it, and it can be merited only through striving to fulfill the divine command. This is the command to love God with all our heart, and all our soul, and all our mind, and to love our neighbor as ourselves.[4] The first part of this commandment cannot be fulfilled unless the second is also fulfilled, for "If a man say, I love God, and hateth his brother, he is a liar: for he that loveth not his brother whom he hath seen, how can he love God whom he hath not seen?"[5] But a man can fulfill the command to love God and therefore his neighbor and his brother only through living in society, not through living in the state of nature. This is the case for two reasons.

The first is that, as we have seen, man in the pure state of nature is merely a natural creature who acts in accordance with laws imposed upon him from without by God or nature and of which he therefore need not be conscious. He is not a moral agent who freely imposes laws upon himself, laws of which he must be conscious if he is to impose them upon himself. But the divine command is not a law of nature, but a divine or moral law.

Men do not naturally, i.e., instinctively or unreflectively, act in accordance with it, but can come to act in accordance with it only by overcoming nature through a consciousness of the divine command and through the subsequent imposition of it upon themselves. It is true that, according to Rousseau, men in the pure state of nature are not afflicted with the flaw of egoism, but, instead, seek merely to do good to themselves with as little evil as possible to others. But the voice of heaven does not command us merely to abstain from egoism, nor does it command us merely to do good to ourselves with as little evil as possible to others. Instead, it commands us to love our brother and our neighbor as we love ourselves—it commands, in other words, that we act in accordance with what Rousseau refers to as "that sublime maxim of rational justice," which is to do to others as you would have them do unto you. But this sublime maxim of rational justice and the divine command to love our brother and our neighbor as we love ourselves cannot be fulfilled merely by doing good to ourselves with as little evil as possible to others. On the contrary, they can be fulfilled only by attempting to do good to others as we attempt to do good to ourselves, for we do not and cannot love others as we love ourselves unless we attempt to do good to them as we attempt to do good to ourselves. But this we do not by nature attempt to do. Instead, as we have seen, even though in the pure state of nature self-love is moderated by compassion, it is still the former that is fundamental. So long, then, as men live in the state of nature, the divine command cannot be fulfilled. Nor can it be fulfilled through attempting to return to this state. Therefore, should someone, unlike Rousseau, have the power to resign his fatal acquisitions, his restless spirit, his corrupt heart and endless desires, to return to the state of nature, he could seek to embark upon the return only if either he has "never heard the voice of heaven" or else, having heard it, has not been persuaded by it.

This brings us to the second reason for saying that the divine command can be fulfilled only through remaining in society, and not through seeking to return to the state of nature. Given the considerations of the preceding paragraph, the man who seeks to make the return is, in effect, directly repudiating the divine command. For in attempting to make the return he would be endeavoring to act in accordance with the principle of self-love, as moderated by the principle of compassion. He would be attempting, in other words, to substitute the principle of self-love for the divine command as the principle of his action. For the principle of self-love, even as moderated by the principle of compassion, does not amount to the divine command. It is true that it is also not equivalent to the principle of egoism—that the person who acts in accordance with it is not thereby necessarily seeking to promote his own good at the expense of the good of others. But he is concerned primarily with promoting his own good and is therefore acting incompatibly with the divine command, which commands us, not first to seek our own good, but to love our neighbor and our brother as we love ourselves.

Indeed, there is perhaps an even more immediate and more serious incompatibility between seeking to return to the state of nature and fulfilling the divine command. This is that the person who attempts the return is, in effect, seeking his own good by abandoning those of his neighbors within society who require his assistance in purging the society and therefore themselves from corruption and injustice. He is, in effect, declaring by his action that he is seeking his own good even though those he abandons rot in corruption and injustice—that he is seeking his own safety even though the rest of the world go up in flames. In thus seeking his own good, the effects of his action approximate those of egoistic action. For even though he would not intend by his action to prevent the attainment of the good of others, he would at least unintentionally inhibit the attainment of their good through failing to concern himself with it, which is in direct violation of the divine command. This can perhaps be put by saying that although he would not be guilty of a sin of commission, he would be guilty of a sin of omission. And we all know that the consequences of sins of omission can sometimes be as grievous as those of sins of commission.

For these reasons, then, those who might seek to return to the state of nature could attempt to do so only because either they have not heard the voice of heaven or, if they have heard it, have not been persuaded by it. Nor will it do to suggest that the command of the voice of heaven could be fulfilled if everyone within society were to return to the state of nature. For, as we have seen, men in the state of nature act in accordance with the principle of self-love, as moderated by natural compassion, and action in accordance with such a principle is not equivalent to action in accordance with the divine command. Nor would it do to suggest that at least the corruption and injustice of society would be avoided if everyone made the return. For should everyone do so there would be nothing to insure that the same transition from the state of nature through pre-civil society to civil society—with the same process of corruption—would not repeat itself. Nor will it do to suggest that an application of the lessons learned through the hard experience of having already gone through this process would prevent its repetition. For it would be possible to make the return only through transforming ourselves into purely natural creatures as opposed to rational beings and moral agents, and thus through re-acquiring the primitive innocence we have long since lost. This would require, not only that we abstain from a rational and moral application of the lessons learned, but also that we endeavor to forget the lessons themselves. Thus the suggestion that we return to the state of nature is idle. Even though some few individuals may be sufficiently free from the attractions of society to attempt the return, it is obvious that the overwhelming mass of men are not. This being the case, a universal return to the state of nature is not merely unlikely—it is impossible.

Indeed, a return to this state by any man is impossible, despite Rousseau's supposition that some men might be capable of making the return. This is so because it is impossible for man in society to recover the primitive innocence of the pure state of nature, since it is impossible for a rational being and a moral agent to transform himself into a purely natural creature, impossible for a man to divest himself of his humanity and transform himself into a brute, impossible for a man to divest himself of the moral freedom and responsibility he ineluctably possesses as a rational being and a moral agent. Having once lost his primitive natural innocence, man is condemned permanently to the status of rational being and moral agent, and therefore to moral freedom and responsibility.

We may therefore take it as established, not only that Rousseau himself did not advocate a return to the state of nature, but also, for the reasons given, that such a return would be impossible. If so, the corruption of actual societies and the concomitant egoism of their members can be eliminated, if at all, not by attempting the impossible task of a return to the state of nature, but, instead, only through transforming these societies into just societies. Since Rousseau's account of the conditions that must be satisfied if this transformation is to be effected is presented most fully in *The Social Contract*, we must therefore now turn to a consideration of the position presented there.

XIII. The Problem of *The Social Contract*

As was noted earlier, Rousseau informs us of his purpose in *The Social Contract* in the very first paragraph of Book One: "I mean to inquire if, in the civil order, there can be any sure and legitimate rule of administration, men being taken as they are and laws as they might be. In this inquiry I shall endeavour always to unite what right sanctions with what is prescribed by interest, in order that justice and utility may in no case be divided." The first thing to be noted in this passage is that Rousseau proposes to take men as they are, not as they might be, and laws as they might be, not as they are. His point here seems to be that although human nature is plastic, it still is not as malleable as law—that although human nature can be changed, at least within limits, it still cannot be changed either as completely or as readily as a system of law, and, in fact, can most effectively be changed only indirectly, through first effecting changes within the systems of law to which men are subject. At the same time, however, the constancy of human nature imposes limits upon the extent to which changes within a system of law can effect changes in man, so that if one is to arrive at a just estimate of the extent to which changes in human nature can be effected by means of changes within systems of law, one must attempt to arrive at a realistic estimate of what is and of what is not constant within human nature. For Rousseau, as we have seen, man is at once both the perfectible and the corruptible animal. Just as he can be corrupted through living under a corrupt system of law, so also he can be perfected through living under a perfect system of law. If, however, a system of law is to be perfect, it must take account of and be grounded in the constant nature of man.

A perfect system of law, however, is not merely a just system—it is also a stable system that makes possible a stable form of political association. Rousseau is not interested in presenting a plan for a utopian society, without regard to the question of whether such a society could ever be actualized on earth, given the actual nature of man. If this were his interest there would be no need to consider the actual nature of man and the extent to which it can be molded through effecting changes in systems of law. Instead, he would be free to construct any system of law that might happen to please his fancy, without considering the question of whether such a system could ever be realized in the actual world. But this is not his interest. On the contrary, it is to discover, by taking men as they are, some form of political association that is at once both legitimate and stable and that is also realizable in the actual world peopled by actual and therefore imperfect men.

It is true, as we have seen, that Rousseau maintains that many of man's blemishes are the effects of life in corrupt forms of society. But, as we have also seen, he claims that self-love, along with natural compassion, is one of the two fundamental natural traits of man. Of the two it is self-love that is the more fundamental, even in the pure state of nature. We have seen also that compassion may be dulled, even deadened, and rendered inoperative and ineffective by corrupt societies, whereas such societies have the opposite effect upon self-love, heightening its operation and transforming it into egoism. But although Rousseau maintains that compassion is frequently dulled and deadened by corrupt societies, he does not suppose that just societies would have the same effect upon self-love. Although such societies would weaken egoism and render it less operative and effective, they would not have such an effect on self-love. On the contrary, self-love remains constant, regardless of whether one lives in the pure state of nature, in pre-civil society, or in civil society, and regardless of how corrupt or how just a society one happens to live in. This is at least part of what is meant by saying that self-love is the fundamental principle of human nature.

Although, then, human nature is indefinitely plastic and can be molded in a variety of ways so as either to corrupt or to perfect it, self-love remains constant throughout all these changes. Both compassion and egoism can be either strengthened or weakened, but not self-love. Compassion is strongest in the pure state of nature, but is weakened and may even be extinguished in corrupt societies, whereas egoism is strongest in corrupt societies and non-existent in the pure state of nature. In just societies compassion would be stronger than in corrupt societies, whereas egoism would be stronger in corrupt than in just societies. But throughout all changes of society and circumstance the strength and operation of self-love remain constant. In the pure state of nature its operation is moderated naturally by the operation of compassion; in corrupt societies, in which the moderation of its operation by compassion and by principles of justice is minimized, it tends through excess of operation to degenerate into egoism; and in just societies its operation is moderated by principles of justice. Yet its operation remains constant regardless of the extent to which it is moderated, either naturally by compassion or morally by principles of justice, and regardless of the extent to which it degenerates into egoism.

The effect of the operation of self-love upon other persons may be either beneficial or baneful. To the extent that its operation is moderated by compassion or by principles of justice, the effect upon others will tend to be beneficial; but to the extent that it is not thus moderated by these other principles and degenerates into egoism, the effect upon others tends to be baneful. But though the operation of self-love can be channeled in directions beneficial rather than baneful to others, its operation cannot be annulled. Being the fundamental principle of human nature, and therefore a constant principle, it cannot be extirpated from the nature of man, regardless of the extent to which its operation may be moderated and of the direction in which its operation be channeled. Therefore, any attempt to establish a form of political association that is both legitimate and stable, if it is to succeed, must begin by taking men as they are, i.e., as constantly moved by self-love, however it may be moderated and channeled, and by framing the system of law, which is to make a stable and legitimate form of political association possible, in such a way as to take account of its constant operation. Unless this is done you may succeed in forming in your imagination a utopian system of law that delights your fancy, but you will not succeed in framing a system of law that makes possible the establishment of a stable and legitimate society within the actual world peopled by flesh-and-blood human beings universally animated by self-love. Thus, although the number of systems of law that you can conjure up in your fancy will be limited only by the extent of your imagination, the number of systems applicable to the actual world in such a way as to make a stable and legitimate form of political association possible will be limited by the constant and universal operation of self-love.

It is because of the constant and universal operation of this principle that Rousseau says that in *The Social Contract* he will attempt "always to unite what right sanctions with what is prescribed by interest, in order that justice and utility may in no case be divided." Right must be united with interest and justice with utility because the existence of a legitimate and stable political association is possible only to the extent that these unions are attained. The legitimacy of a political association is connected with right and justice. These three notions—right, justice, and legitimacy—mutually imply one another, so that each can be realized within a political association only if and insofar as the other two are also realized. Each of these notions is moral or non-natural, as contrasted with the notions with which Rousseau associates them—stability, interest, and utility. These latter notions are natural, in that they are non-moral. We are thus given two sets of concepts—one a set of moral or non-natural concepts, the other a set of natural or non-moral concepts. The problem of *The Social Contract* is to unite the two sets—legitimacy with stability, right with interest, and justice with utility—in short, to unite the moral and non-natural with the natural and non-moral.

This is a problem because these two realms are not given as united, but as standing in opposition to one another. We are presented historically in experience and actuality the separation of the two. As Rousseau attempted to demonstrate in the first two discourses, the realm of the moral has not been actualized historically, at least not adequately, and, conversely, the realm of the actual has not been moralized, at least not adequately. The problem of *The Social Contract* is therefore to show how the opposition between these two realms can be overcome through moralizing the realm of the actual and thereby actualizing the realm of the moral. This can be done by means of reason alone, not by means of the continued operation of nature, undirected by reason. For it is precisely the operation of nature, independent of the direction and demands of reason, that is the source of the bifurcation between the actual and the moral, the natural and the rational. The problem, however, cannot be solved merely by sacrificing the claims of one realm in order to satisfy those of the other, for the claims of each demand satisfaction, each in its own way. The claims of nature and the actual will persist until satisfied, but so will the claims of reason and morality. However, as long as they remain antithetical they cannot both be satisfied; thus if the claims of each are to be satisfied they must be synthesized in some way. Yet a satisfactory or genuine synthesis cannot be effected merely by seeking to impose some arbitrary or artificial solution, but only through showing how the claims of each realm can effectively be satisfied without sacrificing the claims of the other. Unless the fulfillment of the claims of one realm can also constitute the satisfaction of the claims of the other, no genuine synthesis of the two realms is possible, and the problem is therefore insoluble.

Rousseau believes that this problem is soluble, at least theoretically or philosophically—that the claims of both realms can be genuinely synthesized, so that the claims of each are satisfied without sacrificing the satisfaction of the claims of the other. Indeed, he takes the even stronger position that the claims of each can be satisfied *only* through or by means of the satisfaction of the claims of the other. This means that in *The Social Contract* he seeks to show, not only that the stability of a political association is compatible with its legitimacy, but also that its stability depends upon its legitimacy—that a political association is stable only if and insofar as it is legitimate. It also means that he seeks to show, not only that the claims of interest and utility are compatible with those of right and justice, but also that the claims of the former can be satisfied only if and insofar as those of the latter are satisfied. For just as a political association is legitimate only if and insofar as the claims of right and justice are satisfied, so also it can be stable only if and insofar as the claims of interest and utility are satisfied. But since its stability depends not only upon the satisfaction of the claims of interest and utility, but also upon its legitimacy, and since its legitimacy depends upon the satisfaction of the claims of right and justice, it follows that its stability also depends upon the satisfaction of the latter claims. This, however, is to show, or rather to claim, only that the satisfaction of the claims of nature—the claims of stability, interest, and utility—depends upon the satisfaction of the claims of morality—the claims of legitimacy, right, and justice. If, however, a genuine synthesis or union of the two kinds of claim is to be effected, it must be established not only that the satisfaction of the claims of nature depends upon the satisfaction of the claims of morality, but also that the reverse is true—that the satisfaction of the claims of morality depends upon the satisfaction of the claims of nature.

XIV. Self-love and Egoism

Rousseau's argument designed to establish this latter dependence can be understood only by keeping in mind his distinction between self-love and egoism. Self-love, as we have seen, is natural to man, whereas egoism is not. To say that the former is natural is to say that each man instinctively or unreflectively seeks his own good, independent of any of the influences of society upon him, regardless of whether he be in the pure state of nature, in pre-civil society, or in civil society, and regardless of how just or how corrupt the society in which he lives may be. On the other hand, to say that egoism is not natural is to say that men are not instinctively or unreflectively egoistic, but become so only as a consequence of living in society. This, however, is to say only that self-love is natural to man and that egoism is not. It does not specify the essential nature of each, which is what must be done if one is to show that the satisfaction of the claims of morality depends upon the satisfaction of the claims of nature.

The difference between the essence of each may be specified in the following way. Self-love leads a man simply to seek his own good, whereas egoism leads one to seek to possess a greater quantity of some kind of good than others have. Insofar as a man acts solely from self-love he seeks his own good without considering the relation in which his good stands to the good of others—he is concerned, that is to say, only with his own good, not with the good of others. It is true that insofar as self-love is moderated either by natural compassion or by principles of justice the agent considers the good of others as well as his own good, and seeks his own, so far as he can, in a way compatible with the attainment of the good of others. But self-love, considered by itself in abstraction from the effects upon it of natural compassion and principles of justice, leads a man simply to seek his own good without regard to the good of others. It is because of this that self-love can operate in the pure state of nature as well as in society. Since its operation does not require that the agent concern himself with the good of others, it can operate in a situation—such as the pure state of nature—in which one individual is isolated from others and in which his action therefore has no effect upon the good of others. The principle of self-love is thus essentially non-social in nature.

But egoism is different. Insofar as a man acts under the influence of this principle, he does not seek merely his own good in isolation from the good of others; instead, he seeks a good that is greater than that of someone else. He is therefore satisfied or content not merely in attaining his own good, but in attaining a good of some kind that is greater than that of others. The operation of self-love permits a man to be content with a situation in which the good of everyone is attained, so long as his good is also attained, and therefore to be satisfied with a situation in which the good of each man is equally or fully realized, and in which no man has more of a good than is possessed by anyone else. In contrast, the man animated by egoism is not content with such a situation, even though his good be as fully realized as that of anyone else, but, instead, desires to possess more of some kind of good than others possess. Accordingly, if the object of the egoist be the acquisition of wealth, he, in contrast to the man animated by self-love, is not content to possess the same wealth as others possess, and thus is not content with an equality of wealth among men sufficient to enable each to obtain his own good, but, instead, wishes to possess more wealth than others do. Or else, if the object of the egoist be the acquisition of political power, he, in contrast to the man moved by self-love, is not content merely with a voice equal to that of everyone else in determining the law of the body politic, but wishes a voice greater than others have. Or again, the egoist, in contrast to the man motivated by self-love, is not satisfied simply to be treated with the same degree of respect as others receive and to respect others as much as he wishes to be respected by them, but, instead, wishes to be treated with greater respect than that which is granted others and which he is willing to grant them. And so on.

From this it is evident that egoism, unlike self-love, is essentially social in nature, since it necessarily involves a comparison in some way of the amount I possess of some kind of good with the amount of that kind of good possessed by others, and therefore could not exist in a pure state of nature in which individuals are isolated from one another. It is also evident that it takes different forms. It may manifest itself as greed, as in the desire to possess more wealth than others do, or as the lust for power, as in the desire to have a greater voice in the affairs of state than others have, or as vanity, as in the desire to be esteemed more than others are. It is evident also that it is a source of unhappiness, either for the egoist or for those afflicted by his success. For the egoist is dissatisfied to the extent that his egoistic desires are unfulfilled, whereas others suffer, at least at times, if they are fulfilled. It is therefore also evident that egoism is anti-social in nature, since the aim of the egoist, as an egoist, is not a state of society in which the good of each person is attained, but, rather, a situation in which he possesses more of some kind of good than others do, even at the expense of the attainment of their good. It is true that self-love, moderated neither by natural compassion nor by principles of justice, is non-social in nature. For insofar as self-love operates independently of any moderation by either natural compassion or principles of justice, I am concerned only with the promotion of my own good, not with the good of others. Yet self-love, even though moderated by neither natural compassion nor principles of justice, unlike egoism, is still not essentially anti-social. For the man moved by such unmoderated self-love, unlike the egoist, seeks only his own good, not a good greater than that which someone else possesses, and is content insofar as he attains the good he seeks, regardless of whether it be greater than that which someone else happens to possess.

Given these differences between self-love and egoism, certain consequences follow. One is that a harmony or compatibility is possible between the goods sought by a number of men when each is animated by self-love, even though it be moderated neither by natural compassion nor by principles of justice. For if each is concerned only with the attainment of his own good, and not with attaining more of a good of some kind than others possess, then there is no necessity that the good of some always be sacrificed in order that the good of others be attained. It is true that a situation of extreme scarcity may exist such that it is impossible that the good of each person be attained. In such a case the good of some may have to be sacrificed in order that the good of others be attained. But situations of such extreme scarcity are relatively rare. By far a more frequent sort of situation is one in which there is a sufficient abundance of attainable goods so that no one need starve, yet not so great an abundance that each person moved by unmoderated self-love can attain fully the good he seeks. This, of course, is the kind of situation that usually obtains within society. Conflicts are thus likely to occur in such situations to the extent that different persons, even though motivated only by unmoderated self-love and not by egoism, have desires for goods that cannot all be satisfied.

To say, then, that a harmony is possible between the goods sought by a number of men, each animated by unmoderated self-love, is not to say that this harmony will in fact exist. Instead, it is to say only that the good each seeks, insofar as he is moved by self-love alone, is not necessarily incompatible with the goods others seek. The situation is different when we have a number of men, all or some of whom are animated by egoism. In this case some men, at least, are not content merely to seek their own good, but rather seek to possess more of a good of some kind than others do. It is obvious that in such a situation there can be no harmony between the objects they seek—it is impossible for Peter to possess more of A than Paul does while Paul also possesses more of A than Peter does. Egoistic

desires of two or more persons directed toward the same object, in which
each desires to possess more of it than the others do, are therefore necessarily incompatible.

This, however, does not mean that egoistic desires are always incompatible, regardless of what their object may be. For it may happen that Peter
desires to possess more of A, say wealth, than Paul does, but not more of
B, say political power, whereas Paul desires to possess more of B than
Peter does, but not more of A. In this event the satisfaction of the egoistic
desire of Peter might well be compatible with the satisfaction of that of
Paul, since the two desires are directed toward different objects. Neither
must the satisfaction of the egoistic desire of one person be incompatible
with the attainment of the good sought by another who is moved only by
unmoderated self-love. For the person animated by the egoistic desire may
seek only more of some good than the other seeks, without seeking so
much more that the other is deprived of the object of his unmoderated
self-love. Indeed, it may even be plausibly argued that the chances are
greater of an incompatibility occurring between the egoistic desires of
different persons than between the egoistic desire of one person and the
object of the unmoderated self-love of another. If so, then enmities are
more likely to arise between egoists than between egoists on the one hand
and those animated by self-love on the other. For so long as the egoist
desires only to possess more of certain goods than others do, but not so
much more that those moved only by self-love are thereby deprived of the
good they seek, the latter are not likely to be disturbed. But the situation is
different among egoists. So long as they each wish to possess more of
goods of the same kinds than the others do, their desires conflict in such a
way that it is impossible that they should all be satisfied. Such a situation
is likely to constitute a source of enmity among egoists.

This, however, does not mean that this enmity need manifest itself in
such a way that the conflict between egoistic desires erupts into a competition in which the desires of certain egoists are satisfied at the expense of
the satisfaction of the desires of other egoists. Instead, there may exist
such a relative equality of power among egoists that they effect a kind of
truce among themselves, and agree, either expressly or tacitly, to content
themselves with the acquisition of a greater quantity of goods than those
animated by self-love succeed in acquiring. In this way the egoists might
avoid becoming involved in the kind of competition among themselves
that would result in the satisfaction of the aims of certain egoists only at
the cost of the satisfaction of the aims of other egoists. The formation of
such agreements would not mean that the egoists would cease to be egoists
relative to one another. Nor would it mean that occasions would not

continue to occur in which one egoist would take advantage of another. But it would mean that the egoists recognize, at least implicitly, that they have certain interests in common distinct from those of non-egoists.

Should such agreements be entered into, the egoists may proceed to prey upon the non-egoists to such an extent that the latter find it increasingly difficult to satisfy even their most modest non-egoistic desires. Should this occur, the non-egoists eventually become aware of the incompatibility between the promotion of their interests and the aims of the egoists, enmity between the two classes develops, and a class consciousness on the part of the non-egoists arises. Given these developments, the non-egoists may develop sufficient power to prevent the satisfaction of the egoistic aims of egoists at the cost of the satisfaction of their non-egoistic aims. Once the egoists recognize the likelihood, or at least the possibility, of this development, they may content themselves with attempting to attain their egoistic aims without preventing the attainment of the aims of the non-egoistic class, through making concessions to the latter class sufficient to keep its members satisfied and thus pacified. Should the egoists adopt this tactic, we might perhaps refer to them as enlightened egoists. Enlightened egoism, however, is not the same thing as enlightened self-interest, given Rousseau's distinction between egoism on the one hand and self-love or self-interest on the other. The enlightened egoist, as opposed to the unenlightened egoist, is simply the egoist who employs generally effective means of attaining his egoistic ends, whereas enlightened self-interest, as opposed to unenlightened self-interest, is the employment of generally effective means of attaining one's non-egoistic good.

This development of the implications of Rousseau's distinction between self-love and egoism, though not explicit in Rousseau's work, is nevertheless, I believe, a legitimate development of what Rousseau does make explicit about this distinction. What it shows is that the extent to which the pursuit either of egoistic ends or of one's non-egoistic good is compatible with the attainment of the non-egoistic good of others varies with circumstances. In general, the pursuit of one's non-egoistic good is more compatible with the attainment of the non-egoistic good of others than is the pursuit of egoistic ends, and the enlightened pursuit either of one's non-egoistic good or of egoistic ends is also generally more compatible with the attainment of the non-egoistic good of others than is their unenlightened pursuit. It is important, however, to keep in mind that neither the pursuit of one's non-egoistic good nor the pursuit of egoistic ends, regardless of whether either be enlightened or unenlightened, amounts to the pursuit of the non-egoistic good of another as an end in itself. This is to say that neither, whether it be enlightened or unenlightened, amounts either to natural compassion or to action from principles of justice. For the object of natural compassion is always the non-egoistic good of another as an end in itself, and the object of justice is always the non-egoistic good of everyone affected by a given course of action, including both the agent who acts and everyone affected by his action, whereas both self-interested and egoistic action aim ultimately only at the good of the agent, the first at his non-egoistic good and the second at his egoistic good.

XV. Natural Compassion and Morality

Since both self-interested and egoistic action aim ultimately only at the good of the agent, whereas action motivated by natural compassion or by principles of justice aims at the good of others, action of the latter two kinds results more frequently in the attainment of the good of others than does action of the first two types. This, however, is not to say that it necessarily results in the attainment of the good of others, nor is it to say that it necessarily results in more good for others than does self-interested or egoistic action. Just as egoistic action is sometimes more compatible with and productive of the good of others than is non-egoistic self-interested action, so also is each of these kinds of action sometimes more productive of the good of others than is action animated by natural compassion or by principles of justice. This is explained, at least partly, by the fact that in the case of self-interested or egoistic action the production of the good of others is by no means always only an accidental or unintended consequence of such action. For although the agent, insofar as he acts self-interestedly or egoistically, does not aim at the good of others as an end in itself, he can intend their good as means to the attainment of his own good. Moreover, although action animated by natural compassion or principles of justice does aim at the good of others as an end it itself, it may through some accident fail to attain its object, particularly if it be unenlightened. Such action may just as easily be unenlightened as self-interested or egoistic action, and insofar as it is unenlightened it may well, through ignorance, fail to achieve its goal, either through a deficient or mistaken conception of the good of others or, given an adequate conception of the good of others, through a deficient or mistaken understanding of the means necessary for the attainment of its goal.

But although self-interested or egoistic action may sometimes be as effective in promoting the good of others as action motivated by natural compassion or by principles of justice, action of either of the latter two kinds is nonetheless more likely to be effective in doing so than is action of either of the first two types, particularly if it be as enlightened. This is the case for at least two reasons. One is that the ultimate object of both self-interested and egoistic action is the agent's own good, so that if he comes to believe that the promotion of the good of others is neither necessary for nor conducive to the promotion of his own, he ceases, insofar as his action is only self-interested or egoistic, to have any interest in promoting the good of others. This, however, cannot happen in the case of action animated by natural compassion or principles of justice, for in such action the agent seeks to promote the good of others, not as a means to the promotion of his own, but as an end in itself. A second, related, reason is that in the case of self-interested and egoistic action in which the agent seeks the good of others only as a means to the promotion of his own, he is likely to seek some other means should serious difficulties in promoting the good of others present themselves. But, for the same reason as above, this cannot happen in the case of action motivated by natural compassion or principles of justice.

Just as action animated by natural compassion or principles of justice is more likely to promote the good of others than is egoistic or self-interested action, so also action motivated by principles of justice is more likely to do so than is action animated by natural compassion. This, of course, applies only to the condition of society, not to the pure state of nature, since action motivated by principles of justice, like egoism, is possible only in society. Both self-love and natural compassion, as we have seen, are natural, in the sense that both exist in the pure state of nature and are not products of society, whereas both egoism and action from principles of justice are social, not natural, since both are possible only in society. We have already examined Rousseau's reasons for maintaining that egoism is a product of society. We have also examined, at least implicitly, his reasons for maintaining that action based upon principles of justice is possible only in society. But it may be helpful to remind ourselves here of what those reasons are.

Action from principles of justice is moral action, since it involves acting out of respect for a principle which I impose upon myself as a law binding upon myself. The principle of justice can be stated in various ways. It can be stated as the divine command of the voice of heaven: "Love your neighbor and your brother as you love yourself." Or it may be stated as what Rousseau refers to as "that sublime maxim of rational justice": "Do to others as you would have them do unto you." Or, again, it may be stated in any one of the ways in which Kant states the categorical imperative, as for example as follows: "Act always so as to treat humanity, whether in your own person or in that of others, as an end in itself, never merely as a means." Or, finally, it may be stated in this way: "Always act compatibly, not merely with the promotion of your own good, but also with the promotion of the good of everyone affected by your action." But regardless of how it is stated or apprehended, its statement and apprehension presuppose the attainment of a level of reason that makes possible both (1) the apprehension of an abstract universal principle or law, and (2) self-consciousness, since I cannot act out of respect for a principle, which involves imposing it upon myself, unless I am conscious of myself as something upon which I can and ought to impose it. But this level of reason, according to Rousseau, is attainable only in society, not in the pure state of nature. It is therefore society that makes morality possible, not morality that makes society possible, even though, as we shall see, it is morality that makes a just society possible.

Morality, then, like egoism and unlike self-love and natural compassion, is essentially social and rational in nature, since both morality and egoism presuppose the attainment of a level of rationality that is possible only in society. Both self-love and natural compassion are pre-social and pre-rational, since neither presupposes the existence of society nor the level of rationality presupposed by morality and egoism. But although egoism, like morality, is essentially social and rational in nature, there are important differences. One is that egoism, as we have seen, though social in the sense of presupposing society, is also anti-social, whereas morality is not. Another is that morality presupposes the attainment of a higher level of rationality than egoism does. For whereas morality presupposes the attainment of a level of rationality at which the apprehension of universal principles is possible, egoism does not; it presupposes only that relatively low level of rationality at which I am capable of comparing myself with another and desiring to possess more of some kind of good than he does. Still another difference is that morality and egoism are incompatible with one another. The egoist directly violates the fundamental principle of morality or justice, as this principle is stated in any of the four formulations of the preceding paragraph. For he does not love his neighbor and his brother as he loves himself, he does not do to others as he would have them do to him, he does not treat others as ends in themselves, and he does not endeavor to act compatibly with the promotion of the good of everyone affected by his action. This, however, is not to say that the egoist is totally devoid of compassion. In fact, Rousseau supposes that compassion is not completely absent from the souls of even the most complete egoists.[1] But insofar as I am an egoist, the cries of compassion are stifled within me whenever I believe them to be incompatible with the attainment of my egoistic aims.

Morality, on the other hand, is not only compatible with compassion, but is impossible without it. This, of course, does not mean that action that does not issue from compassion may not be outwardly compatible with the requirements of morality or justice, for both self-interested and egoistic action, especially if it be enlightened, may conform outwardly with these requirements. But the outward conformity of such action to these requirements does not transform it into moral action, for moral action is action performed out of respect for principles of morality or justice which I impose upon myself, and neither self-interested nor egoistic action is performed out of respect for these principles. Nor can self-love or egoism generate such respect. All that either can generate is action outwardly compatible with the principles of morality, from the consideration that such action is conducive to the promotion of my own good, and such action does not amount to action performed out of respect for these principles. The only thing that can generate such respect is natural compassion, so that where there is no antecedent natural compassion there can be no subsequent respect for principles of morality. What is perhaps behind Rousseau's thinking here is the consideration that these principles are not ends in themselves, but means toward the attainment of something else that is an end in itself. This ultimate end in itself is the good of each and every human being, insofar as the good of each is compatible with the good of the rest.

This can be seen if we consider the four formulations of the principle of morality presented above. The first commands us to love our neighbor and our brother as we love ourselves; the second to do to others as we would have them do to us; the third to treat each and every human being as an end in himself; and the fourth to act compatibly with the promotion of the good of every human being affected by our action. Each, in one way or another, commands us to treat the good of each and every human being with whom we have anything to do as an end in itself. Although each commands, at least implicitly, unconditional respect for itself, it does so only because it commands unconditionally that we treat the good of each human being as an unconditional end. This is to say that we are not to treat the good of each human being as an ultimate end in itself in order to respect the principles of morality, but, conversely, that we are to respect the principles of morality in order to treat each human being as an end. It is true that respect for these principles is inseparable from treating human beings in this way—that we cannot respect these principles unless we do treat men in this way, and, conversely, that we cannot treat men in this way without in practice respecting these principles, even though we do not consciously or reflectively apprehend them and even though we be unable to formulate them if called upon to do so. Nevertheless, the source of the respect due these principles is the content of what they command. They merit respect because they command us to treat men as ends in themselves. Should they command something incompatible with this they would not merit our respect. It is true that they would be different principles were they to command something different. This, however, does not alter the fact that the obligatory nature of a principle depends upon its content. Should it be a purely formal principle, devoid of content, it would not be obligatory, but could become so only if given some content, and then only if the content is satisfactory. Whether, then, a principle is obligatory depends both upon whether it has content and also upon what its content is.

The mere statement and rational specification of the content of a principle, however, are not by themselves sufficient to induce someone to respect it, impose it upon himself, and act accordingly. Thus each of two men may have a completely adequate intellectual apprehension of the content of some principle, in the sense that each can formulate it as well as anyone else and derive its theoretical and practical consequences as well as anyone. Each, in other words, may be a superb moral philosopher. Yet it may warm the heart of one, who accordingly accepts it, and leave the other cold, who accordingly rejects it. This applies to each of the four formulations of the principle of morality presented above. Two men may have an intellectual apprehension of this principle as adequate as that of anyone else, yet one may accept it and the other may reject it. On Rousseau's view, what leads the one to accept it is natural compassion, and what leads the other to reject it is a deficiency of compassion. Although the first may excoriate the second as having a heart as cold as a stone and a soul as shriveled as a prune (as indeed he may have), he still can present no reason sufficient to compel the second to accept it. In such a situation the intellect runs up against a stone wall (or a stone heart). In the end, after the intellect has completed its task of clarification and exhausted its reasons either for accepting or for rejecting it, either compassion leads me to accept it or it does not, and the intellect has nothing further of any significance to say.

But, the question may arise, if natural compassion alone can lead one to impose the principle of morality upon oneself, what function does an intellectual acceptance of this principle have that natural compassion by itself does not have? The answer is implicit in what has already been said.

Natural compassion is only a necessary condition of the self-imposition of the moral law, not a sufficient condition. It is also necessary that I attain the level of rationality at which the apprehension of a law as abstract and universal as the moral law is possible. Given this level of rationality, I can do two things.

One is to correct the blindness of natural compassion, unenlightened by rationality. Just as unenlightened self-love may move me to perform certain acts that, though immediately beneficial or pleasant to myself, are nonetheless incompatible with my long-range good, so also unenlightened natural compassion may move me to perform certain acts that, though immediately beneficial or pleasant to others, are nevertheless incompatible with their long-range good. Unenlightened compassion, in other words, can have long-range consequences as deleterious as those of unenlightened self-love. But once the level of rationality at which morality is possible is attained, rational action in accordance with the moral law will assist me to restrain, order, and correct the blind impulses of natural compassion. A second thing I can do, given this level of rationality and an acceptance of the moral law, is to extend the range of persons for whom I have compassion to the entire human race, and to order my action accordingly. Prior to the attainment of this level of rationality my unenlightened natural compassion can be directed only to the persons who happen more or less haphazardly to cross my path. Unenlightened natural compassion operates, so to speak, in a way analogous to that of a court of law. It is directed to particular cases alone, and then only when these cases happen to be brought to its attention, so that its operation is passive as compared to that of compassion enlightened by rationality. Once natural compassion is enlightened by rationality, it is transformed from relative particularity and passivity into universality and activity. The person animated by compassion enlightened by rationality no longer occupies a position analogous to a judge in a court of law, who can deal only with particular cases brought to him through the initiative of others, but, instead, is in a position akin to that of a legislator, who can initiate legislation applicable to all men and all cases, without waiting passively for particular cases to be brought to him upon the initiative of others. Once, that is, compassion is enlightened by rationality, I can, to use Kant's language, act as if I were a legislator, the maxims of whose actions are to become law for a universal kingdom of ends.

We may therefore say that implicit within Rousseau's position is a distinction between two kinds of compassion. The first, compassion unenlightened by rationality, is natural compassion, and may also be referred to as non-rational or pre-rational, non-moral or pre-moral compassion or love, or, to use Kant's expression, as pathological compassion or love. The second, compassion enlightened by rationality, may be referred to as non-natural, rational, or moral compassion or love.

XVI. Moral Freedom

This distinction between two kinds of compassion or love is connected with Rousseau's conception of moral freedom or liberty, as contrasted with moral slavery or bondage. He distinguishes between the two in the following way: "moral liberty . . . alone makes man truly master of himself; for the mere impulse of appetite is slavery, while obedience to a law which we prescribe to ourselves is liberty."[1] Rousseau does not, either in the chapter containing this passage or elsewhere in *The Social Contract*, expand upon this distinction between moral freedom or liberty and moral slavery or bondage. It is possible, however, given what has already been said, to elucidate it briefly.

As has been seen, prior to the attainment of rationality and self-consciousness, man is a purely natural creature, subject to various laws imposed upon him by nature. Prior to the attainment of rationality and self-consciousness he is free neither to accept nor reject these laws, since he is conscious neither of them nor of himself as something subject to them. He simply acts or behaves in accordance with them, as does any other animate or inanimate natural thing. Given various impulses or wants, as for food, a mate, or sleep, he simply unreflectively or un-self-consciously endeavors to satisfy them. These impulses, as we have seen, may be classed as falling under the headings of self-love and natural compassion. Those impulses, the satisfaction of which contributes to his own preservation and pleasure, come under the heading of self-love, and he promotes his own good insofar as he succeeds in satisfying them, without any consciousness of himself as something distinct from them, enduring throughout their various occurrences, and continuing to exist after particular impulses are satisfied. Similarly, those impulses, the satisfaction of which contributes to the preservation or pleasure of another, come under the heading of compassion, and he acts or behaves compassionately insofar as he seeks to satisfy them, without being conscious of another as a distinct and enduring ego, self, or person. Although from time to time contrary impulses may pull him in different directions at once, the direction in which he eventually moves is determined either by a conjunction of these impulses or by one giving way to the other, not by a consideration of either his own long-range good or that of others, for as yet he has not reached a level of consciousness at which this kind of consideration is possible. Since his behavior is determined entirely by the impulses that assail him, regardless of whether they come under the heading of self-love or under the heading of compassion, and which pull or push him now in one way, now in another, he may be said to be in bondage to or enslaved by them. And since the laws of nature that describe the occurrence, the causes, and the consequences of these impulses and his behavior are imposed upon him from without, and not through his own act of will or choice, they may be said to be laws of bondage or of slavery, and he to be in bondage to or enslaved by them. They are something to which he is subject whether he wills it or not; indeed, since he has no consciousness of them, he can will neither his subjection to nor freedom from them.

But with the passage of centuries man gradually becomes conscious of himself and of others as relatively enduring or permanent persons, selves, or egos as compared with the evanescence of the various particular impulses that regularly assail him. With this self-consciousness he acquires the ability, so to speak, to stand off from them and hold them in abeyance while he examines them and deliberates about which to satisfy and which to deny. Insofar as he is animated by his long-term good, he decides to satisfy those he believes to be compatible with it and to deny those he believes to be incompatible. Given this ability to stand off from his impulses and to hold them at arm's length, to make them wait in the antechamber of the soul as he deliberates about which to satisfy and which to reject, he is free from subjection to their control. The shoe is now on the other foot. Although he is still subject to their solicitations, they have lost their imperiousness, and the direction in which he moves is no longer determined by them, but by himself. He is now self-determined, not determined by his impulses. It is true that they are still necessary if self-determination is to be possible, for without them and other desires that arise once rationality and self-consciousness appear on the scene there would be no content to fill the concept of one's long-range good. But this means only that the existence of impulses and desires is a necessary condition of self-determination—that without them there could be no self-determination. It does not mean that they determine in which direction I move. It is I who determine this, by deciding which are compatible with my own long-range good and which are not and by choosing to satisfy the former and to reject the latter. Once this stage is attained I am no longer a merely natural creature subject to determination by the natural impulses that assail and solicit me, but a self-determined rational agent free from enslavement to them.

The attainment of this level of freedom, however, does not amount to the attainment of the level of moral freedom. This level of freedom is only what may be referred to as metaphysical or psychological freedom, not moral freedom. For moral freedom, as we have seen, is "obedience to a law which we prescribe to ourselves." The law in question is the moral law, so that moral freedom consists in imposing the moral law upon ourselves and therefore acting in accordance with it. It is important to remember here that the self-imposition of the moral law consists in subjecting myself to it simply out of respect for it, i.e., simply in order to promote the good of everyone affected by my action. Should I act in accordance with it merely in order to promote my own good or that of another regardless of the effect upon others, I am merely using it, not subjecting myself to it.

Since Rousseau regards moral freedom as "obedience to a law which we prescribe to ourselves," it is clear that for him moral freedom may be said to be an achievement, not the mere possibility of an achievement. I am morally free only if I obey a law that I prescribe to myself. I may have the capacity or ability to do so, yet refuse or fail to do so. If so, I am metaphysically or psychologically free, for the capacity to obey a law that I prescribe to myself presupposes such freedom. But I am not morally free, for although moral freedom presupposes metaphysical or psychological freedom, it is not reducible to it, but requires the actual exercise of metaphysical freedom in subjecting myself to the moral law, and not merely the possiblity of or capacity for such an exercise of it.

The relationship of metaphysical freedom to the moral law is somewhat analogous to its relationship to natural impulses. Given the attainment of the level of rationality necessary and sufficient for the attainment of metaphysical freedom, I have the metaphysical freedom to order my impulses and desires in terms of some goal, such as the attainment of my long-range good. But to say that I have the freedom to do this is merely to say that I have the ability to do it—it is not to say that I exercise this ability so as actually to do it. Thus even though I have the ability to do so I may fail to do so, and, if and insofar as I do fail to do so, I am subject to the control of my impulses or desires, and therefore not free from determination by them. I am both metaphysically free, since I have the ability to control and order my impulses and desires, yet am enslaved by or in bondage to them, since I fail to exercise this ability. Moreover, given this ability, I am responsible for its exercise, and therefore praiseworthy insofar as I do exercise it and blameworthy insofar as I do not. Similar considerations apply to the relationship of metaphysical freedom to moral freedom. Given the level of rationality necessary and sufficient for the attainment of metaphysical freedom, and given also a consciousness of the moral law, I am metaphysically free, i.e., I have the ability, to impose the moral law upon myself. If I do impose it upon myself then I am morally as well as metaphysically free. If I do not then I am still metaphysically free, since I have the ability to do so but refuse or fail to do so, but am not morally free, but instead am in moral bondage to something such as impulse or desire, self-love, egoism, immoral compassion that leads me to seek the good of another at the expense of acting compatibly with the moral law, or perhaps simply moral indifference. But regardless of whether I am morally free or not, i.e., regardless of whether I subject myself to the moral law or not, I am still metaphysically free, and am therefore responsible either for subjecting myself to it or for failing or refusing to do so, and praiseworthy if I do so and blameworthy if I do not.

XVII. The Reconciliation of Nature and Morality

We are now in a position to return to a consideration of the relationship of the claims of morality to the claims of nature and to the problem of their reconciliation. We have seen that the fundamental claim of nature is that of self-love—that each man, regardless of whether he be in the pure state of nature, in pre-civil society, or in civil society, endeavors constantly to promote his own good. We have seen also that the fundamental claim of morality is that each man act compatibly with the promotion of the good of every person affected by his action. Each of these claims is ultimate within its own sphere—the first within the sphere of nature, the second within the sphere of morality. In saying that each is ultimate within its own sphere we mean two things. One is that the claims of each will persist until satisfied. Since, however, the claims of neither can be satisfied once and for all, in the sense that after a certain point in time the claims of each will cease, the claims of each will continue and demand satisfaction so long as the human race continues to exist. The second is that the claim of each is legitimate. It is because of this that they are reconcilable with one another, for if the claim of one were legitimate and that of the other illegitimate a reconciliation between them would be impossible.

Since the kind of legitimacy in question here is moral legitimacy, the legitimacy of the claim of nature can be established only by showing its compatibility with the claim of morality. The legitimacy of the latter claim cannot itself be established by appealing to anything other than the fundamental principle of morality itself. There is, of course, a sense in which such an appeal does not establish the legitimacy of the claim of morality, but is either question begging or merely a re-statement of the legitimacy of this claim. This, however, is unavoidable and therefore not to be lamented, for there is nothing more fundamental than the fundamental principle of morality in terms of which its legitimacy could be established. The ultimate or absolute moral legitimacy of this principle is something that can be seen only by someone graced with natural compassion, and then only if and insofar as his natural compassion has been raised to a level of universality, through the operation of reason upon it in such a way that it has a universal object—in such a way, that is, that it is directed toward each and every human being as an end in himself and an object of compassion. Insofar as natural compassion is thus operated upon by reason it is transformed from natural and particular compassion, directed toward certain particular persons to the exclusion of others, into rational and universal compassion, directed toward all mankind. The legitimacy of the claim of nature, i.e., of the claim of self-love, follows immediately from the legitimacy of the claim of morality. This is the case because the object of rational and universal compassion is the non-egoistic good of each human being, insofar as it is compatible with the non-egoistic good of every other human being. This may be put differently by saying that the object of rational compassion is a universal system or order comprising every human being and organized in such a way that each promotes his own non-egoistic good, which he endeavors by nature to do, by acting compatibly with the promotion of the non-egoistic good of everyone else, something that he does not by nature seek to do, but which he is commanded by moral law to do.

But although the legitimacy of the claim of nature—of the claim of self-love—follows from the claim of morality, there is nevertheless a sense in which the claim of morality presupposes the claim of nature. This is the case for two reasons. One is that the very possibility of morality presupposes the existence of something given as actual and natural, which requires moralization. Unless there is something given as actual and natural to which the principles of morality are to apply, then these principles will have no applicability to anything. They would therefore be otiose, and, indeed, would not exist at all. The second reason the claim of morality presupposes the claim of nature is that unless there were some respect in which nature is at least potentially good, then the principles of morality would be purely formal, devoid of content. But if they were purely formal they would be insufficiently directive, if not indeed vacuous. They could direct us always to act consistently and thus never to contradict ourselves in action. But if this were all they could do they would lose much, if not all, of their importance for practice, for the number of ways in which one can act consistently is quite large. The ethical egoist, for example, can avoid inconsistency in his action simply by acting always in accordance with egoistic principles.

Now for Rousseau what is given as good by nature is the happiness or well-being of the individual and the absence of pain or suffering, except in so far as the existence of the latter is conducive to the promotion of happiness or well-being. This is the object of both self-love and natural compassion. Insofar as I am animated by self-love I aim at the attainment of my own happiness, and insofar as I am moved by natural compassion I aim at the production of the happiness of another. To say that the happiness or well-being of the individual is good by nature is to say two different but related things. On the one hand, it is to say that each human being by nature, i.e., independent of any consideration of and therefore independent of being influenced by the moral law, seeks happiness or well-being as a good, his own in the case of self-interested action and that of another in the case of naturally compassionate action. On the other hand, it is to say that the natural goodness of happiness or well-being is presupposed and not established by the moral law. All that the moral law does is to command us to seek our own happiness and that of those upon whom our natural compassion is directed in such a way that we act compatibly with the attainment of the well-being of everyone affected by our action. In giving this command it presupposes that the well-being of each person is good, and does not establish that it is.

The preceding considerations are not to be found, at least not in the form and in the detail in which they are presented here, either in any of Rousseau's three discourses or in *The Social Contract*. But they are, I believe, not only sanctioned by the spirit animating these works and compatible with what he says explicitly in them, but also constitute what seems to me to be a reasonable statement of the considerations that Rousseau himself, if called upon to do so, might well present in defense of his supposition that the claims of nature can be reconciled with the claims of morality. For what these considerations show, if sound, is not only that the claims of nature are reconcilable with the claims of morality, but also that the satisfaction of the claims of either involves or requires the satisfaction of the claims of the other. It is because of this that a form of political association that is at once both stable and legitimate, and in which right and justice are united with interest and utility, is not only possible but necessary. Such a form of political association is possible because of the compatibility of the claims of morality with the claims of nature and because of their mutual involvement with one another, and yet is also necessary, since the satisfaction of the claims of each can be realized adequately only in such an association.

At the same time, however, such an association is attainable only if the realm of actuality—the realm of human nature and human history—is transformed by means of the operation of human reason informed and

directed by the principles of morality. For so long as the realm of the
actual continues to exist and to unfold itself independent of the operation
of a morally informed human reason, human history will continue to
manifest itself as a long litany of lamentations, to use a phrase from Hegel,
in which man sinks ever more deeply into egoism. This is to say that so
long as human history continues to unfold itself independent of the direction of reason informed by morality it moves in a direction precisely the
opposite of that required by the principles of morality, for the growth of
egoism is precisely what is condemned by these principles. The task of
reason informed by morality is therefore to arrest the natural descent of
history into the depravity of egoism and to re-direct its course along the
lines demanded by morality. This is not only the purpose of *The Social
Contract*, but also the function of the social contract, for the natural descent into egoism can be arrested and human history re-directed, re-
formed, and moralized only insofar as the terms of this contract are
fulfilled.

XVIII. Freedom, Nature, and History

Before, however, we turn to discuss in detail the terms of the social
contract, it may be advisable to emphasize that at no place in *The Social
Contract* does Rousseau assert its historicity. Given his view of man in the
state of nature as a natural creature devoid of reason, the formation of the
social contract while man is still in the state of nature would be impossible,
for its formation presupposes the development of a level of reason that
would be impossible so long as he remains in this state. But neither does
Rousseau, in *The Social Contract*, assert the formation of the social contract
as an actual historical event at some point in time after man, through living
in society, has developed the level of reason which would make its formation possible. Instead, he presents the social contract, not as a contract that
men enter into as a means of leaving the state of nature, nor even as a
contract that any men have ever actually entered into at some time after
they have left the state of nature, but rather as an ideal contract the terms
of which must be fulfilled if the claims of nature and the claims of morality
are to be reconciled with each other and if, therefore, a stable and legitimate political association, in which right and justice are united with interest and utility, is to be possible. It is true that he maintains that the terms
of the social contract are "everywhere tacitly admitted and recognized."[1]
This, however, is neither to assert nor to imply its historicity. Instead,
this passage is to be interpreted as a hyperbolic expression of the view that

everywhere certain men, at least, have tacitly admitted and recognized that the claims of nature and of morality can be reconciled only insofar as the terms of this contract are adhered to, even though such a contract has never actually been formed at any time or place. This view may, of course, be exaggerated or even false. But it does not imply that Rousseau is to be interpreted as either asserting or implying the historicity of the contract.

Indeed, in *The Social Contract* Rousseau is not even concerned with the kind of conjectural or philosophical history he dealt with in the second discourse. This he makes clear in the very first paragraph of the first chapter of Book One. "Man is born free; and everywhere he is in chains. One thinks himself the master of others, and still remains a greater slave then they. How did this change come about? I do not know. What can make it legitimate? That question I think I can answer." Here Rousseau is stating that he does not know how the change from the freedom of the pure state of nature to the bondage of society came about, and refuses even to speculate about it in the way in which he had done in the second discourse. In fact, he writes as though he is not even interested in the question of how it came about, but is concerned only with the question of what can legitimize it, a question that, as he says, he thinks he can answer. The fact, however, that he thinks that this change can be legitimized makes this passage somewhat puzzling.

When Rousseau says, in the context of the quoted passage, that man is born free, the word "free" has more than one sense. In one sense it refers to freedom from subjection to the authority of another. Thus one thing that is meant by saying that man is born free is that he has a natural right to freedom and therefore, by virtue of his nature as a man, is not naturally subject to the authority of any other man. Hence no man has any natural authority over any other man, but can acquire authority over another only by being given it by the person over whom it is acquired. Second, to say that man is born free is to say that in the state of nature each man is self-dependent, in the sense that no man depends upon the assistance of others for the satisfaction of his needs. Each man in the state of nature is therefore free from dependence upon others. A third sense of "free" is connected with the second. It is that no man in the state of nature is subject to the power of another, and is thus free from subjection to the power of another.

But in addition to these three senses of "free" there are also, as we have seen, two senses of the word in which he is not born free. For man in the state of nature is not metaphysically or psychologically free, but, instead, is a mere natural creature enslaved by or in bondage to the various natural impulses that constantly assail him, pulling him now in one direction, now in another. Metaphysical or psychological freedom is not something that we have by nature, and thus is not something we should have in the state of nature, but is at most only a natural potentiality that can be actualized only by leaving the state of nature and living in society. Given that man is not born free in the metaphysical or psychological sense, there is a second sense in which he is not born free. He is not born morally free. For since, as we have seen, moral freedom is an achievement the possibility of which presupposes the actualization of metaphysical freedom, and since the latter is possible only in society, moral freedom too is possible only in society. But since man is neither metaphysically nor morally free in the state of nature, there is a fourth sense in which he is born free. He is born free from moral obligation. As a purely natural creature in the state of nature he has no consciousness of moral law and therefore is free from any obligation to impose it upon himself, just as any brute is free from this obligation. The bonds of moral obligation, since they presuppose the possibility of metaphysical and moral freedom, are, like them, possible only in society, not in the state of nature.

Having distinguished between the various senses in which man is and is not born free, we turn now to consider the various senses in which "everywhere he is in chains." First, he is in chains everywhere in the sense that everywhere he lives within a civil society of some sort and therefore has attained the metaphysical freedom that subjects him to the bonds of moral law and moral obligation. These bonds, however, are easily broken. But although they are easily broken, their existence is a necessary condition for the attainment of moral freedom. For just as there can be no moral obligation without moral law, neither can there be moral law without moral obligation, and moral freedom, as we have seen, consists precisely in fulfilling one's moral obligations through subjecting oneself to the moral law. The bonds of moral obligation therefore make possible that which, from the moral point of view, is the highest form of freedom. Although the person who breaks these bonds retains his metaphysical freedom, he nevertheless, in breaking them, rejects the highest form of freedom, and in doing so enslaves himself to desires the satisfaction of which is incompatible with the retention of moral freedom. Given the superiority of moral freedom to other forms of freedom, the transition from the freedom from moral obligation with which man is born to the acquisition of the bonds of moral obligation is a change to be welcomed rather than lamented. Thus regardless of what the actual details of this transition may happen to be (details with which Rousseau does not concern himself in *The Social Contract*), the transition itself is legitimate.

Given the legitimacy of the transition from the freedom from the bondage of moral obligation to the acquisition of such bondage in society, the loss of the freedom of the state of nature, in the other senses specified, can also be legitimized. This is the case because the loss of freedom in these other senses is necessary if the realization of moral freedom is to be a possibility. We have seen that the existence of society is a necessary condition of the acquisition of metaphysical freedom and the attainment of moral freedom. We have also seen that insofar as human history is not directed by human reason informed by the principles of morality it is a progressive descent into egoism in which the self-dependence of the state of nature is lost and replaced by the increasing subjection of some to the power of others to whom they have given no authority. Yet such a descent is necessary before human history and society can be moralized. This is to say that human history must unfold itself independent of the direction of reason informed by the moral law before it can be controlled by moralized reason.

We have seen that reason and morality do not exist in the state of nature. Neither do they appear fully developed on the scene as soon as the state of nature ceases to exist. Instead, they require time to develop, and the same historical process that, undirected by reason and morality, engenders corruption also slowly engenders the reason and morality whose existence is necessary if the corruption it causes is to be eliminated, or at least lessened. On this view the course of history as it develops independent of the direction of reason and morality may be likened to the gestation of a child within the womb. Just as a woman would be silly to expect to have a child of her own without undergoing the discomforts of pregnancy and the violent, painful pangs of delivery, so also would a philosopher be foolish to suppose that human reason and morality could exist ready-made in the state of nature and direct the course of human history from the beginning. The truth of the matter is that the period of history prior to its direction by reason and morality is the gestation period of the latter and must therefore precede their birth. And just as the beauty of the child and the love and joy it brings justify the discomfort and pain of pregnancy and delivery, so also the value of reason and morality legitimize the loss of the freedom of the state of nature and the subsequent bondage of the course of history that make them possible and out of which they develop.

This, however, is not to say that the loss of self-dependence and of freedom from subjection to the power of others has any intrinsic value. On the contrary, it is to say only that it is necessary if the development of the level of reason and morality required for the correction of the corruption of history is to be possible. Did this loss not engender this level of reason and morality it would be unjustifiable and therefore an illegitimate intrinsic evil. But once this level of reason and morality is attained, the corruption of the course of history is to be eliminated. It cannot, however, for reasons already given, be eliminated through returning to the state of nature. Such a return, besides being impossible, would require the sacrifice of reason and morality, and thus the sacrifice of a level of freedom superior to any possible within the state of nature. But if its elimination cannot be achieved through returning to the state of nature, it can be attained only through reforming and restructuring society by means of reason informed by the principles of morality. This means that it can be eliminated only through fulfilling the terms of the social contract.

XIX. Freedom and Justice

The preceding will have to suffice, at least for the present, as a solution to the puzzle of how the transition from natural freedom to the bondage of the chains of society can be legitimized. We turn now to consider a second puzzle, even more difficult to solve than the one just considered. We have seen that in *The Social Contract* Rousseau is not concerned with asserting the historicity of the social contract. Instead, it is to be understood as an ideal contract the terms of which must be fulfilled if the problem of reconciling the claims of nature with the claims of morality is to be solved. In addition to the various statements of this problem presented by Rousseau that have already been discussed, he also states it in the following puzzling terms. "The problem is to find a form of association which will defend and protect with the whole common force the person and goods of each associate, and in which each, while uniting himself with all, may still obey himself alone, and remain as free as before."[1] The problem, stated in this way, is undoubtedly as difficult as any problem any political philosopher has ever set himself to solve, and Rousseau certainly has not made matters easy for himself by stating it in this way. Indeed, one may well argue that it is insoluble, given Rousseau's statement of it. Whether it is or not can be decided satisfactorily only after we have examined Rousseau's heroic effort to solve it.

The difficulty of the problem as Rousseau states it is essentially this: how is it possible for an association of the kind in question to be formed so long as each person obeys himself alone and remains as free as he would be independent of the association? Here we seem to have two incompatible requirements. One is "to find a form of association which will defend and protect with the whole common force the person and goods of each associate." The other is to find a form of association in which each associate, "while uniting himself with all, may still obey himself alone, and remain as free as before." If any two requirements have ever been incompatible with one another, these two would certainly seem to be so. Although we are not yet in a position to render a judgment as to whether they are ultimately incompatible, we are in a position to specify somewhat more precisely just what the problem of reconciling them consists in. It consists, not in reconciling the first requirement with the requirement that each member of the association remain as free as he would be outside the association, but, rather, in reconciling it with the requirement that each member of the association obey himself alone. This is so for the following reasons.

We have seen that in the second discourse Rousseau distinguishes among four stages in the development of man—the pure state of nature, uncorrupt pre-civil society, corrupt pre-civil society, and corrupt civil society. A fifth stage can also be conceived—uncorrupt, or stable and legitimate, civil society. The object of *The Social Contract*, as we know, is to delineate the conditions that must be satisfied if this fifth stage is to be attained. Once this is done a philosophical solution, at least, to the fundamental problem the social contract is designed to solve will have been achieved. But the practical solution to this problem can be attained only if a form of association is established in which each member of the association is as free as he would be outside it. The question therefore arises: to what extent, and in what senses, would each member of the association be free outside it? To this question the essentials of Rousseau's answer have already been presented.

Someone outside a just political association can exist only in one of the four stages distinguished above. In point of fact, however, there are only two real possibilities—either one lives in a just civil society or one lives in a corrupt civil society. These are the only two alternatives, for history and mankind have transcended the stages of the pure state of nature (if indeed this stage ever existed) and of pre-civil society, and there is no likelihood of returning to either. But although the only real alternative to living in a just civil society is to live in a corrupt civil society, it may be helpful to recall here the kinds of freedom possible in the state of nature and in pre-civil society as well as the kinds possible in corrupt civil society. For Rousseau is as concerned in *The Social Contract* (indeed even more concerned) with contrasting the kind of freedom possible in a just civil society with that possible in the state of nature as he is with contrasting it with the kind possible in pre-civil society and in corrupt civil society.

In pre-civil and civil society, whether they be corrupt or uncorrupt, two kinds of freedom are possible, neither of which is possible in the state of nature. These are metaphysical freedom and moral freedom. As far, then, as these two kinds of freedom are concerned, men would be freer in a just civil society than in the state of nature, and as free in a just civil society as in either pre-civil or corrupt civil society. Indeed, as Rousseau seeks to show, they would also have more moral freedom in a just civil society than in either pre-civil or corrupt civil society, since in a just civil society conditions conducive to the realization of moral freedom would be more fully satisfied than in either of the other two types of society. In fact, it is not necessarily an exaggeration to say that there would also be more metaphysical freedom in a just civil society than in either of the other two forms of society, since in the former a higher degree of self-consciousness and of one's possibilities would be actualized among a larger number of persons than in either of the latter two forms of society. But be this as it may, the fact remains that there would be as much metaphysical and moral freedom in a just civil society as in either pre-civil or corrupt civil society, and more than in the state of nature, since in the latter both these forms of freedom would be impossible.

But although in the state of nature neither metaphysical nor moral freedom would be possible, so that in this respect it is inferior to all forms of society, whether pre-civil or civil and whether corrupt or uncorrupt, there is nevertheless, as we have seen, one form of freedom that is possible in the state of nature alone. This is freedom from the bonds of moral obligation. This kind of freedom, however, can be had only at the cost of metaphysical and moral freedom, for it is impossible for one to be both metaphysically and morally free and also free from moral obligation. But since it is only in virtue of his metaphysical freedom that man is more than a brute, and since it is only insofar as a man is morally free that he is what he ought to be, metaphysical and moral freedom are more to be cherished than is freedom from moral obligation. Thus man in the state of nature, in being free from moral obligation, has a form of freedom inferior to the metaphysical and moral freedom that are possible only in society. Man in society, in being metaphysically free and in having the possibility of attaining moral freedom, is therefore in this respect in a position preferable to that of man in the state of nature. Thus, as we have seen, the loss of freedom from moral obligation is not something to be lamented. Moreover, as we have also seen, even if its loss were something to be lamented, it is not something that could be re-acquired, since it is impossible for one who has attained the level of metaphysical freedom to abandon it and return to the innocence of the state of nature.

There are, however, two other forms of freedom that are possible in the state of nature. One is freedom from dependence upon others for the satisfaction of one's needs or desires, the other freedom from subjection to the power and direction of others to whom one has given no authority. Both of these forms of freedom are absent in corrupt societies, whether they be pre-civil or civil. But in uncorrupt societies, whether pre-civil or civil, the second form of freedom exists. The first form of freedom, however, is absent from uncorrupt as well as corrupt pre-civil society. The question therefore arises of whether it would also be absent in a just civil society. If so, then there would be at least one form of freedom available in the state of nature that is not possible even in a just civil society.

If, however, this form of freedom is in fact possible only in the state of nature, then its desirability, as the desirability of freedom from moral obligation, becomes questionable. For if it is possible only in the state of nature, then its realization, as the realization of freedom from moral obligation, is incompatible with metaphysical and moral freedom, since these latter two forms of freedom are possible only in society. But since the possession of metaphysical and moral freedom is the source of man's metaphysical and moral dignity, in the sense that he is something more than a brute only in virtue of his metaphysical freedom and is the kind of man he ought to be only insofar as he is morally free, to choose freedom from dependence upon others at the sacrifice of one's metaphysical and moral freedom, even if it were a choice that could be made, would be to degrade oneself. If, then, freedom from dependence upon others is incompatible with metaphysical and moral freedom, then its loss, like the loss of freedom from moral obligation, is not a loss to be lamented. And, as in the case of freedom from moral obligation, it is not a kind of freedom that could be re-acquired even if its loss were lamentable, for we cannot return to the state of nature.

The outcome of these considerations is that neither form of freedom that might be possible in the state of nature but not in a just civil society is either desirable or possible. Freedom from moral obligation is not possible in society, and is therefore incompatible with metaphysical and moral freedom, both of which are possible only in society. And if freedom from dependence upon others is possible only in the state of nature, then it too is incompatible with metaphysical and moral freedom, neither of which is possible in the state of nature. But if and insofar as these two forms of freedom are incompatible with metaphysical and moral freedom, neither is desirable, for any form of freedom that is incompatible with metaphysical and moral freedom is an inferior form of freedom. And, finally, if either of these forms of freedom is possible only in the state of nature, then

they are inaccessible to us, for we cannot return to the state of nature.
Moreover, given the impossibility of returning to the state of nature, the
consideration of the desirability or lack of it of the forms of freedom
possible only in that state is largely academic. Given that one is already in
a corrupt civil society, the only choice open to him is that of remaining in
it or attempting to establish a just civil society. But although the consideration of the forms of freedom possible only in the state of nature is largely
academic, it nevertheless, properly understood, has the practical effect of
dispelling whatever romantic yearning one might have for a state of affairs
that is neither desirable nor possible.

We still, however, have not answered the question of whether the freedom from dependence upon others that would be possible in the state of
nature would also be possible in a just civil society. As we shall see,
Rousseau's answer is that it is not. But neither is this to be lamented. What
is to be lamented and avoided is not freedom from dependence upon
others as such, but, instead, the kind of dependence upon others that has
an enslaving effect. Accordingly, one of the major problems of *The Social
Contract* is to show how an association can be formed such that the dependence of its members upon one another does not have this effect upon
them, so that in being dependent upon others no one is enslaved to or by
any other person. This, however, seems a minor problem when compared
with the problem of establishing "a form of association which will defend
and protect with the whole common force the person and goods of each
associate, and in which each, while uniting himself with all, may still obey
himself alone."

We have seen that it is possible to reconcile membership in such an
association with the retention of as much freedom as one would have
outside it. For in such an association each person would retain the
metaphysical and moral freedom he would have in either pre-civil or
corrupt civil society, and no one would be either metaphysically or
morally free in the state of nature. And in such an association each person
would be as free from subjection to the power of anyone to whom he has
not granted authority over him as he would be in either the state of nature
or in pre-civil society, and would be freer from such subjection than he
would be in corrupt civil society. And, finally, in such an association each
person would be as free from an enslaving dependence upon others for the
satisfaction of his needs and desires as he would be in either the state of
nature or pre-civil society, and would be freer from such dependence than
he would be in corrupt civil society. But even if all this be granted Rousseau, the problem still remains of how membership in such an association
could possibly be compatible with a situation in which each member of the

association obeys himself alone. I might be able to obey myself alone in the state of nature, and might even be able to do so in pre-civil society. But how could I possibly do so in civil society, regardless of whether it be corrupt or just? For in civil society each person is subject to the civil law of the society, and therefore cannot possibly obey himself alone. It would therefore seem that Rousseau has posed himself an insoluble problem. Yet he thinks that it can be solved, and, in fact, one of the primary purposes of *The Social Contract* is the presentation of a solution to it. We turn now to a consideration of the solution he proposes.

XX. On Obeying Oneself Alone

His solution cannot be understood unless we understand what he means by "obeying oneself alone." We may say at once that it consists of two things. One is moral freedom. The other is subjection only to those laws to which I have consented, and therefore only to the acts of persons that are in accordance with or compatible with these laws. We have already discussed Rousseau's conception of moral freedom, and have seen that it consists in subjecting oneself to the moral law. We have seen also that moral freedom is impossible in the state of nature. From this it follows that in the state of nature I cannot obey myself alone. As we have seen, man in the state of nature has no conception of himself as something distinct from his impulses and enduring throughout their occurrence and satisfaction. Having no conception of himself as something distinct from his impulses, he cannot obey himself alone, but is subject to or enslaved by his impulses. In short, he obeys his impulses, not himself. He can come to obey himself, as something distinct from his impulses, only after he enters society, for it is only then that he acquires self-consciousness. But we have also seen that self-consciousness is only a necessary, not a sufficient, condition of moral freedom. Although I cannot be morally free unless I am conscious of myself as something subject to the moral law, I can nevertheless be conscious of myself without in fact imposing this law upon myself. In attaining this level of consciousness I am metaphysically free, but I am morally free only insofar as I do in fact subject myself to the moral law. In thus subjecting myself to this law I endeavor to seek my own good, which I seek naturally, independent of any consideration of the moral law, only in ways that are compatible with the promotion of the good of everyone affected by my action. This requires that I refrain both from succumbing to impulses the satisfaction of which is incompatible with the moral law and also from succumbing to egoistic inclinations insofar as their satisfaction conflicts with the moral law. It requires, in short, that I master these impulses and inclinations—that I subject them to my control rather than permit them to subject me to their control. It is a question of who is to be master—I or the impulses and inclinations that solicit me. Insofar as I impose the moral law upon myself I succeed in mastering my contrary impulses and inclinations; but insofar as I fail to impose this law upon myself I surrender to my impulses or inclinations, and am thereby enslaved by them.

But the attainment of moral freedom is only a necessary condition of my obeying myself alone—it is not a sufficient condition. Instead, it is also necessary that I be subject only to those laws to which I have consented to subject myself. For even though I be morally free I still do not obey myself alone if I am compelled to submit to commands or edicts to which I have not consented. In this case I obey, not myself alone, but those who issue or who enforce such commands or edicts. If, however, I am to obey myself alone, it is not sufficient that I consent to obey the commands of another person or of a group of which I am not a member. Should I consent to do so I do not obey myself alone, but, rather, enslave myself to the person or group whose commands I agree to obey. Thus the person who consents to obey the commands of a Hobbesian sovereign does not thereby obey himself alone, but, instead, enslaves himself to the sovereign. The extent to which I thereby enslave myself to another depends upon the extent to which I consent to obey his commands. Should I agree to obey them without limit, regardless of what they might be, then I completely enslave myself. But even though I place limits upon the extent to which I shall obey the commands of another, I nonetheless enslave myself to him to the extent to which I do consent to obey his commands. Rousseau's point here is related to a point that we discussed earlier. Insofar as I consent to will what another wills that I will, I will to surrender my own will to that person's will and to have him will for me, and thereby enslave myself and my will to him and his will. If, then, I am to obey myself alone, I cannot surrender or enslave my will to that of another person or to that of a group of which I am not a member, and to the extent that I do, I do not obey myself alone.

We therefore seem to be confronted with a dilemma. The only way, it seems, in which we could obey ourselves alone, in the sense of not being subject to the will of others, is through returning to the state of nature. But such a return is impossible for reasons already given. Yet the only alternative to the state of nature, it seems, is a society in which certain persons are subject to the will of certain other persons, in which case they do not obey themselves alone. This dilemma can be escaped only if there is some third alternative. But is there? Rousseau thinks there is. It consists in forming an association such that each person who is subject to its laws has a voice equal to that of every other person subject to them in determining what they shall be. In such an association, no person would be subject to the will of another or of a group of which he is not a member. Instead, he would be subject only to the will of the association of which he is a member, as determined by the vote of each person who is to be subject to its laws. But still the problem remains. How can each member of the association obey himself alone if he is subject to the will or the law of the association? If this problem is soluble at all, its solution depends upon an identity between the object of the will of the association on the one hand and the object of the will of each of its members on the other. Only then would each of its members obey himself alone in obeying the will or the laws of the association. But is such an identity possible, and, if so, how is it possible?

To answer this question we must turn again to Rousseau's distinction between nature and morality and to his conception of the relation between the two. We have seen that according to Rousseau each man naturally, i.e. independent of reason and morality, seeks his own good. We have seen also that for Rousseau nature is good—that the claims of nature and the claims of morality are compatible with each other. Not only does each man naturally seek his own good—the claims of morality require that the good of each man be promoted. All that morality forbids is that any man seek his own good at the expense of the good of others when it is possible for him to seek it in a way compatible with the good of others. What it forbids is egoism, not self-love, and thus insofar as I seek my good in ways compatible with the promotion of the good of others I act compatibly with the claims of morality. I fulfill these claims perfectly, however, not merely by seeking my good in ways compatible with the good of others, but by seeking to promote the good of everyone affected by my action fully as much as I seek to promote my good. It is only to the extent that I do so that I become morally free. Here, however, there is a tension between nature and morality. For by nature I seek only to promote my good in ways compatible with the promotion of the good of others. Natural self-love leads me to seek my own good, and natural compassion leads me to seek it in ways compatible with the promotion of the good of those affected by my action. But neither natural self-love nor natural compassion leads me to concern myself with the good of others fully as much as I concern myself with my own good, which is what morality does require of me. At the same time, however, this tension between nature and morality is not an opposition between the two in the sense in which there is an opposition between egoism and morality. For morality forbids egoism, or the attempt to seek my good at the expense of the good of others when I can obtain it in ways compatible with the promotion of the good of others.

Now the kind of association in which each person obeys himself alone is precisely an association in which both the claims of nature and the claims of morality are satisfied. It is an association whose laws are such that each person, by acting in accordance with them, not only promotes his own good, but also acts compatibly with the promotion of the good of every other member of the association. It is therefore a moral association in which the claims of nature, i.e., the claims of self-love and of natural compassion, and the claims of morality are united or reconciled with each other. The members of such an association therefore obey themselves alone in two senses. First, they obey themselves alone in the sense that they are subject only to those laws that they collectively impose upon themselves. Each person subject to the law of the association is to have an equal voice in the determination of what the law is to be, so that no person is to be subject to laws imposed upon him by others, in the enactment of which he has been denied an equal voice. Second, each person, to the extent that he seeks his own good in ways compatible with the promotion of the good of the other members of the association, obeys himself alone. This is so for two reasons. The first is that a man would obey himself alone even in the state of nature insofar as he sought his own good in ways compatible with the promotion of the good of others, and thus does not cease to do so as a member of a political association whose laws require him to seek his own good in these ways. The second reason is that the laws of such an association are not felt as restrictions or constraints by the man who seeks his own good in these ways, but, instead, may be regarded as instruments assisting and enabling him to do what he wills to do. They are felt as constraints only insofar as I seek my good at the expense of the good of others. In this case, however, it is through my fault, not through that of the laws, that I do not obey myself alone. Given the existence of the laws, I can come to obey myself alone simply through willing my good in ways compatible with the attainment of the good of the other members of the association.

It may be helpful here if we apply Locke's distinction between liberty and license to the problem Rousseau is dealing with.[1] The problem is to discover a form of association in which the claims of both nature and morality are satisfied and in which each member of the association obeys himself alone and remains as free as he would be outside it. It is important to remember that the claims of nature include only the claims of natural self-love and natural compassion. They do not include the claims of egoism. The claims of morality are compatible with the claims of nature and, indeed, are inseparable from them because the former are satisfied only insofar as the latter are satisfied. This is to say that an association is a moral association only if and insofar as its laws are such that the good of each member of the association will be promoted as long as each acts in accordance with them. But neither the claims of morality nor the claims of nature are compatible with the claims of egoism. For what the egoist seeks is to promote his good at the expense of the good of others, and in doing so he violates both the claim of morality, which requires that the good of each person be promoted, and also the claim of nature, since he seeks to prevent others from obtaining the good they naturally seek. But not only are the claims of egoism incompatible with the claims of morality and nature—they are also incompatible with liberty. For liberty, as distinct from license, is possible only insofar as each man acts compatibly with the good of every person affected by his action. This can perhaps be put by saying that the liberty of one man is possible only insofar as it is compatible with the liberty of every other man. Liberty and slavery are therefore not only incompatible in the sense that it is impossible for one and the same man to be both free and enslaved—they are also incompatible in the sense that it is impossible for one man to be free so long as another is enslaved because of the so-called "freedom" or "liberty" of the first. It is only license, not liberty, that is compatible with slavery.

Given that liberty consists in acting compatibly with the promotion of the good of every person affected by one's action, what the egoist seeks in attempting to promote his good at the expense of the good of others is not liberty but license. The laws of an association are laws of liberty insofar as they are such that action in accordance with them is compatible with the promotion of the good of every member of the association. This means that the laws of a moral association are laws of liberty, and that they are not felt as constraints by the members of such an association so long as they are content to act compatibly with the promotion of the good of others. They are felt as constraints only insofar as I seek to promote my good at the expense of the good of others. But in seeking release from these restrictions what I seek is license, not liberty, for I can have liberty only by acting in accordance with them. If, then, the association compels me to act compatibly with its laws, it is compelling me to refrain from acting licentiously and to act in accordance with principles of liberty. This is to say that if I do not voluntarily or willingly act in accordance with laws of liberty, then the association, if it be a moral association, must compel me to do so. In doing so it forces me to be free.[2]

It is easy to ridicule Rousseau's contention that a man may be forced to be free. Such ridicule, however, seems to issue either from overlooking or from rejecting Locke's distinction between liberty and license. For what Rousseau means by compelling a man to be free is simply compelling him to act in accordance with laws of liberty. It does not mean that the man who is compelled to act compatibly with such laws will not feel the compulsion as compulsion. He undoubtedly will so long as he has inclinations he is prevented from satisfying. Nor does it mean that he is compelled to become morally free, i.e., to act in accordance with laws of liberty out of respect for these laws. No one can compel anyone else to impose moral law upon himself out of respect for it. But although the man who is compelled to act compatibly with laws of liberty may well feel the compulsion as compulsion, and although it is impossible to compel a man to act out of respect for moral law, it is nonetheless also true that the man who is compelled to act in accordance with laws of liberty may eventually, as a consequence of such compulsion, reach a point at which he no longer needs to be compelled to do so, but instead does so independent of such compulsion, simply out of respect for the moral law. This is to say that although it is impossible to compel a man directly to act out of respect for moral law, it is nevertheless possible to compel him indirectly to do so, through initially compelling him to act in accordance with it from fear of the consequences of failing or refusing to do so.

But Rousseau not only believes that it is possible indirectly to compel men to act out of respect for the moral law—I think it no exaggeration to say that he conceives the highest function of a political association to be the moralization of its members. Its function is not merely to establish laws of liberty that enable each person in the association to seek and attain his own good, but to establish laws such that each person acts compatibly with the moral law out of respect for it. The attainment of such a goal is undoubtedly an ideal that can never be perfectly attained in any society, and, as we shall see, Rousseau does not suppose that it can be so attained. But it is nevertheless still an ideal to be aimed for, and one that can be more or less closely approximated. This position is in keeping with Rousseau's view of the plasticity of human nature and the social character of morality. We have seen that for Rousseau neither metaphysical nor moral freedom is natural to man, except in the sense that man naturally has the potentiality of or the capacity for acquiring such freedom as a consequence of living in society. Man is not born free in either the metaphysical or the moral sense of the word, but attains both kinds of freedom only in society. But if the corrupt societies of history have been such as to make metaphysical and moral freedom possible, then it is also possible, Rousseau argues, to organize society in terms of laws that will make possible a closer approximation to the ideal of a society in which each man freely imposes upon himself laws of liberty, and in which such laws are no longer felt as restrictions. The entire *Social Contract* may be read as an attempt to set forth the conditions that must be satisfied if such a society is to be possible. To the extent that an approximation is made toward attaining such a society an approach is thereby also made toward attaining a situation in which each of its members no longer feels its laws as restrictions upon his liberty, but, instead, regards them as what in fact they are, i.e., as laws of liberty.

XXI. The Terms of the Social Contract

The fundamental condition that must be satisfied if such a society is to be attained or approached is that the terms of the social contract be observed. This contract, when we exclude from it everything that is not essential to it, reduces to the following terms. "Each of us puts his person and all his power in common under the supreme direction of the general will, and, in our corporate capacity, we receive each member as an indivisible part of the whole."[1] The various clauses of this contract reduce to "the total alienation of each associate, together with all his rights, to the whole community" which comes into being as a consequence of the contract. Since, however, each person party to the contract gives himself absolutely to the community, "the conditions are the same for all." This being the case, "no one has any interest in making them burdensome to others." Moreover, since the alienation of himself and all his rights and power to the community is made without reserve, "the union is as perfect as it can be, and no associate has anything more to demand." In this connection Rousseau repeats Hobbes' contention that the state of nature would continue "if the individuals retained certain rights," since then "there would be no common superior to decide between them and the public," and "each, being on one point his own judge, would ask to be so on all;" so that "the association would necessarily become inoperative or tyrannical." It would become inoperative if the individuals retain certain rights in such a way that they alone are to be the judge of whether their rights have been violated, and it would become tyrannical if, the individuals reserving the right to judge for themselves whether certain of their rights have been violated, the association nevertheless compels them to accept its judgment as to whether they have in fact been violated. "Finally, each man, in giving himself to all, gives himself to nobody; and as there is no associate over which he does not acquire the same right as he yields others over himself, he gains an equivalent for everything he loses, and an increase of force for the preservation of what he has."[2]

The formation of the social contract creates immediately, "in place of the individual personality of each contracting party, . . . a moral and collective body, composed of as many members as the assembly contains voters," and receiving from the act of association "its unity, its common identity, its life, and its will." The "public person" formed by the union of the persons party to the contract is called a "republic" or "body politic," and once was called a "city." Each of these names is appropriate, particularly the first and the last: the first because the association thus formed is a *res publica*—a public thing— and the last because it is composed of citizens.[3] There is a difference between a town and a city: a town is composed of houses, whereas a city is composed of citizens. Not every town is peopled by denizens who are also citizens, for its houses may be occupied only by persons who are the subjects of some government and not also citizens.[4] The body politic is called "sovereign" when active, "state" when passive, and "power" when related to other bodies politic. The persons associated in it are called collectively "*people*, and severally are called *citizens*, as sharing in the sovereign power, and *subjects*, as being under the laws of the *State*."[5]

Since Rousseau's position cannot be adequately understood unless the preceding terminology is understood, it may help to dwell a moment longer on these terms. As a consequence of the social contract a body politic comes into being. This body politic has two sides or aspects. As active, i.e., as imposing law upon itself, it is sovereign; as passive, i.e., as being that upon which laws are imposed, it is the state. Thus the sovereign and the state are not two separable and distinct things, but the same thing, namely the body politic, regarded from two different points of view. Similarly, the citizens and the subjects of the body politic are not two separable and distinct classes of persons, but the same persons regarded in different ways. As active, i.e., as imposing law upon themselves, the members of the body politic are citizens; as passive, i.e., as being the persons upon whom law is imposed, they are subjects. This can be expressed differently by saying that as citizens the members of the body politic constitute the sovereign, whereas as subjects they constitute the state. The individuals who constitute the sovereign are therefore identical with the individuals who constitute the state, which is to say that the individuals who enact laws are identical with the individuals who are subject to the laws enacted.

What this means is that the terms of the contract are such that no one has an obligation to subject himself, as a member of the state, to the laws enacted by the sovereign unless he is also granted membership, as a citizen, in the sovereign. No one, that is, has an obligation to become or to remain a member of the state unless he is also granted membership in the sovereign, and, correspondingly, no one has an obligation to become or to remain a subject unless he is granted the status of citizen. An acceptance of either role or status morally requires an acceptance of the other. Thus no one has a right to attempt to acquire the status of citizen and membership in the sovereign unless he is willing also to accept the status of subject and membership in the state, and as a subject and member of the state to subject himself to the laws that, as a citizen and a member of the sovereign, he participates in enacting. For if he seeks the status of citizen and membership in the sovereign while seeking to avoid the status of subject and membership in the state he is, in effect, seeking to participate in the enactment of laws to which others but not he are subject, and therefore to tyrannize over and to enslave those who are to be subject to the laws he participates in enacting. And, conversely, no one has a right to accept the status of subject and to reject the status of citizen should he have the opportunity of acquiring it, for to do so would in effect be to enslave oneself, and no man, as we saw earlier, has a right to enslave himself.

Unless these considerations are kept in mind Rousseau's contention that the terms of the contract are such that each party to it totally and absolutely alienates or gives himself and all his rights and all his power to the community can be quite misleading. For this contention, taken by itself, makes it seem as though the individual gives everything to the community and receives nothing in return. The meaning of this contention, however, is not that the individual alienates to the community his natural right to life and to liberty, i.e., his natural right to free life, but is rather the following. In placing himself and all his power and possessions under the direction of the sovereign, what he does is to alienate to the community two things. The first is the freedom from subjection to civil law that he would enjoy in the state of nature. The second is any societal rights or privileges that may have been granted to or conferred upon him by some society in which he has lived prior to his entrance into the association formed in accordance with the terms of the social contract. Whether he is to retain any of these rights or privileges or not and, if so, which ones, is something to be determined neither by himself alone nor by a consideration of his previous status in the earlier society, but, instead, by the sovereign under the direction of which he places himself as a subject and of which he becomes a member as a citizen. The freedom from subjection to civil law which he would enjoy in the state of nature is, of course, something that he must alienate absolutely in becoming a member of the body politic. But in return for this alienation he acquires moral freedom, civil liberty, and a voice, as a citizen and a member of the sovereign, in determining the character of the laws to which he will be subject as a member of the state.

In point of fact, however, the individual who becomes a party to the social contract alienates to the community only those rights and privileges, if any, that have been granted to or conferred upon him by the society of which he is a member at the time of the formation of the contract. He does not alienate to the community the freedom from subjection to civil law which he would enjoy in the state of nature. The reason he does not do so is implicit in our previous considerations. For despite the fact that at places in *The Social Contract* Rousseau writes as though men could form the social contract while still in the state of nature, the account of this state that he presents in the second discourse makes it clear that the formation of the contract while men are still in this state would be impossible. This is so because, as was seen earlier, the formation of the contract presupposes the attainment of a level of rational development that could not be attained so long as men remain in the state of nature. On the contrary, its formation presupposes that men have already lived in some form of pre-civil society, if not also in some form of civil society, long enough to enable them to attain the level of rational development at which they can conceive of the terms of the contract. And since, moreover, *The Social Contract* is addressed to readers whose ancestors have long since abandoned the state of nature, and who are themselves in civil society, there is no question of their alienating their freedom from subjection to civil law in order to form the contract. Although our ancient ancestors living in the obscure recesses of pre-history may have been free from such subjection, we are not. We therefore cannot alienate our freedom from it, for we can alienate only what we have, not what we do not have. Therefore all that we, who live in civil society, can alienate to the community is not our freedom from subjection to civil law, for this is a freedom we do not have, but the rights or privileges that have been granted to or conferred upon us by the society in which we live.

It is important also to keep in mind that the only rights we alienate to the community in forming the social contract are the civil and societal rights conferred upon us by the society in which we happen to live. We do not alienate our natural rights to life and to liberty. Rousseau is at least as insistent as Locke that these rights cannot legitimately be alienated. Rousseau's insistence on this point, like Locke's, has two consequences. The first is that the only way in which any person or body can acquire political authority is by having it granted by those over whom it is acquired. This means that Rousseau, like Locke, derives a doctrine of consent from his assertion of a natural right to liberty. Indeed, Rousseau's doctrine of consent is merely a repetition of Locke's and adds nothing to it. Like Locke, he distinguishes between express and tacit consent, and maintains that continued voluntary residence within the territory subject to the jurisdiction of a given sovereign constitutes tacit consent to that jurisdiction, provided that I am offered the status of citizen and membership in the sovereign as well as that of subject and membership in the state. "When the State is instituted, residence constitutes consent; to dwell within its territory is to submit to the Sovereign."[6] The second consequence issuing from Rousseau's insistence that the natural rights to life and liberty cannot be alienated is that Rousseau, like Locke, maintains that the individual has a right to subject himself to political authority and, conversely, that authority can be acquired over the individual, only if certain conditions are satisfied. For Rousseau these conditions may be summed up by saying that the individual has a right to alienate himself to the community and thereby to assume the status of subject and membership in the state only if he is also granted and accepts the status of citizen and membership in the sovereign. And, conversely, the community has a right to compel the individual to submit to it as a subject only if it also grants him the status of citizen. Given the natural right to liberty, no one can legitimately be a subject unless he is also a citizen, which is to say that no one can legitimately be a member of the state unless he is also a member of the sovereign. The expressions "subject" and "citizen" on the one hand and "member of the state" and "member of the sovereign" on the other are correlatives, and neither member of either pair can legitimately be applied to any individual unless the other is also applied.

Given these considerations, the meaning of Rousseau's contention that the clauses of the social contract "are so determined by the nature of the act that the slightest modification would make them vain and ineffective"[7] becomes clear. It is that the clauses or terms of the contract are natural in the sense in which the rights to life and liberty are natural. Just as these rights are not conventional, neither are the terms of the contract conventional. Just as an individual or group can neither confer any natural rights upon either themselves or others nor legitimately deprive either themselves or others of any natural rights they possess, neither can any individual or group alter the terms of the contract. Just as the natural rights of men are determined by their nature as men, and thus are not subject to alteration as a consequence of any human decision, so are the terms of the contract fixed by the nature of man and not subject to alteration by man. This is to say that the terms of the contract are determined by, or follow from, the natural rights to life and liberty. Given these rights as natural, no man or group can legitimately be subjected to the laws of a community unless they are given a voice equal to that of every other person in the community in determining what they are to be, and no man has a right voluntarily to subject himself to them unless he is also granted and accepts the status of citizen. It is because each and every man has a natural right to life and liberty that the expressions "citizen" and "subject," "member of the sovereign" and "member of the state," are strict correlatives, and that their correlativity is expressed in the terms of the contract. Thus although the formation of the contract is a voluntary act, the terms of the contract are not alterable at the will of any individual or group. They are as unalterable and as fixed, as universal and as eternal, as the natural rights that determine them.

But although the terms of the contract are universal and eternal, and thus are not subject to alteration or variation, as human customs, conventions, and laws are, the sovereign, i.e., the collectivity of citizens, is free, within the limits of the terms of the contract, to impose upon the state, i.e., the collectivity of subjects, any and every law that in its judgment is conducive to the promotion of the good of the body politic. It is also free, within the limits of the terms of the contract, to rescind any law, the repeal of which, in its judgment, promotes the good of the body politic, which is to say that it is never bound by any law it enacts in such a way that it cannot repeal it. Instead, any law it can legitimately enact it can also legitimately repeal. In Rousseau's words, it is "against the nature of the body politic for the sovereign to impose on itself a law which it cannot infringe."[8] Like Hobbes, Rousseau argues that to suppose that the sovereign can impose a law upon itself which it cannot later repeal is analogous to supposing that an individual can enter into a contract with himself.[9] Both suppositions are absurd, for contracts are possible only between two or more distinct persons. It is true that an individual can resolve in the present to perform a certain act in the future. But such a resolution is in no sense a contract with oneself, and he can later resolve not to perform the act in question without violating any contractual obligation he may have acquired as a consequence of the first resolution, for, again, to resolve to perform an act is not to enter into a contract with oneself. Precisely similar considerations apply to an act of sovereignty. The sovereign, in enacting a law, does not thereby incur an obligation never to repeal it, and may legitimately rescind it whenever in its judgment the good of the body politic can most effectively be promoted through its repeal. This, however, is not to say that the body politic cannot enter into contracts. For just as an individual can bind himself through entering into a contract with another person, so also the body politic, as a corporate person, can enter into contracts with persons, either natural or corporate, distinct from or external to it, since "in relation to what is external to it, it becomes a simple being, an individual."[10]

But although the sovereign can enact and repeal any laws, the enactment or repeal of which it judges to be conducive to the promotion of the good of the body politic, and although the body politic can enter into undertakings with others, Rousseau is clear in his insistence that these acts are legitimate only if they are compatible with the terms of the contract. Just as for Locke the natural rights to life, liberty, and property constitute fixed limits within which the government must operate, so also for Rousseau the natural rights to life and liberty, and the terms of the contract that emanate from them, constitute fixed limits upon the authority of the sovereign within which it must operate. "The body politic or the Sovereign, drawing its being wholly from the sanctity of the contract, can never bind itself, even to an outsider, to do anything derogatory to the original act, for instance, to alienate any part of itself, or to submit to another Sovereign. Violation of the act by which it exists would be self-annihilation; and that which is itself nothing can create nothing."[11] What Rousseau particularly has in mind here is that the body politic has no more of a right to subject itself to another in such a way that its members become subjects but not citizens of the other than an individual has to subject himself to a sovereign in which he is not granted membership as a citizen. Just as an individual would enslave himself if he did so, so also would a body politic, and a body politic can no more legitimately enslave itself than an individual can. Should it nevertheless do so, it would violate the terms of the contract in such a way as to dissolve itself. For it would, in effect, be seeking to enslave its subjects, and they would thereby be freed from any obligation to obey it.

XXII. The Termination of the Contract

This, however, does not mean that the body politic cannot legitimately dissolve itself. It can. Rousseau states its right to do so somewhat misleadingly in these words: "there neither is nor can be any kind of fundamental law binding on the body of the people—not even the social contract itself."[1] This seems at first to run directly counter to the contention that the terms of the contract constitute a fixed or unalterable limit upon the authority of the sovereign. This, however, is not what this passage means. Its meaning can be understood only if taken in conjunction with a passage occurring in the final paragraph of Book Three. "There is in the State no fundamental law that cannot be revoked, not excluding the social compact itself; for if all the citizens assembled of one accord to break the compact, it is impossible to doubt that it would be very legitimately broken."[2] This makes it clear that when Rousseau says that there is no law, not even the social contract itself, that is binding upon the body of the people, he means only that the contract itself can be terminated should the citizens decide to do so, and therefore is binding upon them only so long as they do not decide to terminate it. But until or unless they do decide upon its termination, its terms constitute fixed and unalterable limits within which they must operate in the enactment of law. Should any of their enactments violate these limits they would not have the authority of law, and the subjects would be under no obligation to obey them.

A question arises, however, as to what proportion of the assembled citizens must agree to terminate the contract if it is legitimately to be terminated. We have just seen that Rousseau maintains that "if *all* the citizens assembled of one accord to break the compact, it is impossible to doubt that it would be very legitimately broken." This would seem to mean that unanimous agreement to terminate it is necessary if its termination is to be legitimate. If so, then the agreement of a majority that falls short of unanimity to terminate it would not be sufficient to render its termination legitimate, and the refusal of a minority of only one citizen to agree to its termination would suffice to make its termination illegitimate. On the other hand, Rousseau maintains that the only law that requires unanimous consent is the social contract itself, and that its terms are such that those who consent, either expressly or tacitly, to become a party to the contract thereby also consent to be bound by the will of the majority of the citizens when votes are taken as to what the laws of the body politic are to be. The social contract requires unanimous consent because of the natural right to liberty. "Every man being born free and his own master, no one, under any pretext whatsoever, can make any man subject without his consent."[3] But in consenting to the terms of the contract, I thereby consent to abide by the will of the majority of the citizens as to what the law of the body politic is to be, provided that what the majority wills does not violate the terms of the contract. Thus although the will of the majority of an association is morally binding upon each member of the association, this is only because each member, in consenting to become a member, thereby consents to be bound by the will of the majority. The citizen, in consenting to the terms of the contract, thereby "gives his consent to all the laws, including those which are passed in spite of his opposition, and even those which punish him when he dares to break any of them."[4]

We therefore seem to have an inconsistency. On the one hand Rousseau seems to say that the contract can be terminated only through the unanimous consent of those who are parties to it. Yet on the other hand he says that in consenting to the contract one thereby consents to accept the will of the majority as to what the laws of the association are to be. This apparent inconsistency, however, is possibly only that—an apparent and not a real inconsistency. For there seem to be two ways in which it can be resolved.

First, one could deny that the decision to terminate the contract is a law. The ground of this denial would be that the laws enacted by the citizens bind them all as subjects, at least until they vote to repeal them, whereas the decision to terminate the contract frees them from it. Such a decision, instead of subjecting the citizens as subjects to the laws of the association, would free them from such subjection, and thus would neither constitute nor have the effect of a law. But since Rousseau maintains only that consent to the contract implies consent to accept the will of the majority as to what the *laws* of the association are to be, and since the decision to terminate the contract does not amount to the enactment of a law, he is not inconsistent in maintaining that it requires the unanimous consent of all the citizens. Second, one could argue that the act of terminating the contract is analogous to the act of instituting it, in the sense that it annuls the latter act and therefore the body politic it creates. But since the contract can be formed only through the unanimous consent of everyone who is to be party to it, so also can it be terminated only through their unanimous consent. One could go on to argue that this is so because a contract can legitimately be terminated in only two ways. One is through the fulfillment by each party of the obligations he acquires as a consequence of the contract. The other is through the consent of each party to the contract to terminate it. The social contract could be terminated only in the latter way. For the social contract, unlike most contracts, is a continuing contract, in the sense that the persons party to it, in becoming parties to it, acquire obligations that cannot be fulfilled once and for all, but that, instead, continue either so long as they live or else until the time at which they consent unanimously to terminate it.

But although the apparent inconsistency in question can perhaps be resolved in either of these two ways, the question of whether the contract can be terminated only through the unanimous consent of those who are party to it has a somewhat academic air about it and appears to be of little practical importance. This is the case for the following reasons.

First, should a majority, or even a considerable minority, of the citizens vote to terminate it, it would be extremely probable that its terms would already have been so grossly and persistently violated that it has already ceased to serve its purpose significantly. In this case, the association structured in terms of it has already begun to die, and the vote to terminate it, whether this be the vote of a majority or of a considerable minority, may be looked upon simply as an issuance of a death certificate certifying the death of something already dead or about to die. A healthy body politic that is fulfilling its purpose, and in which the terms of the contract are generally fulfilled, has not degenerated to such an extent that a considerable portion of its members, either a majority or a large minority, are eager to declare its death by terminating the contract. Should such an association die, its death comes not from within but from without, at the hands of an external power or association that attacks and kills it. Second, it is extremely doubtful that the members of a body politic would ever will unanimously to terminate the contract. There would always be some who benefit, or at least believe that they do, from the contract and thus would not agree to its termination. It is never the people, simply and as such, who seek to overthrow a government or to dissolve a political association, but, at most, only a large part of the people, perhaps a majority. Third, should a majority of the body politic will to terminate the contract, it will be effectively terminated even though its termination is not agreed upon unanimously. But should they succeed in terminating it, they could not, for reasons already given, return to the state of nature. Their only alternative would be to establish another political association. But if they do so it would be legitimate only if structured in terms of the conditions specified by the social contract, for only an association so structured can be legitimate. This is to say that the only alternative, given the impracticability if not also the impossibility of returning to the state of nature, to living in a political association structured in terms of the social contract is to live in one that is illegitimate. This amounts to saying that the only alternative to living in a legitimate society is to live in one that is illegitimate.

Given these considerations, the following conclusions seem to follow. First, despite Rousseau's contention that "if all the citizens assembled of one accord to break the compact, it is impossible to doubt that it would be very legitimately broken," the contract cannot legitimately be terminated. This is the case because, given the impracticality or impossibility of returning to the state of nature, the only alternative to living in a society organized in terms of the contract is to live in an illegitimate society. This means that Rousseau's contention that the contract may legitimately be terminated is incompatible with his more fundamental theses concerning the nature of man and society and the conditions of a just society, and must therefore be rejected if these more fundamental theses are accepted. Second, given the illegitimacy of terminating the contract, a body politic can legitimately be dissolved only if two conditions are satisfied. The first is that it has ceased either to be organized in terms of or else to operate in accordance with the contract. In either event, those responsible for its departure from the terms of the contract have already acted illicitly in causing this departure to occur. The second condition is that it is probable that a more legitimate state of affairs can be brought about through dissolving the body politic than through continuing to permit it to exist in its corrupt state. Third, the dissolution of the body politic under such conditions does not amount to a termination of the contract. On the contrary, it amounts either to an attempt to re-institute it, in those situations in which its terms were once fulfilled by the body politic in question, or else to an attempt to institute it, in those situations in which its terms were never fulfilled by the body politic in question. Fourth, the dissolution of the body politic does not involve, or at least need not involve, the return of its members to the state of nature. Instead, it involves only restructuring its laws, its form of government, and its institutions in such a way as to make them conform to the requirements of the contract. It therefore does not involve a dissolution of the society, but rather involves only a dissolution of the constitution, the government, and certain institutions. Indeed, it may not even require their dissolution, but only their alteration or reformation. The question, however, of when a body politic is dissolved as distinguished from being only reconstituted or restructured is not one to which an easy answer can always be given. This, however, is not a question that need detain us here. For here we are interested only in pointing out that the dissolution or reconstitution of a body politic is by no means identical with the termination of the social contract, and that whereas the former is sometimes justifiable in terms of Rousseau's fundamental theses, the latter never is, despite his inconsistent contention that the contract may legitimately be terminated.

The only argument Rousseau presents in support of his contention that the contract may legitimately be terminated is the following. He cites with apparent approval the position of Grotius that "each man can renounce his membership of his own state, and recover his natural liberty and his goods on leaving the country," and then goes on to assert that "it would be indeed absurd if all the citizens in assembly could not do what each can do by himself."[5] This argument, however, fails, for the following reasons.

First, there is an obvious difference between, on the one hand, the renunciation by an individual of his citizenship and his emigration from the body politic and, on the other, the termination of the contract by means of a simultaneous act on the part of all or a majority of the citizens.

For the former is an act performed by an individual, whereas the latter is an act performed by all or a majority of the citizens; the former is only an act of renunciation of citizenship and emigration from the body politic, whereas the latter is an act of terminating the social contract; and, finally, the effect of the first act is not the termination of the contract, whereas the result of the latter is its termination. It is true that the body politic would be dissolved, or at least would disappear, and that the social contract would be terminated, at least as far as the organization of the body politic in question is concerned, if all its citizens successively renounced their citizenship and emigrated. But even if they should do so (and that *all* the citizens of any body politic would ever do so is unlikely in the extreme), the act of renouncing one's citizenship and emigrating is still the act of an individual distinct in kind from the collective act of terminating the contract. From the fact, then, that the first act is legitimate it does not follow that the second is.

Second, there is a question as to whether even the first act would be legitimate. We have seen that Rousseau accepts, at least implicitly, Locke's distinction between express and tacit consent. Locke argues that those persons who expressly consent to a government thereby obligate themselves to a lifelong obedience to it on the condition that it does not violate the natural rights of its subjects, and are free to separate themselves permanently from its jurisdiction only if it grants them this freedom. It is only those who give merely their tacit as distinguished from express consent to a government who have the natural right to separate themselves from it whenever they choose to do so.[6] Rousseau, however, although he accepts the distinction between express and tacit consent, does not draw the same conclusion as Locke does. Instead, he writes as though any individual, regardless of whether he has expressly or only tacitly consented to the terms of the contract, has the right to separate himself from the body politic whenever he pleases, provided that "he does not leave to escape his obligations and avoid having to serve his country in the hour of need." In such a case his departure "would be criminal and punishable, and would be, not withdrawal, but desertion."[7]

But who is to determine whether his departure is simply a withdrawal or a criminal and punishable desertion? Is the individual who wishes to separate himself to make the determination, or is the community or its agents to make it? The answer seems clear from the terms of the social contract itself. For, as we have seen, the individual, in becoming a party to the contract, places himself and all his powers, possessions, and rights under the direction of the general will of the community. He therefore alienates to the community the right to decide whether his separation of himself from it is simply a withdrawal or a criminal and punishable desertion. If the community or its agents decide that it is only a withdrawal, then it may permit him to emigrate. But if it should decide that his separation would be a criminal and punishable desertion, then it has the right, according to the terms of the contract, to forbid and to prevent it. The terms of the contract are therefore such that the question of whether any of the members of the body politic may legitimately separate themselves from it on any given occasion is a question to be answered by the community or its agents, not by the individual. This being the case, Rousseau cannot legitimately argue that the members of the body politic may legitimately terminate the contract on the ground that an individual may legitimately separate himself from the body politic whenever he chooses to do so.

If the preceding argument is sound, we must conclude that Rousseau is inconsistent with his fundamental theses in maintaining that the contract may legitimately be terminated and that individuals may legitimately separate themselves from the body politic whenever they choose. For his fundamental theses are, first, that the terms of the contract are permanently binding upon those who are party to it in such a way that it cannot be terminated, and, second, that every person party to the contract is permanently subject to the laws of the body politic so long as their enactment, their content, their application, and their enforcement are compatible with the terms of the contract, and therefore can legitimately separate themselves from the body politic only if its laws permit them to do so. Although a body politic, or at least its constitution and government, may legitimately be dissolved when its structure and operation are hopelessly incompatible with the terms of the contract, the dissolution of the body politic is not equivalent to a termination of the contract. But so long as the structure and operation of the body politic are compatible with the terms of the contract, it can no more be legitimately dissolved than the contract can legitimately be terminated, and none of its members can legitimately separate themselves from it unless its laws permit them to do so. These are fundamental theses of Rousseau's, and the passages in *The Social Contract* that run counter to them may be dismissed as inconsistent aberrations resulting from his failure to develop consistently the implications of these theses.

XXIII. Equality and Democracy

We have seen that the terms of the contract are such that no one may legitimately be compelled to subject himself as a member of the state to the laws of the body politic unless he is granted the status of citizen and

membership in the sovereign, and, conversely, that no one may legitimately acquire or retain the status of citizen and membership in the sovereign unless he subjects himself as a member of the state to the laws enacted
by the sovereign. The membership of the state, i.e., the subjects of the
body politic, is therefore identical with the membership of the sovereign,
i.e., the citizens of the body politic. Each person as a subject is to be
equally subject to the laws of the body politic, and each person as a citizen
is to have one and only one vote in determining what the laws are to be.
Should any person be denied citizenship, i.e., membership in the sovereign, then he will be under no obligation to obey the laws of the body
politic, and, conversely, should any person granted citizenship refuse to
subject himself to the laws that he participates in enacting, he will thereby
forfeit the status of citizen. One of the fundamental principles of the social
contract is therefore the principle of equality. Each person party to the
contract is to be equally subject to the law of the body politic on the
condition that he is granted a voice as a citizen equal to that of every other
person in the body politic in determining its law. The terms of the contract are therefore such that equality must be the principle of law in a
double sense. Each person in the body politic must be equally subject to
the law, and each must have an equal voice in determining the law. Its
terms therefore constitute an expression of the essential nature of natural
justice, and are thus unalterable.

It is no exaggeration to state that Rousseau, more than any other great
political philosopher, takes seriously the relationship between equality on
the one hand and justice and morality on the other. More than any other
great political thinker, he assiduously endeavors to ground his entire political philosophy upon the contention that there is an essential connection
between equality and justice. He sees, as clearly as any other thinker, that
to say that each man has a natural right to something, say life or liberty, is
to say that each has an equal right to it. This can be put by saying that if
any man has a natural right to anything, then he has a natural right to
equality of treatment. It can also be put by saying that each man has a
natural obligation to subject himself to laws of equality. But Rousseau is
also convinced, as we have already seen and as we shall presently see more
fully, that most men are naturally partial to themselves, and therefore that
if all men are to subject themselves to laws of equality it is necessary that
each participate in the enactment of these laws. This is the best, if not the
only, guarantee that the laws enacted will be genuine laws of equality and
apply equally to everyone subject to them. For should any one man or
group within the body politic, to the exclusion of others, be granted the
authority to enact law, the temptation to enact laws favoring
themselves—or some one or a few groups—at the expense of the rest of the

members of the association might easily be too great for them to resist.

Even if there were some one man or group excelling so in wisdom and justice that they would unfailingly enact only wise and just laws of equality, the purpose of the social contract and political association would still not be fully attained. For at least part of their purpose is the moralization of men, and this is something that can be adequately achieved only when men act in accordance with laws of justice and equality that they freely impose upon themselves. This is to say that the moralization of a person or a people is adequately attained only when they have the responsibility of moralizing themselves. So long as a person or a people act in accordance with laws prescribed to them by some wise and just legislator or group of legislators, they are under a kind of tutelary bondage to their legislators. The content of the laws prescribed to them may be wise and just, and may even be identical in content to the laws they themselves would impose upon themselves were they to legislate for themselves. But there would still be something missing—the presence of conditions under which they are fully responsible for moralizing themselves, through being responsible for freely imposing upon themselves laws of justice and equality.

Here we are touching upon one of the fundamental sources of Rousseau's democracy and of his repudiation of intellectual aristocracy. His insistence upon democracy (or republicanism, as he would probably term it) does not rest merely upon his conviction that a natural right to something such as life or liberty is an equal right to it, or upon his conviction that if there is a natural right to anything there is a natural right to equality of treatment. Nor does it rest merely upon a belief that wise and just legislators who can be trusted to enact wise and just laws are never to be found. Indeed, he supposes that such legislators are necessary, not to enact laws, but to enlighten the citizens through proposing wise and just laws to them.[1] Instead, it rests also upon the conviction that so long as men are subject to laws prescribed to them by others, and do not accept the responsibility of freely imposing laws of justice and equality upon themselves, they remain in tutelary bondage to their legislators and fail to develop fully their capacities as free and responsible moral agents. This, I believe, is part of the source, not only of his insistence upon the moral necessity of democracy as opposed to intellectual aristocracy, but also of his admiration for John Calvin and Calvinistic Protestantism and his dislike for the intellectual and ecclesiastical aristocracy of Roman Catholicism, a religion, which, in his opinion, "is so clearly bad, that it is a waste of time to stop to prove it such."[2] Whether, however, his admiration for the former and dislike for the latter forms of religion are justifiable is, of course, another matter.

Given, then, (1) the natural right to liberty and to equality of treatment,

(2) the fact that most if not all men are partial to themselves and their families and friends, and (3) the supposition that the full moralization of men requires that they be responsible for freely imposing laws of justice and equality upon themselves, the terms of the social contract are such that each subject and member of the state be also a citizen and member of the sovereign, and that laws apply equally to each person within the body politic and be enacted only through taking a vote in which each person who is to be subject to the law has one and only one vote. Indeed, Rousseau defines the term "law" in such a way that an enactment is to count as a law only if (1) each person who is to be subject to it has a voice equal to that of every other person who is to be subject to it in determining whether it is to be enacted and (2) no person has a voice in determining whether it is to be enacted unless he is to be subject to it on the same terms as every other person to whom it applies. "When the whole people decrees for the whole people, it is considering only itself; and if a relation is then formed, it is between two aspects of the entire object, without there being any division of the whole. In that case the matter about which the decree is made is, like the decreeing will, general. This act is what I call a law."[3] Given this definition of "law" there is an analogy between moral law and the law of the body politic on the one hand and between moral freedom and political and civil liberty on the other. Just as moral freedom consists in acting in accordance with the moral law which I freely impose upon myself, so political or civil liberty consists in or depends upon action by the subjects of the body politic in accordance with the law of the body politic, which they as citizens freely impose upon themselves. Given this analogy, the body politic may be regarded as a person possessing a will, just as an individual is a person possessing a will. This is in fact how Rousseau does regard the body politic, both in *The Social Contract* and in the *Discourse on Political Economy*.

XXIV. Natural Persons and the Corporate Person

We have seen that Rousseau maintains that once the terms of the social contract are agreed to, what he refers to as "a moral and collective body" and as a "public person" possessing life and a will is created.[1] This is to say that when men incorporate themselves into an association structured in terms of the social contract they create a moral entity that may be referred to as an "artificial," a "collective," a "public," or a "corporate" person. This person is artificial as opposed to natural because it is an artifact made by human art through the operation of human reason and will, and does not arise through the operation of nature alone independent of the operation of human reason and will. It is collective as opposed to singular because it is a person consisting of an association or union of a multiplicity of natural persons. It is public as opposed to private because its operation is of concern to and subject to the direction of all its members. It is corporate because it results from an act of incorporation on the part of the natural persons who become its members. And, finally, it is moral both in the sense that it is a moral agent, in virtue of its personality and possession of will, and also in the sense that it wills the common good of all its members.

The differences between the body politic as a corporate person and the human individual as a natural person are, of course, much more obvious than their similarities are. It may therefore be helpful to dwell for a moment on their similarities, both as Rousseau explicitly states them and as they may be inferred from what he explicitly says. He states them more fully in the *Discourse on Political Economy* than in *The Social Contract*. In the former work he states explicitly that "the body politic, taken individually, may be considered as an organized, living body, resembling that of man,"[2] and goes on to draw the following analogies.

Just as the health and proper functioning of the human body depends upon or consists in the health and proper functioning of its various related parts, so also the health and proper functioning of the body politic depends upon or consists in the health and proper functioning of the various natural persons constituting it. Thus in the case of both the human body and the body politic the health and the proper functioning of the entire body and of the other members of the body may be affected adversely, even to the extent that the entire body dies, should one or some of its members become diseased or fail to function properly. And just as no part of the animal body "can be damaged without the painful impression being conveyed to the brain, if the animal is in a state of health,"[3] neither can any part of the body politic be damaged without causing the damage to be felt by the entire body politic, if it is in a state of health. This is to say that just as it is the person himself who feels and suffers from the pain in his foot when he steps upon a nail, so also the corporate person suffers when one of its members is afflicted. Moreover, just as a natural person, in order to preserve his life or health and the health of the other parts of his body, may be compelled to amputate some diseased part of his body, such as a gangrenous foot, so also the body politic, in order to preserve its life or health and that of its members, may have to kill or banish some diseased member. And finally, just as a natural person, in willing his own good, wills, at least implicitly, the health and proper functioning of the various parts of his body, in the sense that his good depends upon their health and proper functioning, so also the body politic, in willing its own good, wills the good of each of its members, from which its own good is indistinguishable and to which it is therefore reducible. The body politic, like the human body, is therefore a living thing that cannot be understood so long as its parts are regarded merely as standing in spatial and temporal juxtaposition to one another. "The life of both bodies is the self common to the whole, the reciprocal sensibility and internal correspondence of all the parts. Where this communication ceases, where the formal unity disappears, and the contiguous parts belong to one another only by juxtaposition, the man is dead, or the State is dissolved."[4]

This analogy between the body politic and the human body is obviously "in some respects inaccurate," as Rousseau himself recognizes.[5] One of its chief defects is that the members of the body politic are natural persons each of whom wills his own good, whereas the parts of the human body are not persons at all, and therefore will nothing. Another is that the body politic is an artificial or corporate person, depending for its existence and will upon the will of its members, whereas a human being is a natural person. Still another, following from the first two, is that the good of the body politic is not something distinct from and over and above the good of the natural persons who constitute it, but is reducible to or identical with their good, whereas only the grossest of materialists would think of maintaining that the good of a natural person is reducible to or identical with the health and proper functioning of his body. This may also be put by saying that the members of the body politic are each ultimate ends in themselves and not mere means to the attainment of the good of the body politic, as though its good were something distinct from and superior in value to that of its members, whereas the health and proper functioning of the parts of the human body is not an ultimate end in itself, but rather derives its value from that of the good of the person to which it contributes.

But despite these obvious defects in the analogy, it nevertheless illustrates the fact that the body politic may reasonably be looked upon as an organism whose members are organically related to one another and to the whole in such a way that the health and proper functioning of the whole and of each of its members depends upon the health and proper functioning of the other members. It therefore also serves the purpose of illustrating that the body politic, in willing its own good, is also thereby willing the good of each of its members. Its will is therefore general, as distinct from the particular wills of each of its members.

The preceding considerations imply that the body politic is a moral being in at least three senses. First, as we have seen, it is a moral being in the sense that any being with a will is such. This is to say that any being with a will, whether it be a natural person or a corporate person, is a moral being in the sense that it is a moral agent, capable of acting either rightly or wrongly and thus of freely willing a moral good. Second, the body politic is a moral being in the sense that it is an artificial body created to solve the moral problem of establishing conditions under which each natural person can most effectively promote his own good, which by nature he seeks, only by acting compatibly with the promotion of the good of every other person in the body politic. Third, the body politic is a moral being in the sense that in constantly willing its own good it thereby also constantly wills the moral good, since in willing its own good it thereby wills the good of each of its members. This may also be expressed by saying that the will of the body politic, which is the general will, is always what it ought to be, since its object is always the general or common good, which is the good of each of its members. Thus the general will of the body politic, "which tends always to the preservation and welfare of the whole and of every part, and is the source of the laws, constitutes for all the members of the State, in their relations to one another and to it, the rule of what is just or unjust."[6]

The concept of the general will is a complex notion and has probably caused readers of Rousseau more difficulty than any other concept he employs. It is also one of the central notions in his political philosophy, if not the most central, so that his political philosophy cannot be adequately understood unless this notion is understood. It is therefore of some importance that we attempt to understand it.

XXV. Particular Wills and the General Will

We begin by contrasting the source and the object of a will, both of which may be either particular or general. The source of a will is particular whenever it is the will of an individual or natural person. Thus if there be ten men at a given place there are ten particular wills, if there be a hundred there are a hundred particular wills, if there be a thousand there are a thousand particular wills, and so on. There are, in short, at least as many particular wills as there are natural persons, and, as we shall see in a moment, there are in fact even more particular wills than there are natural persons. The source of the will of a natural person is particular because the natural person himself is its source, and he is a particular individual in virtue of his being a natural person. But the object of a will whose source is particular may be either particular or general, depending upon whether this object is itself either particular or general. If the object of a will whose source is particular is the good of some natural person, it is a particular object; but if it is the good of some collection or group of natural persons, it is a general object. A natural person may will his own good or else the good of some other natural person. In either case, both the source and the object of his will are particular. On the other hand, he may will the good of some group of natural persons, either some group of which he is a member or else some group of which he is not a member. In this event the source of his will is particular, since he is its source, but its object is general, since it is the good of some group.

We have seen that the two fundamental natural principles of human nature are self-love and compassion. Insofar as a man acts simply out of self-love both the source and the object of his will are particular. The source is particular because he is its source, and the object is particular because his own good is its object. The same applies to an individual insofar as he acts out of egoism. This is the case even though the individual who acts out of self-love or egoism may also will the good of some group as a means toward the attainment of his own good. For in this event the ultimate object of his will is his own good, not that of the group. The good of the group is only the proximate object of his will, not the ultimate object, and should he come to believe that the good of the group is not a means to his own good it would cease to be even the proximate object. On the other hand, if and insofar as an individual acts out of natural compassion, his will, though particular in its source, may be either particular or general in its object, depending upon whether his compassion is directed toward an individual or toward a group of individuals. But insofar as an individual acts out of respect for the moral law, his will, though particular in its source, is necessarily general in its object, since he endeavors to seek his own good and that of others only through acting compatibly with the promotion of the non-egoistic good of everyone affected by his action.

Although, then, the will of a natural person may be either general or particular in its object, it is necessarily particular in its source. This means that the only will that can be general in its source as well as in its object is the will of a group. But it does not mean that either the source or the object of the will of a group is necessarily general, regardless of the relationship in which the group stands to other groups and to individuals. Instead, both the source and the object of the will of a group may be either particular or general, depending upon the relationship of the group to other groups and to individuals. Indeed, they may be at once both particular and general—particular in relation to one group and at the same time general in relation to some other group. This is the case because there are groups that are sub-groups of larger groups. Thus suppose that there are three groups, A, B, and C, which are groups or sub-groups included in some larger group G. Suppose also that group A is composed of the natural persons f, g, and h, that group B is composed of the natural persons p, q, and r, and that group C is composed of the natural persons x, y, and z. The individual members of one group may also be members of some other group. Thus f may be a member of groups B and C as well as A, q may be a member of group A as well as group B, and z may be a member of group B as well as group C. For the sake of simplicity, however, let us suppose that no individual is a member of more than one of these groups. But although each may be a member of only one of these sub-groups, each is a member, not only of his sub-group, but also of the larger group G that comprehends or includes the sub-groups A, B, and C.

Given these suppositions, the will of each of the three groups A, B, and C is general, both in its source and in its object, relative to the particular wills of the natural persons included in each group. Thus the will of group A is general relative to the particular wills of its members f, g, and h; the will of B is general relative to the wills of p, q, and r; and the will of C is general relative to the wills of x, y, and z. The will of each of the groups A, B, and C is general in its source relative to the particular wills of its members because it is the will of a group of which they are the members, and is general in its object because the object of the will of each group is the good of the group and therefore the good of each member of the group. At the same time, however, the will of each group is particular, both in its source and in its object, relative (1) to the wills of individuals outside the group, (2) to the wills of the other groups, and (3) to the will of G, the comprehensive or all-inclusive group. Thus, for example, the will of group A, though general relative to the wills of its individual members, is particular relative (1) to the wills of the individuals included in groups B and C, (2) to the wills of B and C, and (3) to the will of the comprehensive group G. The same of course applies also, with the necessary changes, to the wills of B and C. The source of the will of each group is particular relative to the wills of individuals outside it, to the wills of other groups, and to the will of G because its source is simply the group in question, and neither the individuals outside it, nor the other groups, nor G. Similarly, the object of the will of each group is particular relative to the objects of the wills of the individuals outside it, of the other groups, and of G because the object of the will of each group is its own good, not the good of either the individuals outside it, the other groups, or G. But the will of G, the comprehensive group, is necessarily general both in its source and in its object, for it comprehends groups *A*, *B*, and *C* and all the individuals included in either *A*, *B*, or *C*. It is general in its source because its source is the comprehensive group, including all the individuals and sub-groups it comprehends, and general in its object because its object is the good of the comprehensive group, including the good of each individual and sub-group included in the comprehensive group.

The comprehensive group stands at the opposite extreme from the individual natural person. Whereas the source of the will of a natural person is necessarily particular, the source of the will of the comprehensive group is necessarily general. Standing in between natural persons and the comprehensive group are the various sub-groups of the comprehensive group. The source of the will of a sub-group is at once both general and particular—general in relation to its members and particular in relation to the comprehensive group, to other sub-groups, and to individuals outside it. The object of the will of the comprehensive group is also, like its source, necessarily general, since its object is the good of the comprehensive group, and therefore the good of each individual and sub-group included in the comprehensive group. The object of the will of an individual and of a sub-group, on the other hand, may be either particular or general. The object of the will of an individual is particular if he wills the good of an individual, either himself or some other individual, and general if he wills the good of some group, either one of which he is a member or one of which he is not a member. The object of the will of a sub-group, on the other hand, is general insofar as it wills the good of a group, either its own good, that of some other sub-group, or that of the comprehensive group, and particular insofar as it wills the good of some sub-group, either its own or that of some other sub-group, as contrasted with the good of some other sub-group or with that of the comprehensive group.

Rousseau clearly maintains that an individual may will the good of some natural person other than himself, for, as we know, he maintains that natural compassion is one of the two fundamental principles of human nature. But whether he would admit that a sub-group could ever will the good of some other sub-group, except as a means of attaining its own good, is not clear from what he explicitly says in *The Social Contract* and the *Discourse on Political Economy*. But that they not only can do so but, in fact, often do is obvious from the following considerations. First, some sub-groups are expressly formed for charitable purposes of one kind or another, and expressly will the good of other sub-groups independently of willing their own good. Second, groups that are not expressly formed for such purposes sometimes come to the aid of other groups as an end in itself, and not merely as a means to the promotion of their own good. It is therefore not only possible that an individual should will as an end in itself the good of another individual or of a group of which he is not himself a member, but also that one group should will as an end in itself the good of some other group.

From the preceding considerations it follows that the object of the will of an individual or a group—though general insofar as either wills the good of a group as distinguished from the good of an individual—is at the same time nonetheless particular insofar as either wills the good only of some sub-group within the comprehensive group, as contrasted with the good of other sub-groups and with the good of the comprehensive group. Thus should some individual, f, will the good of some sub-group A of which he is a member, or else the good of some sub-group B of which he is not a member, the object of his will is general rather than particular, since it is the good of a group rather than the good of an individual. Yet insofar as he wills only the good of some sub-group within the comprehensive group, and not the good of the comprehensive group itself, the object of his will is particular rather than general. Precisely similar considerations apply to the object of the will of a sub-group. Should some sub-group A will either its own good or the good of some other sub-group B, the object of its will is general rather than particular, since it wills the good of a group rather than the good of an individual. Yet insofar as it wills only the good of some sub-group within the comprehensive group, and not the good of the comprehensive group itself, the object of its will is particular rather than general.

This means that the object of a will, regardless of whether its source be particular or general, can be absolutely or unqualifiedly general only if it is the good of the comprehensive group. Thus the object of the will of an individual and of any sub-group within the comprehensive group is absolutely general only if they will the good of the comprehensive group. Although it is possible for individuals and sub-groups to will the comprehensive good, they do not constantly do so, but instead frequently substitute some particular or less general good for the comprehensive good, often in ways incompatible not only with the attainment of the comprehensive good, but also with the attainment of some good that, though less general than the comprehensive good, is nevertheless still more general than the good they seek. Indeed, as we shall see, Rousseau maintains that the more constricted or particular the object of a will is, the stronger the will is, in the sense that its object is more assiduously sought by the person, whether natural or corporate, who seeks it. Thus a natural person more assiduously seeks his own good than he does the good of some group of which he is a member, and the members of a sub-group more diligently seek the good of this sub-group than they do the good of the comprehensive group. This means that the natural order is precisely the reverse of the moral order.

According to the moral order the comprehensive good takes precedence over the good of any sub-group within the comprehensive group, and the good of a sub-group, insofar as it is compatible with the comprehensive good, takes precedence over the particular good of any of its members. This means that individuals ought to will first the comprehensive good, next the good of the sub-groups of which they are members—so far as the good of these sub-groups is compatible with the comprehensive good— and finally their own particular good. This can be expressed also by saying that an individual ought to will his own particular good in ways compatible with the attainment of the good of the sub-groups of which he is a member, so far as the good of these groups is compatible with the comprehensive good, and that sub-groups ought to will their good in ways compatible with the attainment of the comprehensive good. But the natural order is just the reverse of this moral order. Self-love, as we have seen, is the fundamental natural principle in man, and insofar as it operates independent of the influence of natural compassion and morality men seek their own particular good first, the good of the sub-groups of which they are members next, and the comprehensive good last of all, if indeed they seek it at all. And, similarly, sub-groups seek their own good before they seek the comprehensive good, if indeed they seek the latter at all.[1]

The moral order, however, is the reverse of the natural order only insofar as nature operates independent of the direction of reason and morality. We have seen that the antithesis between nature on the one hand and reason and morality on the other cannot be overcome by attempting to stifle or extirpate the claims of nature. Neither can it be overcome by ignoring the claims of morality. The only way in which it can be overcome is through establishing conditions such that the claims of nature can most effectively be satisfied only through satisfying also the claims of morality. This is to say that the only way it can be overcome is through establishing conditions such that the good of individuals and of sub-groups can most effectively be attained only through also attaining the good of the most comprehensive group, which is the absolutely general good and the object of the absolutely general will.

In the *Discourse on Political Economy* Rousseau identifies the most comprehensive of groups with the human race. Thus after writing that the general will of the body politic "constitutes for all the members of the

State, in their relations to one another and to it, the rule of what is just or unjust," he goes on to say that

this rule of justice, though certain with regard to all the citizens, may be defective with regard to foreigners. The reason is clear. The will of the State, though general in relation to its own members, is no longer so in relation to other States and their members, but becomes, for them, a particular and individual will, which has its rule of justice in the law of nature. This, however, enters equally into the principle here laid down; for in such a case, the great city of the world becomes the body politic, whose general will is always the law of nature, and of which the different States and peoples are individual members.[2]

Taking this passage in connection with what has already been said, the only will that is absolutely general in its source, and the only good that is absolutely general, is that of the entire human race. This absolutely general will and the absolutely general object—its constant object—therefore constitute the law of nature in terms of which the will of any body politic is to be assessed as just or unjust in its relation to the good of other powers. Thus although the general will of any given body politic constitutes the rule of justice for the individuals and lesser partial associations within it, since the object of this will is the good of the entire body politic and thus of each person within it, it is only a particular will in relation to the general will and general good of humanity. As such, it may be either just or unjust, depending upon whether it is compatible or not with the general will and the general good of humanity, which comprehends the good of each and every human being, regardless of what state he happens to be a member of.

In *The Social Contract*, however, there is no mention of the general will and the general good of "the great city of the world." Instead, the absolutely general will and absolutely general good are there identified with the will and the good of the body politic. This does not mean that in *The Social Contract* Rousseau has abandoned his position in the *Discourse on Political Economy*. On the contrary, it means only that in *The Social Contract* he is concerned only with the internal constitution of the body politic, not with relations between independent powers. He tells us in the foreword that *The Social Contract* is part of a longer work that he had begun years before without realizing his limitations, and that he had long since abandoned. And in the concluding chapter he writes that he ought to go on to consider the external relations of the body politic, only to end by saying that this would form a new subject too vast for his narrow scope. Had he completed the longer work he doubtlessly would have retained in it the view of the *Discourse on Political Economy* that the only absolutely general

will and general good are that of the entire human race, so that the will and
the good of any particular body politic are only particular in comparison
with that of humanity. Thus when he implies in *The Social Contract* that
the absolutely general will and general good are those of the body politic,
this is to be understood as meaning only that its will and good, taken in
abstraction from that of the entire human race, are absolutely general in
comparison with the will and good of any natural person and partial
association within the body politic. In this work he is concerned only to
argue that the will of any natural person and partial association within the
body politic is what it ought to be only insofar as what they will is
compatible with the general will of the body politic. He is not concerned
to argue that the latter will is what it ought to be only insofar as it is
compatible with the general will of humanity. This question he does not
consider at all, for the reasons already given. If he entertained it at all in
writing *The Social Contract*, it was only to assume, without explicitly asserting, that the general will of the body politic, in being what it ought to be,
is compatible with the general will of humanity.

The most comprehensive association that Rousseau considers in *The
Social Contract* is therefore that of the body politic, not that of humanity.
The body politic is a comprehensive association composed of a multiplicity of natural persons and lesser or partial associations. Each of these
smaller societies has its own interests and its own rules of conduct. The
number of these partial associations is quite large—indeed so large that it
would be extremely difficult if not impossible to enumerate them all. For

those societies which everybody perceives, because they have an external and
authorized form, are not the only ones that actually exist in the State: all individuals who are united by a common interest compose as many others, either transitory
or permanent, whose influence is none the less real because it is less apparent, and
the proper observation of whose various relations is the true knowledge of public
morals and manners.[3]

There are thus two kinds of lesser society within the body politic—those
that have a relatively formal organization and those that do not. The
former, because of their relatively formal organization, are rather readily
recognized; the latter, because of their lack of formal organization, are
sometimes more difficult to recognize, and are sometimes so transitory that
they come into being and pass away almost imperceptibly. The existence
of these associations exerts an influence upon the determination of the
general will of the body politic. "The influence of all these tacit or formal
associations causes, by the influence of their will, as many different

modifications of the public will."[4] This being the case, the question arises of how the general will is to be determined.

XXVI. The Determination of the General Will

In dealing with this question it is important to distinguish between the general will on the one hand and the will of all on the other. We shall be concerned, at least for the moment, only with the general will of the body politic, not with the general will of humanity. Leaving aside, then, the relationship of the body politic to humanity, we may say simply that the general will of the body politic is general both in its source and in its object. It is general in its source because its source is simply the body politic itself, which is an association of individuals and not an individual, and general in its object because its object is the good of the body politic, which comprehends the good of each individual included in the body politic, and not the good of some individual or partial association within the body politic to the exclusion of other individuals or partial associations. The will of all, on the other hand, is simply the sum of particular wills within the body politic.[1] There are as many particular wills within it as there are natural persons and partial associations. These wills are particular both in their source and in their object. The will of an individual, as we have seen, is necessarily particular in its source, since its source is the particular individual whose will it is. And the source of the will of a partial association, though general in relation to the source of the wills of any of its members, is nonetheless particular in relation to the source of the will of the body politic. Similarly, although the object of the will of an individual and of a partial association may be general, it is not always or wholly general, but is sometimes also particular. For although each individual may will the good of the body politic and of the partial associations of which he happens to be a member, he also by nature, in virtue of the principle of self-love, wills his own good, and in doing so the object of his will is particular rather than general. Similarly, although the object of the will of a partial association is general in relation to the object of the will of any of its members insofar as they each will their own good, and although a partial association may will the good of the body politic, it also wills its own good, and in doing so the object of its will is particular in relation to the good of the body politic.

Given this distinction between the general will and the will of all, we may now proceed to consider Rousseau's account of how the general will is determined. He presents two distinct accounts, the first in Chapter III of Book II, the second in Chapter II of Book IV. The first may be said to be an account of the determination of the general will as a consequence of the operation of individuals and partial associations merely as natural agents, the second to be an account of its determination as a consequence of the action of individuals as moral agents. At first glance these two accounts seem to be incompatible, but, as I hope to show, they are in fact complementary rather than incompatible. We shall first examine the first account.

The general will, Rousseau says, "considers only the common interest," whereas the will of all "takes private interest into account, and is no more than a sum of particular wills: but take away from these same wills the pluses and minuses that cancel one another, and the general will remains as the sum of the differences."[2] What is the meaning of this puzzling passage? More specifically, what does Rousseau mean by taking away from particular wills "the pluses and minuses that cancel one another" and by "the sum of the differences" that remain when this is done? Some light can be thrown on these questions by considering Rousseau's quotation from the Marquis d'Argenson that "the agreement of two particular interests is formed by opposition to a third" and Rousseau's addendum that "the agreement of all interests is formed by opposition to that of each." To this Rousseau adds that "if there were no different interests, the common interest would be barely felt, as it would encounter no obstacle; all would go on of its own accord, and politics would cease to be an art."[3] Politics is an art because the common interest must be made to emerge from the opposition of particular interests and the general will from the clash of particular wills. But how is this to be done? What is there in the opposition of particular interests and wills to one another that enables the common interest and the general will to emerge? The answer, I think, runs as follows.

For the sake of simplicity, let us restrict our attention to a hypothetical situation in which there are only three natural persons, x, y, and z. These three persons constitute a group, a society, or an association, G. Each of them by nature—in virtue of the operation of the fundamental natural principle of self-love—wills his own good. If each always wills his good in a way compatible with the attainment of the good of the other two, there is then no clash among their wills. A conflict of wills can occur only if one person wills an object the attainment of which is incompatible with the attainment of the object that another person wills. And if no conflict of wills occurs, the political problem of resolving such conflicts does not arise; "all would go on of its own accord, and politics would cease to be an art." Since, that is, politics is the art of resolving conflicts between wills, there is no need for the practice of this art when such conflicts do not occur. But such conflicts do occur. They may arise either accidentally or intentionally. Thus some individual, x, who is animated only by self-love as distinct from egoism, may seek his good in a way that is in fact incompatible with the attainment of the good that another individual, y, seeks, even though he is unaware of the incompatibility and does not intend to prevent y from attaining the good y seeks. In this case the conflict of wills occurs accidentally. On the other hand, some individual, z, who is animated by egoism as distinct from self-love, may seek not merely his own good, as he would if he were moved only by self-love, but instead may intentionally seek to prevent another individual, y, who is animated only by self-love, from attaining the object y seeks. In this case the conflict of wills may be said to arise intentionally, since the intention of z is to prevent y from attaining the object y seeks. But regardless of whether conflicts of wills occur accidentally or intentionally, the fact is that they do occur.

But not only does each of these three individuals, in virtue of the natural principle of self-love, naturally will his own good. Each also, in willing his own good, is also thereby at least implicitly willing, although he may not explicitly or consciously realize that he is doing so, that he not be prevented from attaining the good he wills by the action of any other person or group. Thus x wills implicitly that neither y nor z either singly or conjointly prevent him from attaining his good, y that neither x nor z singly or conjointly prevent him from attaining his good, and z that neither x nor y prevent him from attaining his good. This being the case, x and y both will that z not prevent them from attaining their good, x that z not prevent him from attaining his good and y that z not prevent him from attaining his good; x and z both will that y not prevent them from attaining their good, x that y not prevent him from attaining his good and z that y not prevent him from attaining his good; and, finally, y and z both will that x not prevent them from attaining their good, y that x not prevent him from attaining his good and z that x not prevent him from attaining his good.

The question now arises: do these considerations mean that any two of these individuals will anything in common? It might seem at first that they do not, any more than the fact that each wills his own good means that they all will something in common. For x, in willing his good, is not also willing the good of y and z; y, in willing his good, is not also willing the good of x and z; and z, in willing his good, is not also willing the good of x and y. Similarly, one might argue, x and y, in willing that z not prevent them from attaining their good, are not willing anything in common. For x is willing only that z not prevent him from attaining his good, not that z not prevent y from attaining his good; and y is willing only that z not prevent him from attaining his good, not that z not prevent x from attaining his good. The same applies to the members of the other two pairs, x and z, and y and z. Each is willing only that the third individual not prevent him from attaining his good, not that he not prevent the other member of the pair from attaining his good.

Such an argument, however, though perhaps appealing at first glance, does not succeed. For each individual, in willing his good, may be said to be at least implicitly willing also that no individual or group prevent the members of a class into which he can be grouped from attaining the good they seek. Thus x and y without z constitute a class; x and z without y constitute a class; and y and z without x constitute a class. This being the case, each member of each of these classes may be said to be implicitly willing, in virtue of his willing his own good, that no person or group outside some class of which he is a member prevent every member of that class from attaining the good they seek. For if each member of some class to which an individual belongs is prevented from attaining the good he seeks, then that individual is also prevented from attaining the good he seeks. Thus the members of the class consisting of x and y but not z each will implicitly, in virtue of their willing their own good, that z not prevent all the members of that class from attaining the good they seek. This is to say that x, in willing his good, implicitly wills that z not prevent both x and y from attaining the good they seek, and that y, in willing his good, implicitly wills that z not prevent both x and y from attaining the good they seek. If so, then both x and y will something in common, namely, that z not prevent both x and y from attaining the good they seek. The same applies, with the necessary changes, to each of the members of the other two classes, x and z, and y and z . Thus both x and z will in common that y not prevent them both from attaining their good, and y and z will in common that x not prevent them both from attaining their good. Precisely similar considerations apply to the comprehensive group, G, consisting of x, y, and z. Each member of this group, in virtue of his willing his own good, is thereby implicitly willing that no individual or group outside G prevent all the members of G from attaining the good they seek.

It is true that each member of any of these classes, insofar as he is animated only by self-love, wills only his own good as an end in itself, not that of any other individual or of any class of which he happens to be a member. This, however, does not mean that the members of any given class do not implicitly will something in common—that the members of

THE DETERMINATION OF THE GENERAL WILL   147

the class consisting of x and y, for example, do not will in common that z not prevent all the members of this class from attaining the good they seek. Instead, it means only that they implicitly will the good of the class of which they are members as a means to the attainment of their own individual good, not as an end in itself. This can be put by saying that the good of the class of which they are members is only the proximate object of their will, not the ultimate object. But from this it does not follow that they will nothing in common. All that follows is that the ultimate object of the will of each is distinct from the ultimate object of the will of the rest, not that the proximate object of their will cannot be identical. So long as the good sought by x and that sought by y is attainable only so long as z does not prevent them both from attaining the good they seek, each does implicitly will in common that z not prevent them both from attaining the good they seek. Although the latter is not the ultimate object of the will of either x or y, it is the proximate object of both. Moreover, in saying that x and y both will implicitly that z not prevent them both from attaining the good they seek, I am not saying that either x or y explicitly or consciously wills that z not do so. I am saying only that each can attain the good he seeks only if z does not prevent them both from doing so. They may or may not be sufficiently enlightened to see that this is the case. In the former case they may come to will explicitly or consciously that z not prevent them both from attaining their good; but in the latter case they continue to will this only implicitly.

Given the preceding considerations, it is evident that even in a group consisting of only three individuals it is possible that three partial associations exist, one consisting of x and y, one of x and z, and one of y and z. These associations may be either formal or informal, depending upon whether or not their members recognize their existence. A necessary but not a sufficient condition of their existence as formal associations is that their members recognize that they have some interest in common. Given such recognition, the members of one of these associations, say that consisting of x and y, may explicitly or consciously agree formally to form an association or alliance. Thus x and y, each willing explicitly that z not prevent him from attaining his good, may agree to come to the assistance of the other should z attempt to prevent either from attaining his good. In this event x and y may be said to will explicitly in common not only that z not prevent them both from attaining the good they seek, but also that he not prevent either of them from doing so. There would then exist a formal partial association consisting of x and y which has a general will the object of which is identical with what its members will in common, namely, that z not prevent either from attaining the good he seeks. A conflict between the will of this association and of its members on the one hand and of the will of z on the other would occur should z will to prevent either x or y from attaining the good he seeks.

Not only is it possible that x and y should form an association of the sort just specified; it is also possible that they should form an association for the egoistic purpose of preventing z from attaining his non-egoistic good. In this case also there would arise a conflict between the will of this association and the will of z. But not only is it possible that conflicts occur among the wills of individuals as individuals and among the wills of individuals and the wills of associations; it is also possible that they should arise among the wills of associations. These conflicts also may occur either accidentally or intentionally, just as those between individuals may arise in either way.

We are now in a position to present the answer of Book II, Chapter III, to the question of how the general will and the common interest emerge from the conflicts of particular wills and interests. If the conflict between wills is removed, what remains is the good of each individual that each wills by nature insofar as he is animated simply by self-love. To return to our hypothetical example: the individuals x, y, and z, insofar as each is moved solely by self-love, will their own good—x wills his own good, y his own good, and z his own good. Remove the conflicts among their wills that prevent any one or more of them from attaining the good he wills, and each thereby is enabled to attain his good. In this way the object of the general will of the comprehensive group, G, is attained, since its object is the general or common good of the group of which x, y, and z are members, and this general good of the group is nothing other than and therefore reducible to the good of each of its individual members. It is true, of course, that any of them might be prevented from attaining his good even though the conflicts among their wills be removed, through the occurrence of unpreventable circumstances that arise even though no conflicts of wills occur, such as the occurrence of accidents or natural catastrophes. The complete prevention of the occurrence of such circumstances is of course impossible; all that can be done is to attempt to minimize their occurrence and their baneful effects. Even so, the fact remains that no one is prevented from attaining the good he wills as a consequence of conflicts of wills if such conflicts are eliminated. Eliminate these conflicts and what emerges or remains is the general or common good, which, again, is nothing other than the non-egoistic good of each and every member of the group.

This is as far as the answer of Book II, Chapter III, goes. So far as it goes it is, I think, both intelligible and sound. But it is not the complete answer, nor does Rousseau present it as such. For it fails to respond to the question of how conflicts of wills are to be eliminated. Even though we agree with Rousseau that the general or common good emerges when all conflicts between wills are eliminated, we still do not know how these conflicts can be eliminated. We may grant that they, like the occurrence of the undesirable situations mentioned above, cannot be entirely eliminated. But how can their occurrence and undesirable consequences be minimized?

We saw above that conflicts of wills may arise either accidentally or intentionally. They arise accidentally when one or more individuals, animated by self-love as contrasted with egoism, seeks his good in a way that conflicts with the attainment of the good some other individual seeks. Insofar as such conflicts occur accidentally their occurrence can be minimized through an increase of enlightenment. Insofar as an agent acts from self-love, as distinct from egoism, he seeks only his own good and is not concerned with the good of others, much less with preventing others from attaining the good they seek. And insofar as he is influenced by natural compassion he seeks to avoid preventing others from attaining their good. Given, then, the operation of self-love and natural compassion upon him and the absence of egoism, he will seek his good in ways that do not conflict with the attainment of the good of others if he is shown how he can do so. But conflicts between wills do not only arise accidentally. They also arise intentionally, as a consequence of the action of egoistic individuals. These individuals are not content to seek merely their own non-egoistic good. On the contrary, they sometimes seek intentionally to prevent others from attaining the good they seek, even though they could attain their non-egoistic good in ways compatible with the attainment of the good of others, and know that they could do so. Indeed, egoism may reach such a peak of intensity that the egoist positively delights in preventing others from attaining their good even though by doing so he does not in the least contribute to the attainment of his own non-egoistic good. In such a case he may be said to make the prevention of the attainment of the good of others a constituent of his own good, and thus to make evil his good. If, then, the problem of eliminating or minimizing conflicts of wills, and thereby enabling the object of the general will to be attained or approached, is to be solved, two other problems must be solved. One is the problem of enlightening non-egoistic individuals. The other is the problem of eliminating egoism or, if this prove impossible, of lessening it and its influence.

The essentials of the solution to these problems have already been presented. We have seen that each of the individuals, x, y, and z, in willing

his own good, is at least implicitly, if not explicitly, also thereby willing
that neither of the other two, either singly or conjointly, prevent him from
attaining the good he seeks. We have also seen that two of them, say x and
y, may form an association designed to prevent z from preventing either of
them from attaining his good. In this way x and y will in common that z
not prevent either of them from attaining his good. But if x and y can form
such an association, then all three can form an association the conditions of
which are such that each agrees to seek his own good only in ways that are
compatible with the attainment of the good of the other two and to come
to the defense of the others should some other association or some individual outside their association seek to prevent any of them from attaining
his good. Should one of them agree to the conditions of the association, yet
seek to act incompatibly with the good of either or both of the other two,
then he may rightly be restrained or punished by the others. Or should
one of them not agree to the terms of the association, yet remain in the
presence of the others even though they do not compel him to do so, his
continued presence among them constitutes his tacit consent to the conditions of the association, and he too may rightly be restrained or punished
by the others if he violates or seeks to violate these conditions.

An association formed by all the members of a group is essentially
different from one formed by only some members to the exclusion of
others. The latter kind of association constitutes only a partial association
or sub-group within the comprehensive association or group consisting of
all the individuals within a given group. Thus x and y, for example, may
form an association the purpose of which is to prevent z from preventing
either of them from attaining his good, and may refuse to widen the
association to include z. They may refuse, that is, to form a comprehensive association containing all three as members, the conditions of which
are such that each agrees to seek his good only by acting compatibly with
the attainment of the good of the others. If so, they form only a partial
association. But such an association, as we have seen, may not restrict
itself merely to preventing z from preventing either of its members from
attaining his good. Instead, it may proceed to seek its good, i.e., the good
of its members, at the expense of the good of z, and may do so not
accidentally, but intentionally. If so, it becomes what may be referred to
as an egoistic association, since it intentionally seeks its good at the expense of the good of someone outside it, even though it would be possible
for it to include the excluded person within its membership and seek his
good along with that of its other members. A comprehensive association,
on the other hand, is essentially non-egoistic in nature, in at least two
senses or for at least two reasons. The first is that there is no one outside

the association, as there is in the case of a partial association, toward whom the association as a whole can act egoistically. For it includes every individual within a given group within its membership. The second is that it requires its members to act non-egoistically toward one another. For it includes them within its membership only on the condition that each agree, either expressly or tacitly, to seek his good in ways compatible with the attainment of the good of every other person within the association. Each person accepted into the association, in agreeing to this condition, is in effect agreeing to act non-egoistically toward the other members of the association. Thus should any of its members act or seek to act egoistically, he may rightly be punished or restrained by the association.

The body politic is a comprehensive association relative to any of the partial associations within it. But, as we have seen, it is not an absolutely comprehensive association. There is only one such association. This is that of the entire human race, including each and every human being. We have seen that Rousseau recognizes this in the *Discourse on Political Economy*, despite the fact that in *The Social Contract* he makes no mention of it and treats the body politic as a comprehensive association. Since the only absolutely comprehensive association is that of the entire human race, it is the only association that cannot act egoistically. For since the entire human race includes each and every human being, there is no human being or group of human beings outside it toward whom it can act egoistically. But since any particular body politic is a partial association within the absolutely comprehensive association consisting of the entire human race, any body politic can act egoistically toward individuals outside it and toward other powers. But since the body politic is a comprehensive association relative to the individuals and partial associations within it, it cannot act egoistically toward them. Although individuals and partial associations within the body politic can act egoistically toward one another, it cannot itself act egoistically toward any of its members. This means that if it wills anything at all it can will only the general or common good, not the particular good of some of its members or partial associations to the exclusion of the good of others.

But although the body politic cannot act egoistically toward any of its members and can will only the general or common good of the entire body politic, the general will and the common good can be prevented from emerging as a consequence of the action of various individuals and partial associations within the body politic. We have seen that the common good, which is the object of the general will, is nothing other than the non-egoistic good of each and every member of the body politic. We have also seen that this good is what remains after the conflicts between particular wills have been eliminated. Such conflicts occur either accidentally or intentionally. They occur intentionally insofar as individuals and partial associations act egoistically, and they occur accidentally insofar as individuals and partial associations, even though animated only by self-love or natural compassion or respect for the moral law as contrasted with egoism, are unenlightened. If, then, the object of the general will is to emerge from conflicts of particular wills, enlightened moral action is necessary. This means that each individual, in voting upon the laws of the body politic, must ask himself the right question. The question is not whether a proposed law is merely compatible with or conducive to the promotion of his own particular good or that of some partial association of which he happens to be a member, but is rather whether it is compatible with or conducive to the promotion of the common good, which includes the non-egoistic good of each and every member of the body politic. Insofar as each citizen asks and answers the latter question rather than the former in voting, the object of the general will emerges when a vote is taken. This is the answer of Chapter II of Book IV as to what must be done if the common good is to emerge. The discussion of this section shows that this answer, rather than being incompatible with that of Book II, Chapter III, supplements it.

XXVII. Partial Associations

The answer of Chapter II of Book IV to the question of what must be done if the object of the general will is to emerge from the conflicts of particular wills makes it clear that this object can emerge only insofar as individuals act as enlightened moral agents, both as citizens and as subjects. They act as such agents as citizens only insofar as they concern themselves in voting primarily with the enactment of laws conducive to the promotion of the common good, and not merely with the enactment of legislation that promotes only their own particular good or that of the partial associations to which they belong. And they act as such agents as subjects only insofar as they subject themselves to the laws that they as citizens participate in enacting. But to say that the common good is attainable only insofar as individuals act as enlightened moral agents is one thing; to establish conditions conducive to their doing so is another. One such condition is the elimination, or at least the control, of partial associations that have a morally corruptive influence upon individuals through leading them to substitute either their own egoistic good or that of the partial associations to which they belong for the common good of the entire body politic.

Individuals animated only by self-love tend to comply with the laws of the body politic insofar as they believe that compliance is compatible with the promotion of the common good. For the common good is nothing other than the non-egoistic good of each and every member of the body politic, and thus individuals, insofar as they are not animated by egoism, generally tend to obey such laws simply out of self-love, independently both of natural compassion and of any concern for the promotion of the common good. Rousseau, somewhat hyperbolically, says something like this in these words: "Why is it... that all continually will the happiness of each one, unless it is because there is not a man who does not think of 'each' as meaning him, and considers himself in voting for all? This proves that equality of rights and the idea of justice which such equality creates originate in the preference each man gives to himself, and accordingly in the very nature of man."[1] But a single powerful partial association, or a combination of several such associations, may succeed in gaining control of the political machinery of the body politic. It may then go on to substitute its own particular will and good for the general will and good of the body politic, and fashion the laws in such a way that compliance with them contributes to the promotion of its particular good at the expense of those members of the body politic who are outside it. If so, then the laws of the body politic come increasingly to be disobeyed as various individuals come to recognize that by obeying they are promoting the particular good of one or a few partial associations at the cost of the common good in general and their own particular goods in particular. Hence although the body politic itself, taken as a single comprehensive association of each of its members, cannot, as such, act egoistically toward any of its members, powerful partial associations within it can use its political institutions, designed to promote the common good, for the attainment of their own particular egoistic ends, at the expense of the good of its other members.

Should such a situation arise, the laws of the body politic, rather than being an expression of the general will and such that compliance with them promotes the attainment of the common good, become only an expression of the particular wills of a single or of several powerful partial associations and such that compliance with them serves only to promote the egoistic particular goods of such associations at the sacrifice of the promotion of the common good.

when factions arise, and partial associations are formed at the expense of the great association, the will of each of these associations becomes general in relation to its members, while it remains particular in relation to the State: it may then be said that there are no longer as many votes as there are men, but only as there are associations. The differences become less numerous and give a less general result. Lastly, when one of these associations is so great as to prevail over all the rest, the result is no longer a sum of small differences, but a single difference; in this case there is no longer a general will, and the opinion which prevails is purely particular.[2]

This means that the existence of such partial associations tends to weaken and corrupt the general will. The individual members of such associations tend to think of themselves first as members of the association and only second as members of the body politic. This is reflected in the way they vote on what the laws of the body politic are to be. Instead of considering first what the common good of the entire body politic is and voting accordingly, their vote is determined by considering first what the particular good of the partial associations of which they are members happens to be.

The existence of such partial associations therefore increases the tension already existing between the natural order and the moral order. We have seen that the fundamental principle of human nature is self-love—that what each man naturally wills most strongly and most insistently is his own good. But we have also seen that the principle of morality requires that the common good be placed first. These two principles—that of self-love and that of morality—can be reconciled only insofar as each man wills his own good in a way compatible with the promotion of the common good. This reconciliation requires only the sacrifice of egoism, not of self-love; it requires, that is, not that one cease altogether to seek one's own good, but rather only that one seek one's good only by acting compatibly with the attainment of the non-egoistic good of others. But insofar as I act from self-love alone, i.e., independent of any consideration of the requirements of morality, I seek only my own good, and do not attempt to restrict the ways in which I seek it so that my acts are compatible with the attainment of the non-egoistic good of others.

Rousseau's point is that membership in a partial association tends to strengthen the operation of the principles of self-love and egoism at the expense of the operation of the principle of morality. For partial associations, like individuals, naturally seek their own good, often at the sacrifice of the common good and of the particular goods of individuals outside themselves and of other partial associations. But since the good of a partial association, like the good of the body politic, is nothing other than the good of its individual members, the members of such an association, in seeking its good, are also seeking their own good. Indeed, insofar as individuals are animated only by self-love or by egoism, they seek membership in such associations only in order to promote their own good. Thus so far as the operation of nature alone is concerned, i.e., so far as the operation of the principle of self-love alone as distinct from the principle of morality is concerned, the individual seeks first his own good, then the good of the partial associations of which he is a member, and only last the common good of the body politic, whereas the principle of morality requires that he seek first the common good of the body politic, since this comprehends the non-egoistic good of every person within it.

Given the corruptive influence of partial associations, it becomes

essential, if the general will is to be able to express itself, that there should be no partial society within the State, and that each citizen should think only his own thoughts.... But if there are partial societies, it is best to have as many as possible and to prevent them from being unequal.... These precautions are the only ones that can guarantee that the general will shall be always enlightened, and that the people shall in no way deceive itself.[3]

Here Rousseau makes it clear that in his view the best thing is to have no partial associations at all. This, however, is impossible. For, as we have seen, "all individuals who are united by a common interest" compose a partial association that is either formal or tacit and either relatively permanent or relatively transitory, and it is impossible that two or three individuals to the exclusion of others should never be united by certain common interests. Indeed, given Rousseau's account of partial associations, families are such associations, and yet he neither explicitly nor by implication advocates the abolition of the family. Thus when he writes that it is essential that "there should be no partial society within the State" his words are to be taken as hyperbolic if we understand him to be referring to any and every partial association, regardless of its size and character. But if they are taken literally they are to be understood as referring only to those associations the size and character of which exert a corruptive influence. This interpretation is supported by Rousseau's quoting with evident approval these words from Machiavelli: "there are some divisions that are harmful to a Republic and some that are advantageous. Those which stir up sects and parties are harmful; those attended by neither are advantageous."[4] It is therefore neither possible nor desirable that all partial associations, regardless of their size or their character, be eliminated. This being the case, it is desirable that there be as many as possible, all fairly equal in power, so that none, and no larger association formed through an alliance of several, be able to impose its will upon the others and to substitute its will for the general will of the body politic. This both requires and justifies the prevention of the growth of concentrations and monopolies of power within the body politic.

Rousseau, as we have seen, draws an analogy between individuals and associations. Just as an individual by nature wills his own good, so also an association wills its own good. Indeed, Rousseau sometimes writes as though the will of an association as particular, i.e., as standing in relation to the wills of other associations and to the wills of individuals outside it, is always either self-interested or egoistic. The fact that he does so may be interpreted in either of two ways. It may mean that he believes that the will of every partial association is always either self-interested or egoistic, and is never either disinterested or else animated by compassion or principles of morality or justice. On the other hand, it may mean merely that he is concerned only with the effect upon the body politic of self-interested and egoistic partial associations, and is not concerned with denying that certain partial associations may be either disinterested or else animated by compassion or principles of morality. The second interpretation seems to be the more reasonable. There are two reasons why this is so. One is his quoting, with evident approval, Machiavelli's view that only those associations that lead to sects and parties are harmful to the body politic, whereas those that do not are beneficial. If he does in fact agree with Machiavelli on this point, and he certainly seems to, his agreement may perhaps be taken as indicating a recognition on his part that certain associations are neither self-interested nor egoistic. The second reason is that it seems unlikely that someone with as profound an insight as Rousseau's into the nature, operation, and effects of partial associations should overlook so obvious a distinction as that between those associations that are either self-interested or egoistic and those that are neither. It was maintained earlier that partial associations as well as individuals may be animated by compassion and by principles of morality as well as by self-love and egoism. To this we may add that just as an individual may be animated by a disinterested, i.e., a non-self-interested and non-egoistic, interest in philosophy, literature, the arts, or the sciences, so also partial associations may be formed for the disinterested study and promotion of these areas of interest and activity.

The preceding, however, does not mean that the existence of self-interested associations is always incompatible with the common good of the body politic, nor does it mean that the existence of associations which are neither self-interested nor egoistic is always compatible with the common good. Just as the fact that an individual is motivated by self-love does not necessarily mean that his self-interested action is incompatible with the promotion of the common good, neither does the fact that an association is self-interested mean that its self-interested action is incompatible with the common good. Self-interested action, whether it be that of an individual or that of an association, is wrong only if and insofar as it needlessly conflicts with the attainment of the common good. Thus insofar as the laws of the body politic are expressive of the general will, so that compliance with them is conducive to the promotion of the common good, self-interested action in accordance with them, whether on the part of individuals or associations, is both legally and morally right. The fact that such action is not morally good, i.e., is not performed out of respect for the moral law, does not mean that it is neither legally nor morally right. Moreover, action that is morally good may be either legally or morally wrong. For an individual or an association that seeks, out of respect for the moral law, to act in accordance with it may nonetheless act wrongly by acting incompatibly with its specific requirements in concrete circumstances, through insufficient enlightenment as to precisely what its specific requirements in these circumstances are. In this case, their action, though morally good, is nevertheless morally wrong. It is also legally wrong if the law of the body politic requires conformity with these specific requirements of the moral law.

Similar considerations apply to individuals and associations animated by compassion. Just as the compassionate action of an individual may or may not be legally and morally right, depending upon whether it is compatible or not with the requirements of the moral law and the law of the body politic, so also the compassionate action of an association may be legally and morally wrong. It is therefore possible that the activities and even the existence of certain associations formed for compassionate purposes be incompatible with the promotion of the common good. For such associations, like self-interested or egoistic individuals and associations and like compassionate individuals, may seek, albeit innocently or unknowingly, to promote the good of certain individuals or groups in ways that are incompatible with the attainment of the good of certain other individuals or groups, and thus with the attainment of the common good. The existence and the activities of such associations are therefore subject to regulation by the body politic.

Similar considerations apply also to associations formed for the disinterested study and advancement of philosophy, literature, the arts, or the sciences. An interest in these areas may lead both individuals and associations formed for their study and advancement to fail to act compatibly with the common good. This can happen in various ways. First, individuals and associations may spend time and energy in the study and advancement of these areas that could more profitably be spent in attempting to alleviate the suffering of others. Indeed, it may even happen that one cultivates an interest in these areas precisely in order to distract one's attention from social injustices and the misery of others. Second, large sums of money may be spent in pursuing an interest in these areas that could more profitably be spent in alleviating the suffering of the poor. Third, the concern to develop or to indulge one's intellectual or aesthetic interests may lead to intellectual or aesthetic amorality or immorality. It may lead, that is, to an inversion of the order of value—to giving intellectual or aesthetic values priority over moral values, whereas in fact it is the latter that take priority over the former. This may manifest itself in various ways. It may lead me, as it led the young Augustine at Carthage, to a greater concern over my enunciation of the word "charity" than over whether I manifest charity toward every person with whom I come in contact, and to a contempt for those whose enunciation of it is less than impeccable, even though their manifestation of charity in their lives ought to put me to shame. Or it may lead me to convince myself that I, because of my intellectual or aesthetic interests or attainments, am no longer subject to the laws of morality, particularly those having to do with sexual matters, to which ordinary folk are subject. In this way I can use my exquisite intellectual or aesthetic interests or attainments as an excuse for giving free rein to my animal lusts; a convenient excuse is at hand for engaging in precisely the same outward behavior as that of the simplest peasant who seduces a servant girl, but who, because of his dull ignorance, lacks the convenient excuse and justification that my intellectuality and aesthetic sensitivity afford me. Fourth, the intellectual attainments of an individual or a learned society or association may lead to intellectual arrogance. Thus an individual or a learned group may so preen itself on its intellectual attainments that it seeks to substitute its own private or particular wisdom for the collective wisdom of the people. This in turn may lead either to an attempt to exempt itself from the rules that the people in their lack of wisdom impose upon themselves or else to an attempt to impose its own superior wisdom, by violence and bloodshed if necessary, upon the unenlightened masses.

In all these ways an initially disinterested interest in philosophy, literature, the arts, or the sciences can finally lead both individuals and associations to act incompatibly with the common good. This is one of the major themes of Rousseau's *Discourse on the Arts and Sciences,* in which he seeks to show, not only that the development of the arts and sciences can have a corruptive effect upon man and society, but also that it has in fact had such an effect historically. Their development not only can but also often has, in fact, led to a kind of intellectual and aesthetic amoralism or immoralism that manifests itself as conceit, arrogance, and heartlessness, as contempt for those of lesser intellectual attainments and less refined aesthetic sensibility, and as indifference toward the common good of the body politic and the non-egoistic good of each and every person within it, regardless of how humble he may be, of how modest his intellectual attainments may be, and of how limited the development of his aesthetic sensitivity may be.

Given not only the possibility but also the actual occurrence of antitheses between intellectual and aesthetic interests on the one hand and the claims of morality and justice on the other, a decision is necessary as to which kinds of values take precedence. Rousseau's answer, as we know by now, is that moral values take precedence over all others, including those that are intellectual or aesthetic. If and insofar as the pursuit of intellectual or aesthetic values is incompatible with the attainment of the common good, their pursuit must be abandoned. This, of course, does not mean that it must be totally abandoned. Instead, it means only that they may legitimately be pursued only insofar as their pursuit is compatible with the common good, and that their pursuit, both by individuals and by associations formed to foster the arts and sciences, is subject to regulation by the general will of the body politic. Nor does the primacy of moral values as contrasted with those that are intellectual or aesthetic mean that Rousseau is anti-intellectual. The fact that he maintains that the pursuit of intellectual and aesthetic values must be regulated by consideration for the common good no more means that he is anti-intellectual than the fact that he maintains that non-egoistic self-interested action and compassionate action must also be regulated by consideration for the common good means that he is opposed to compassion and to the promotion of the non-egoistic good of individuals.

From the preceding considerations, then, it seems clear that partial associations as well as individuals may be animated both by disinterested motives and by compassion as well as by considerations of self-interest. It also seems clear that just as the disinterested or compassionate action of an individual may conflict with the common good, so also may the disinterested or compassionate action of an association, and, therefore, that such action by an association as well as by an individual is subject to regulation by the general will of the body politic. Given these considerations, the analogy that Rousseau draws between individuals and associations is even more complete than it would be if associations were capable only of self-interested action. The parallel between the two, however, is still not as complete as Rousseau sometimes seems to imply. For whereas an individual is by nature a natural rather than a moral person, an association may by nature be a purely moral rather than a natural association. This is the case for the following reasons.

An individual is a natural person. As such, the fundamental natural principle that animates him is self-love—each natural person by nature seeks his own good. It is true that a natural person may also be a moral person—that he may be animated by principles of morality as well as by self-love. But he is not a moral person by nature. Instead, he is first or by nature a natural person, and can become a moral person only through first being a natural person. He becomes a moral person only through acting in accordance with moral principles that he imposes upon himself. The extent to which natural persons become moral persons varies from person to person, so much so that some natural persons may be motivated by principles of morality only in the very slightest degree, if indeed they are moved by such principles at all. But regardless of the extent to which a natural person is motivated by principles of morality, he is also animated by the natural principle of self-love. A partial association, on the other hand, may from its inception be a moral rather than a natural association.

The distinction intended here between a natural and a moral association may be explicated as follows. The principle of a natural association is self-love. Two persons, Peter and Paul, insofar as they are each animated by self-love, seek their own good—Peter his own good and Paul his own good. But it may happen that each can attain the good he naturally seeks only by acting compatibly with the attainment of the good the other naturally seeks. If so, there is an interest or good common to both that consists in each acting compatibly with the attainment of the good of the other. This common interest or good does not depend for its existence upon its recognition by either of them. Regardless of whether or not either recognizes it, it is in the interest of each to act compatibly with the attainment of the good of the other, since it is only by doing so that each can attain his own good, which he naturally seeks. Should either or both fail to recognize the interest or good they have in common, one or both may act incompatibly with the attainment of the good of the other, and thereby prevent the attainment of his own good. But should they both recognize that they have a common interest in acting compatibly with the attainment of the good of the other, they both will do so, insofar as each is animated by self-love, in order to attain the good he naturally seeks. This is not to say that each will in fact act compatibly with the attainment of the good of the other, for one or both may be so animated by egoism that he willingly forgoes the good he naturally seeks merely in order to prevent the other from attaining the good he seeks. That men are sometimes so consumed by egoism that this does in fact happen is, I think, fairly evident. But it does not always happen, and men sometimes act compatibly with the attainment of the good of others through recognizing that it is only through doing so that they can each attain the good they naturally seek.

Given the recognition by each that they can attain their own good only by acting compatibly with the attainment of the good of the other, they may form an association. The association thus formed is a natural rather than a moral association because the principle of its formation is the natural principle of self-love rather than a moral principle. Each, that is, enters into the association only in order to attain his own good, and acts compatibly with the attainment of the good of the other only as a means of attaining his own good. Should one of them come to believe that membership in the association is no longer compatible with the attainment of his own good—should, that is, either come to believe that acting compatibly with the attainment of the good of the other is no longer compatible with the attainment of his own good—then, so far as each is animated only by self-love, the association and understanding or agreement between them is at the point of dissolution.

The principle of a natural association is thus self-love. The principle of a moral association, on the other hand, is respect for principles of morality. The members of such an association assume membership in it, not merely as a means to the promotion of their own particular good, but, instead, in order to promote either the common good of the association or the good of some more comprehensive association or of some individual or group outside the association. It is true that an association may be neither simply natural nor merely moral, but both natural and moral at once. Some of its members may assume membership from considerations of self-interest, others from moral considerations, and still others from considerations of both sorts. The body politic itself, insofar as its laws are such that action in accordance with them is conducive to the promotion of the common good of all its members, may be said to be both a natural and a moral association, and its members may act in accordance with its laws either from self-love, from respect for the principles of morality, or from both motives.

But the fact that some associations, such as the body politic, are both natural and moral whereas others are wholly natural does not mean that none are purely moral. Instances of such purely moral associations would be certain associations formed for charitable, religious, educational, or patriotic purposes. Even in these, of course, various of their members may assume membership from considerations of self-interest rather than from moral considerations, and others from considerations of both sorts. Such associations, however, are still nonetheless purely moral insofar as their object is the promotion, not of their own good or that of their members, but, instead, that of individuals or groups outside themselves or that of some more comprehensive association of which they form only a part.

These associations may fail to persist in the pursuit of the purposes for which they are formed, and may degenerate into self-interested or even egoistic associations, or even into mere instruments used by various of their members only for the purpose of pursuing their own private self-interested or egoistic goals. This may of course occur. But then it may also happen that some of these associations persist for some time in actually promoting the moral purposes for which they are formed.

A natural person is never a purely moral person animated from the beginning and throughout the entirety of his life solely by respect for moral principles. Instead, he is animated by self-love before he is motivated by moral principles, and continues to be animated at least in part by self-love even after he attains the status of a moral person. His nature as a self-interested animal is something given the individual at birth, whereas his status as a moral person acting out of respect for the moral law is not, but is an achievement that can be accomplished only through an effort of will, through willing to subject himself to the moral law and its demands. A moral association, on the other hand, need not first be a natural association before it can become a moral association. On the contrary, it may be a moral association from its inception, since it may expressly be formed for the attainment of certain charitable purposes, and from its inception its action may be purely moral rather than self-interested, as contrasted with that of a natural person, whose action is always self-interested before it becomes moral. Moreover, its action may continue to be purely moral throughout its existence, whereas that of a natural person is not, but to some extent at least continues to be animated by self-love even after he has become a moral person. The only exceptions to this would be those self-sacrificing acts of saints or heroes in which the saint or the hero entirely sacrifices his own natural good in order to satisfy what he takes to be some demand of morality or love. But such supererogatory acts are clearly exceptional, and the morality of the ordinary moral agent consists simply in his endeavoring to promote his own good in those ways sanctioned by principles of morality—it consists, that is, in his seeking his good in ways compatible with the attainment of the non-egoistic good of every person affected by his action.

From these considerations it seems clear that the parallel which Rousseau draws between individuals and associations is not complete. An individual is a natural person before he is a moral person and is therefore animated by considerations of self-interest as well as by moral considerations, whereas an association, from its inception and throughout its existence, may be purely moral, and as such motivated only by moral considerations to the exclusion of any considerations of self-interest. As a member of a purely moral association, an individual may be moved by moral considerations alone, to the exclusion of any considerations of self-interest. Moral considerations alone may lead him to assume membership in such an association, and his actions as a member of such an association may be animated exclusively by such considerations. At the same time, however, his membership in such an association is only one aspect of his life as an individual, and what he does in virtue of his membership in it is by no means identical with what he does as an individual and as a member of other associations. As an individual he is concerned with promoting his own good as well as the good of others, and in order to attain his own good he may assume membership in various self-interested associations the object of which is the promotion of the good of their own members.

Thus the fact that an individual is a member of some purely moral association and, as such, is animated by non-self-interested moral considerations, does not mean that he is not, as an individual, motivated by self-love, nor does it mean that he may not be a member also of some self-interested association the sole object of which is the promotion of the good of its own members. Indeed, individuals generally assume membership in purely moral associations and participate actively in their affairs only after they have attempted to assure themselves of the attainment of their own good through their individual action and their membership in self-interested associations. And sometimes they assume membership in purely moral associations primarily to assuage their consciences and to atone for acts they have performed as individuals and as members of self-interested associations in pursuit of their own good. It is by no means an accident that the rich constitute a larger proportion of the membership of purely moral associations than of the entire body politic, and that these associations often depend heavily upon the rich for contributions of money. But rarely are such acts of atonement or such efforts to lessen the painful pangs of a guilty conscience as thorough as those of a St. Francis of Assisi. For membership in and contributions to purely moral associations are not the same thing as a cessation of self-interested and egoistic action as an individual, nor do they amount to a resignation from self-interested and egoistic associations.

Given these considerations, the fact that the parallel Rousseau draws between associations and individuals is not complete appears relatively unimportant. As we have seen, for Rousseau the natural order is precisely the reverse of the moral order. This means that by nature individuals seek their own good before they seek the common good and that they assume membership in self-interested associations before they assume membership in purely moral associations. This in turn means that the self-interested action of individuals and of self-interested partial associations has a greater effect upon the body politic than does the moral action of individuals and of purely moral partial associations. It means also that an individual's membership in a self-interested association naturally tends to have more importance for him than his membership in some purely moral association, so that if membership in one of these associations comes to be felt to be incompatible with membership in the other, membership in the moral association is more likely to be abandoned than is membership in the self-interested association.

Thus although the analogy Rousseau draws between individuals and associations is not perfect, its point is nevertheless relatively clear. This is that the body politic must concern itself more with the self-interested and egoistic actions of individuals and associations than with their moral and compassionate action if the common good is to be attained. This does not mean that it need never concern itself with those actions of individuals and associations that are animated by compassion or by moral considerations, for, as we have seen, such action may sometimes, even if unintentionally, conflict with the common good. Instead, what it means is that there is a greater likelihood that the self-interested and egoistic action of individuals and associations will conflict with the common good, and thus that it is with these that the body politic must especially concern itself. Indeed, purely moral associations and disinterested associations formed to foster the arts and sciences may well be among those associations the existence of which is beneficial rather than baneful to the body politic, so that the latter may well encourage their formation, provided that it regulate their activity to insure its compatibility with the common good. But if it is important that the body politic regulate the activities of such associations, it is even more important that it regulate the activities of self-interested and egoistic associations and that it prevent the formation of associations whose very existence is incompatible with the common good and abolish them once they come into existence.

XXVIII. Property and the Common Good

Among self-interested and egoistic associations those that are economic in character are of particular importance. We have already seen something of the importance Rousseau ascribes to economics, for in the second discourse he maintains that the institution and recognition by society of private property in land is the ultimate origin of inequality among men. So long as the economy of a society consisted merely in hunting, fishing, and gathering fruit, nuts, and berries no great social inequalities could arise. Nor could they arise so long as activities of these kinds were supplemented only by the possession of grazing animals. Nor could they arise even in an agricultural society, as long as the land was held in common by the society. But once the private ownership of land is recognized and sanctioned by a society, and inequalities in the possession of land permitted, then great inequalities of wealth may rapidly appear. And once these inequalities of wealth appear and receive the legal sanction of society, then other inequalites also appear, such as differences in political power and influence, differences of educational opportunity, and social inequalities in general.

Given the effect upon society of an inequality of property, it might seem that Rousseau would simply advocate the abolition of private property, particularly property in land. But this is precisely what he does not do. On the contrary, in the *Discourse on Political Economy* he specifically maintains that "the right of property is the most sacred of all the rights of citizenship, and even more important in some respects than liberty itself."[1] He gives three reasons in support of this position. First, property "more nearly affects the preservation of life" than liberty does. Second, since property is "more easily usurped and more difficult to defend than life, the law ought to pay a greater attention to what is most easily taken away." Third, "property is the true foundation of civil society, and the real guarantee of the undertakings of citizens: for if property were not answerable for personal actions, nothing would be easier than to evade duties and laugh at the laws."[2] This last reason Rousseau presents in defense of the sacredness of the right of propety is interesting, since it consists in defending this right by arguing that the possession of property can be used as a means of insuring obedience to the laws, through providing that violators of the law be punished through depriving them of their property. If private property is not permitted, compliance with the laws can be insured only through punishing violators by depriving them of their life or liberty; but if it is permitted then a third form of punishment is possible, and thus a third means of insuring compliance with the laws.

It is especially interesting to observe the somewhat unusual interpretation Rousseau here places upon the relationship of the possession of property to the individual's degree of dependence upon the body politic. One might be inclined to suppose that the relationship is precisely the reverse of what Rousseau takes it to be. One might be inclined, that is, to suppose that the greater an individual's property, the greater his independence of the body politic, and go on to argue that one of the most important devices that can be employed to protect the individual against the excesses of a despotic government is the institution of private property. For if the individual depends upon the government to supply him the means of subsistence, then the government can compel him to obey its edicts by threatening to withhold his means of subsistence; but if the individual, through the possession of property, is not dependent upon the government for his subsistence, then he has sufficient economic independence to resist what he believes to be tyrannical government excesses. One of the chief safeguards of political liberty is therefore economic independence.

This argument, however, is not always consistently or completely carried through. There are two points in particular that its proponents sometimes overlook. The first is that political liberty, insofar as it depends upon economic independence, is the possession only of those who possess such independence, not of those who do not. Thus although those who are economically independent may thereby have some protection against despotic government excesses, those who do not enjoy such independence do not have this protection, and, indeed, the protection of the economically independent class from government tyranny may well be bought at the cost of the economic dependence of others within the body politic. The second point is that those who have sufficient economic independence to guard themselves against tyrannical government excesses may also have sufficient economic power to tyrannize over those who do not enjoy such independence. For the latter class may be economically dependent upon the former, and thereby subject to even greater despotic excesses at their hands than either class would be subject to at the hands of government if neither were economically independent. If, then, economic independence is a means of protecting political liberty, the political liberty of everyone within a given society can receive this protection only if all, not merely some, are economically independent. Should some possess such independence to the exclusion of others the excluded class may well be tyrannized over by either the government or the class of the economically independent, depending upon which of the two it depends upon for its subsistence.

Rousseau's justification of private property, however, is just the reverse of that presented by the argument in question. Instead of justifying it by arguing that economic independence is a source of political independence, he argues in precisely the opposite way—the possession of private property makes the individual more dependent upon the body politic than he would be if he had no property. For if he had no property he could be compelled to comply with the laws of the body politic only by such means as threatening to deprive him of his life or his liberty; but if he has property he can also be compelled to comply by threatening to deprive him of his property. Thus if a man possesses property he has a motive for obeying the laws that he would not otherwise have. Hence the possession of property, rather than simply providing protection against the excesses of a despotic government, provides the individual with an additional motive for obeying the laws. If and insofar as the rich are more law abiding than the poor, it is not simply because they do not, like the poor, need to resort to crime for the acquisition of certain goods, but also because they have more to lose by violating the laws than do the poor. Accordingly, poverty ought to be eliminated, so far as possible, not only because there is a correlation between economic independence and political liberty, if indeed there is such a correlation, but also because the property owner has a motive for obeying the laws which the man who has no property does not have.

There are thus two opposing positions that may be taken concerning the relationship of the possession of property to political liberty. The question of which position contains more truth is one to which no simple answer can be given. Instead, Rousseau's position may be more applicable to certain political situations, the opposing position to certain others. Rousseau's position would be more applicable to a situation embodying the principles of justice, as these are conceived by Rousseau. In such a situation the laws of the body politic are enacted by the sovereign, each member of which, as a subject, is equally subject to these laws, and each member of which, as a citizen, has one and only one vote in determining the laws. In this situation, provided that the laws enacted are also enforced, the possessor of property would be subject to the laws to precisely the same extent to which the propertyless person is subject to them, so that his possession of property would afford him no greater political liberty than that enjoyed by the person who owns no property. Both the propertied person and the propertyless person would have the same political liberty as a citizen and be subject to the same laws as subjects. In this situation the property holder would have a motive for obeying the laws which the person who holds no property would not have, provided that the laws provide for the deprivation of property as punishment for their violation, and provided also that they permit the subjects of the body politic to separate themselves permanently from it only on the condition that they leave behind in the body politic all property they may have accumulated beyond a specified amount. This second proviso is necessary for rather obvious reasons, for without it, the wealth of the rich man would provide him a certain exemption from the laws that the poor man does not enjoy, since it would enable him to separate himself permanently from the community in certain cases in which the poverty of the poor man would prevent him from doing so. But if no one is permitted, when separating himself from the political association, to take with him property beyond a specified amount, then each has more or less the same liberty to emigrate, and each to that extent is therefore equally subject to the laws.

To the extent, then, that the laws of the body politic are compatible with principles of justice, the possession of property, rather than being a source of political liberty, provides an additional motive for complying with these laws. This being the case, we have ground for arguing that the body politic ought to insure that everyone willing to work possess some property at least, if for no other reason than as a means of providing everyone an additional motive for complying with the laws. Historically, however, the laws of political associations either have not been perfectly compatible with principles of justice or else have not been administered perfectly in accordance with such principles. The result has been that the possession of property has often had either or both of two results. One is that propertied persons or classes have often succeeded in getting legislation enacted that promotes their good at the expense of those persons or classes who possess no property. A simple example would be legislation requiring the possession of property as a necessary condition of citizenship or voting. Another result has been that the possession of property has often enabled the propertied person to receive certain exemptions from the laws that the propertyless person, because of his lack of property, has been denied. In both cases economic independence has historically served as a source of political liberty, in the first case through enabling the propertied classes to control the character of legislation, and in the second case through enabling them to obtain certain exemptions from the laws. But in both cases it has served as a source of political liberty only for those persons and classes who possess property, not for those who do not.

Yet justice is possible, according to Rousseau, only insofar as each and every person within the body politic is equally subject to its laws and has an equal voice in determining them. If the laws are unjust, the injustice is compounded if only some, the possessors of property, can obtain exemption from them, whereas others, those who possess no property, must subject themselves to them. But if the laws are just, then propertied persons and classes act unjustly in seeking to obtain exemption from them. The implication of Rousseau's position is therefore that a necessary condition of the justice of both the content of the laws and of their administration is that the possession of property, rather than serving as a means of controlling the content of the laws or of obtaining exemptions from them, serve instead as an additional motive for subjecting oneself to them. This being the case, a necessary condition of the justice of the laws and of their administration is that their content and their execution be such that everyone willing to work be assured of possessing some property at least.

But not only does Rousseau defend the sacredness of the right of property—he also maintains that "the goods of a family should go as little out of it and be as little alienated as possible." One reason he presents in support of this contention is that "the right of property would be quite useless" to children "if the father left them nothing." But another reason he adduces is particularly interesting, even surprising, in view of the depth of his obvious democratic convictions. It is that

nothing is more fatal to morality and to the Republic than the continual shifting of rank and fortune among the citizens: such changes are both the proof and the source of a thousand disorders, and overturn and confound everything; for those who were brought up to one thing find themselves destined for another; and neither those who rise nor those who fall are able to assume the rules of conduct, or to possess themselves of the qualifications requisite for their new condition, still less to discharge the duties it entails.[3]

From this it is evident that not only does Rousseau in the third discourse argue for the sacredness of the right of property, but also that he argues in support of the inheritance of property and of something that is at least akin to, if not identical with, a class system based on differences of inherited property, on the ground that there are certain rules of conduct and duties of the rich that can adequately be learned and observed only through being trained from childhood. Not only is it surprising to find so thorough a democrat as Rousseau propounding such a position—his doing so also seems inconsistent with his contention in the second discourse that labor alone gives a title to property, with his condemnation in that discourse of the evils of inherited wealth, and with his awareness, both in the third discourse and in *The Social Contract*, of the evils attendant upon the existence of powerful partial associations within the body politic.

But although the passage in question certainly seems to be inconsistent with the general democratic tenor of Rousseau's thought, it is nonetheless only a relatively minor aberration, and seems to reduce to the following considerations. In addition to the obligations that everyone has in virtue of his nature as a person and in virtue of his status as a citizen-subject, there are other obligations which a person has in virtue of his position or station in society. Thus to some extent the duties of a soldier differ from those of a farmer, the duties of a priest from those of a teacher, the duties of a physician from those of a carpenter, and so on. So also the duties of the rich differ to some extent from those of the non-rich. But not only do the obligations of various classes of persons differ to some extent, depending upon the nature of the position or station the person occupies. It is also the case that it takes time to learn what the specific duties of one's station are, and an even longer time to acquire the ability, the habit, or the virtue of fulfilling them well and with ease. The length of time it takes varies depending upon the nature of the station one occupies. These rather obvious points seem to be implicit in what Rousseau is saying. But he also seems to be saying that the duties of the rich are such that they can be fulfilled well and with ease only by those who from childhood have been educated and trained to fulfill them. Those who have not received such education and training from childhood are ill prepared, should they happen to acquire wealth, to fulfill the obligations its possession entails, and may therefore proceed to practice the vulgar ostentation to which the new rich are sometimes prone.

Although there is perhaps something to this argument, there is not as much as Rousseau seems to think. For it often happens that the children of the rich do not in fact receive the education and training that would enable them to fulfill the duties of their station, or else, if they do receive them, that they do not in fact go on to fulfill these duties. On the contrary, the children of the rich, rather than receiving such education and training, often acquire from childhood a tendency to look upon themselves as a class apart, superior to other classes, and a concomitant snobbishness and distaste and contempt for the non-rich that leads them to tyrannize over the latter rather than to fulfill the duties of their station. This being the case, Rousseau's argument for the inheritance of wealth and against the shifting of rank and fortune is not particularly strong insofar as it rests upon the contention that the duties of the rich can be fulfilled well only if one is educated and trained from childhood to fulfill them. Indeed, Rousseau may justly be accused of conflating two distinct and independent positions. One is the position that, as far as possible, children ought to be permitted to inherit the property of their parents. The other is that shifts of rank and fortune ought to be prevented. Although one way to limit, though perhaps not to prevent, such shifts is to permit the transmission of property from parents to children by inheritance, it is still possible to permit both the inheritance of property and shifts of rank and fortune. If, then, Rousseau wishes to argue for permitting the inheritance of property and against permitting such shifts of rank and fortune, he must present distinct arguments. For one may argue consistently in favor of permitting both the inheritance of property and the shifting of rank and fortune.

But although the passage in question has some importance as showing that Rousseau argues not only in support of the possession of private

PROPERTY AND THE COMMON GOOD

property but also in favor of permitting the inheritance of property and against encouraging shifts of rank and fortune, it still remains something of an inconsistent aberration. This is the case for the following reasons.

The terms of the social contract require each person party to it to place not only himself but also all his powers and possessions "under the supreme direction of the general will." The terms of the contract are such that each person alienates himself totally, "together with all his rights," including any rights he may have to the goods he possesses, "to the whole community."[4] "Each member of the community gives himself to it . . . just as he is, with all the resources at his command, including all the goods he possesses," and hence "the State, in relation to its members, is master of all their goods by the social contract, which, within the State, is the basis of all rights."[5] Yet

in taking over the goods of individuals, the community, so far from despoiling them, only assures them legitimate possession, and changes usurpation into a true right and enjoyment into proprietorship. Thus the possessors, being regarded as depositaries of the public good, and having their rights respected by all the members of the State and maintained against foreign aggression by all its forces, have, by a cession which benefits both the public and still more themselves, acquired, so to speak, all that they gave up.[6]

This supposes that the persons party to the contract already have possessions at the time they enter into the contract.

It may also happen that men begin to unite one with another before they possess anything, and that, subsequently occupying a tract of country which is enough for all, they enjoy it in common, or share it out among themselves, either equally or according to a scale fixed by the Sovereign. However the acquisition be made, the right which each individual has to his own estate is always subordinate to the right which the community has over all: without this, there would be neither stability in the social tie, nor real force in the exercise of Sovereignty.[7]

These passages make it clear that for Rousseau the possession of property is subject to the approval and control of the general will. For Rousseau property is essentially social both in the sense that its possession depends upon social recognition and also in the sense that its possession has social consequences. Thus if a solitary individual, completely isolated from any form of society, possesses something, his possession of it consists only of his ability to control or to use it, and does not amount to property. It is true that Rousseau says that "every man has naturally a right to everything he needs,"[8] so that an individual isolated from society has a natural right not only to what he does in fact possess, provided that he needs it, but also to certain goods that he needs but does not in fact possess. But thus to have a natural right to what I need, regardless of whether I possess it or not, does not mean that what I need is my property. The notions of need and property are two entirely distinct notions. The fact that I need something, and thus have a natural right to possess it, does not mean that it is my property, regardless of whether I possess it or not. On the contrary, property is possible only within society, since it depends upon recognition by society. To enclose a piece of ground and to claim it as my own is not sufficient to make it my property; it becomes my property only if the society of which I am a member concedes my claim and thus recognizes it as mine.[9]

But not only is property essentially social in nature in the sense that its possession depends upon social recognition. It is also essentially social in nature in the sense that its possession has social consequences. We have seen that a man acts rightly only insofar as he acts compatibly with the promotion of the non-egoistic good of those affected by his action, that the terms of the social contract are such that the laws enacted by the sovereign specify how each person party to the contract must act if he is to act compatibly with the common good, and, finally, that each person, in becoming a party to the contract, thereby consents to act in accordance with these laws. Precisely similar considerations apply to the possession of property. Its possession is legitimate only insofar as it is compatible with the promotion of the non-egoistic good of everyone affected by its possession, and each person party to the social contract, in becoming party to it, consents to accept the will of the sovereign, as expressed in the laws of the body politic, as determining the extent, if any, to which the possession of private property is compatible with the promotion of the common good. Thus the questions of whether the possession of private property is compatible with the common good, and, if so, the extent to which it can be accumulated by individuals and partial associations without conflicting with the common good, are questions to be answered by the sovereign. The sovereign must particularly guard against and prevent the division of the body politic into partial associations consisting of the rich on the one hand and the poor on the other. Rousseau takes seriously Aristotle's warning that a city divided into classes consisting of the rich and the poor ceases to be one city, but becomes two separate cities. For Rousseau the consequences of such a division for the body politic are as baneful as, if not worse than, those of any other division.

Associations that are economic in nature are natural rather than moral. They develop from considerations of self-interest and from egoistic considerations rather than from moral considerations, and the claims of nature, as we have seen, are naturally more powerful than the claims of morality. But in addition to this, economic interests are among the most fundamental and powerful of all natural interests, so that when conflicts occur between the economic interests of an individual or association on the one hand and the claims of morality on the other, the economic interests naturally tend to prevail at the expense of the satisfaction of the claims of morality. This means that the rich naturally tend to think of themselves first as rich, or as members of an association or class consisting of the rich, and only second as members of the body politic, and thus to have as their first interest the promotion of the good of the rich rather than, and even at the expense of, the good of the body politic. Thus to the extent that the rich control or influence the legislation of the body politic this legislation tends to promote the interests of the rich rather than, and also at the expense of, the good of the body politic. Similar considerations apply also to the poor. They naturally tend to think of themselves first as members of the class or association of the poor, and only second as members of the body politic, and thus to have as their first interest the promotion of the good of the poor rather than that of the entire body politic.

This analogy, however, between the rich and the poor is incomplete. There are at least three reasons why this is so. First, historically the rich have not only exercised a far greater influence on the enactment of legislation than the poor have, but have also succeeded much more than the poor in obtaining unjust exemptions from its equitable administration. Rousseau makes this clear in the following magnificent passage, which I cannot refrain from quoting at length.

The social confederacy . . . provides a powerful protection for the immense possessions of the rich, and hardly leaves the poor man in quiet possession of the cottage he builds with his own hands. Are not all the advantages of society for the rich and powerful? Are not all privileges and exemptions reserved for them alone? Is not the public authority always on their side? If a man of eminence robs his creditors, or is guilty of other knaveries, is he not always assured of impunity? Are not the assaults, acts of violence, assassinations, and even murders committed by the great, matters that are hushed up in a few months, and of which nothing more is thought? But if a great man himself is robbed or insulted, the whole police force is immediately in motion, and woe even to innocent persons who chance to be suspected. . . . If his coach is met on the road by a wagon, his servants are ready to beat the driver's brains out, and fifty honest pedestrians going about their business had better be knocked on the head than an idle jackanapes be delayed in his coach. Yet all this respect costs him not a farthing: it is the rich man's right, and not what he buys with his wealth. How different is the case of the poor man! the more humanity owes him, the more society denies him. Every door is shut against him, even when he has a right to its being opened: and if ever he obtains justice, it is with much greater difficulty than others obtain favours. If the militia is to be raised or the highway to be mended, he is always given the preference; he always bears the burden which his richer neighbor has influence enough to get exempted from. On the least accident that happens to him, everybody avoids him: if his cart be overturned on the road, so far is he from receiving any assistance, that he is lucky if he does not get horse-whipped by the impudent lackeys of some young duke: in a word, all gratuitous assistance is denied to the poor when they need it, just because they cannot pay for it. I look upon any poor man as totally undone, if he has the misfortune to have an honest heart, a fine daughter, and a powerful neighbor.[10]

There is, of course, some exaggeration in this passage. But there is also much truth in it, particularly when it is applied to the society in which Rousseau lived and to non-democratic societies in general. Its meaning is summed up in the following passage, which also contains some hyperbole: "laws are always of use to those who possess and harmful to those who have nothing: from which it follows that the social state is advantageous to men only when all have something and none too much."[11]

Second, the rich act egoistically, and not merely from self-love, insofar as they seek to promote their interests at the expense of the common good and, in particular, at the expense of the poor. But this is precisely what the rich commonly do when, as rich, they act economically or politically. They do not seek to promote their own good only in those ways that are compatible with the attainment of the good of every person within the body politic, nor are they content to possess sufficient goods to enable them to attain their own non-egoistic good. Instead, they seek to possess more than others have, even at the cost of impoverishing others, despite the fact that they need no more than others do in order to attain their own non-egoistic good. Nor can it legitimately be argued that a rich man needs more to attain his non-egoistic good than a poor man does, for "a grandee has two legs just like a cowherd, and, like him again, but one belly."[12] A rich man is one man with one body, just like a poor man, and therefore by nature has no greater needs than a poor man has. The rich therefore seek to retain and to increase their wealth, not in order to promote their non-egoistic good, but for the egoistic purpose of possessing more than others have. "As long as there are rich people in the world, they will be desirous of distinguishing themselves from the poor;"[13] half the joy would be taken out of being rich if there were no poor people with whom the rich man could contrast himself. Given, then, the egoistic nature of the rich and the fact that the rich historically have tended to exercise a greater influence than the poor on the enactment and administration of legislation, laws historically have tended to favor the egoistic good of the rich at the expense of the common good, and especially at the expense of the poor.

But, third, the poor, insofar as they seek merely to escape their poverty, do not act egoistically, but, instead, seek only to attain their non-egoistic good. It is true that various individuals and groups among the poor some-times seek to promote their interests at the expense of the interests of others, and thus act egoistically, and, in particular, that one way in which they sometimes endeavor to do so is to become members of the class of the rich at the expense of their fellows within the class of the poor. Yet insofar as the poor as a class seek merely to escape their poverty they do not act egoistically, even though in order to effect the escape it may be necessary that they deprive the rich of their excess wealth (the excess wealth of the rich being that wealth that impoverishes the poor and prevents them from attaining their non-egoistic good). Thus whereas the action of the rich in seeking to maintain and increase their wealth, and in seeking to acquire the political power necessary or conducive to enabling them to do so, is neces-sarily egoistic insofar as it involves impoverishing others, the action of the poor in seeking to escape their poverty, and in endeavoring to acquire the political power to enable them to do so, is not egoistic. This may be put by saying that the particular good of the rich as a class or partial association is incompatible with the common good of the body politic insofar as it is incompatible with the particular good of the poor as a class or partial association, whereas the particular good of the poor is compatible both with the common good of the body politic and with the non-egoistic particular good of the rich.

The preceding considerations mean that the existence of a class of rich men within a society is justifiable only if it does not also entail the exis-tence of a class of poor men, and that the existence of a class of poor men is never justifiable if their poverty can be prevented. They mean also that the aim of the poor in seeking to abolish their poverty is always legitimate provided that they do not seek to impoverish others in order to escape their own poverty, and that the aim of the rich in endeavoring to retain and increase their wealth is legitimate only on the condition that they do not attempt to do so by impoverishing others. This can be expressed by saying that the aim of the class of the poor in seeking to abolish itself altogether is always legitimate, although the means employed to attain this end may sometimes be mistaken or illegitimate, whereas the aim of the class of the rich in seeking to perpetuate itself is not always legitimate, but depends for its legitimacy upon the compatibility of its perpetuation with the elimination of the class of the poor. The existence of a class of poor men is always evil when their poverty is preventable or eliminable, whereas the existence of a class of rich men is good only if it does not rest upon the existence of a class of poor men. The existence of a partial association comprised of the poor may thus be said to be an absolute evil, whereas the existence of a partial association comprised of the rich, if good at all, is only a conditional good. Given the absolute evil of poverty, it is the obligation of the body politic to attempt to eliminate it.

Rousseau, however, argues not only for the elimination of poverty, but also for preventing those concentrations of wealth that enable the rich to tyrannize over others.

What is most necessary, and perhaps most difficult, in government, is rigid integrity in doing justice to all, and above all in protecting the poor against the tyranny of the rich. The greatest evil has already come about, when there are poor men to be defended, and rich men to be restrained. . . .

It is therefore one of the most important functions of government to prevent extreme inequality of fortunes; not by taking away wealth from its possessors, but by depriving all men of means to accumulate it; not by building hospitals for the poor, but by securing the citizens from becoming poor.[14]

But not only is it necessary to protect the poor against the tyranny of the rich—it is also necessary to protect the middle classes against both the rich and the poor. "It is on the middle classes alone that the whole force of the law is exerted; they are equally powerless against the treasures of the rich and the penury of the poor. The first mocks them, the second escapes them. The one breaks the meshes, the other passes through them."[15] The wealth of the rich enables them either to control the character of legislation or else, failing this, to buy exemption from being subjected to it equally with others. In either case, their wealth enables them to tyrannize over both the middle classes and the poor. The poor, on the other hand, being unable to provide adequately for themselves by acting in accordance with the laws, and possessing neither the property nor the respectability required to provide a motive for complying with the laws from fear of losing either their property or their respectability, proceed to violate the laws in order to provide for themselves. But those who suffer most from the lawlessness of the poor are the middle classes, not the rich, both because they constitute a more accessible prey than do the rich, and also because what might be only an insignificant loss of property to a rich man might well be disastrous to a member of the middle classes. The middle classes are thus caught in the middle and preyed upon from two directions—by the poor as well as by the rich. Yet it is precisely they who constitute the most law-abiding class within the body politic. More than the rich, they are generally content with such property as they can acquire through complying with the laws, and the modest property they possess, combined with their concern for respectability, provide them motives for such compliance, through fear of losing both should they refuse to comply.

What Rousseau therefore recommends is not merely the elimination of poverty, but also the prevention of great concentrations of wealth. But he does not advocate the total abolition of private property. We have seen that he maintains that "the right of property is the most sacred of all the rights of citizenship," and elsewhere he asserts that "the foundation of the social contract is property," and that "every one should be maintained in the peaceful possession of what belongs to him."[16] His position, in short, is that the common good can be attained "only when all have something and none too much." This means that he advocates a society in which there are no distinct economic classes such as those of the rich, of the poor, and of the middle classes, but an economically classless society in which there is only, so to speak, one great middle class in which "all have something and none too much." It is only when such a society exists that its general will can be readily expressed and the common good of the entire body politic attained.

XXIX. Rousseau and Marxism

Rousseau's insistence upon the importance of the existence of an economically classless society if the common good of the body politic is to be attained or approximated is clearly anticipatory of Marxism. Indeed, Engels goes to the extreme of maintaining that in Rousseau's second discourse

we find not only a sequence of ideas which corresponds exactly with the sequence developed in Marx's *Capital*, but that the correspondence extends also to details, Rousseau using a whole series of the same dialectical developments as Marx used: processes which in their nature are antagonistic, contain a contradiction, are the transformation of one extreme into its opposite; and finally, as the kernel of the whole process, the negation of the negation.[1]

Although this passage doubtlessly contains some exaggeration, it nonetheless also contains some truth, as most Marxists, I believe, would agree. Given that Rousseau does anticipate Marxism in certain respects, it may be helpful to consider briefly some of the similarities and differences between the philosophy of Rousseau and that of Marxism. (By "Marxism" in this discussion I intend to designate simply the general position espoused by Marx, Engels, Lenin, and their disciples. Although there are differences and disagreements between individual Marxists, considerations of space require that I ignore them. But since I am interested only in briefly discussing certain aspects of what may, I believe, with some propriety be referred to simply as "Marxism," these differences and disagreements may reasonably be prescinded from.) We turn first to the similarities.

Both Rousseau and the Marxists distinguish between a pre-historical stage of society and a historical stage. For Rousseau, as we saw in our discussion of the second discourse, the pre-history of man is divisible into two stages—the pure state of nature and pre-civil society. The latter stage in turn is divisible into two stages, an uncorrupt and a corrupt stage. While Marxists do not generally postulate or discuss a pure state of nature, they do sometimes postulate a pre-historical pre-civil stage of society. This is the stage of primitive communism. This stage of pre-civil society corresponds more or less to Rousseau's first stage of pre-civil society. There is no private ownership of land either in the Marxist stage of primitive communism or in Rousseau's first stage of pre-civil society. Both Rousseau and the Marxists maintain that the absence of private real property in the first stage of society means that this stage was free from corruption and that the introduction of private property is the ultimate source of the corruption of man and society and the transformation from pre-civil to civil society. For Rousseau the institution of civil society is preceded by the corrupt stage of pre-civil society, whereas Marxists, insofar as they deal with pre-history at all, tend to write as though the introduction of private property leads immediately to the institution of the state, i.e., civil society. But the important point is that both agree that ultimately it is the introduction of private property into society that leads to its corruption and to the institution of civil society or the state.

Rousseau also anticipates the Marxists in his account of history. He and they both find the actual history of mankind to be a depressing tale of continuing corruption, in which those with economic power use it to acquire political power and to oppress the mass of men. It is true that Marxists present a more thoroughgoing economic interpretation of history than Rousseau does, so much so that they maintain that the state is merely the instrument used by the dominant economic class or combination of classes to oppress other classes. But Rousseau by no means overlooks the importance of economic factors and motives as contributing to the shaping of social and political history. For him, as for Marxists, legal and political institutions have historically been used by the rich to oppress the non-rich, even though he does not go so far as to characterize the state as being merely an instrument of oppression. Moreover, although both regard the actual societies of history as corrupt, both believe in the possibility of establishing just societies and present plans for doing so that involve the establishment of economically classless societies. Finally, both Rousseau and the Marxists take an essentially moralistic stance toward history and society, even though the latter generally look upon themselves as realistic, even positivistic, scientific socialists and scorn the moralism of those they condemn as utopian socialists. But they as well as Rousseau regard the actual societies of history as morally corrupt, as being preceded by morally uncorrupt classless pre-historic societies, and as subject to being transformed into morally uncorrupt and just economically classless societies.

A third possible similarity has to do with socialism. Marxism, of course, is explicitly socialistic, whereas Rousseau is not. But a question arises as to whether socialism is implicit in his position, even though he may not have recognized that it is. We have seen that he maintains that the general will can readily be expressed and the common good attained only in an economically classless society composed of one large middle class in which there are no extremes of wealth and poverty and in which "all have something and none too much." Yet in the absence of concentrations of private wealth it is doubtful that sufficient private capital could be accumulated to finance large-scale industrial enterprises. The rich have sufficient wealth both to meet their consumer needs and also to save or invest. But if wealth were more or less equally distributed it may well be doubted that a sufficient number of persons would be able to accumulate savings sufficient to constitute a source of capital for financing large-scale industrial enterprises. Instead, it might very well be the case that almost all, if not indeed all, of their income would be spent for consumer goods and services designed to meet their daily needs. If so, then the only way in which large-scale industrial enterprises could be financed would be through using funds acquired by the state through taxation. This would mean that a system of private industrial capitalism would have to be replaced with a socialist system in which the state finances large scale industrial enterprises with funds accumulated through taxation.

It might, however, be objected that if sufficient funds can be accumulated through taxation to finance such enterprises, then they could also be accumulated through voluntary savings and investments on the part of individuals, even though wealth be more or less evenly distributed. This objection, however, overlooks two points. The first is that in a society in which wealth is more or less equally distributed larger funds for capital investment can be accumulated through taxation than through voluntary savings. The second point is that if capital were accumulated only through voluntary individual savings, the approximate equality of wealth advocated by Rousseau would eventually be destroyed. Other things being equal, those who spend a smaller proportion of their income on consumer goods and services and, correspondingly, accumulate larger savings for capital investment would eventually acquire greater wealth than those who spend all or almost all their income on consumer items.

Given these considerations, it would seem that in a society such as that advocated by Rousseau, in which there is an approximate equality of wealth among its members, sufficient capital for large-scale industrial investment could be accumulated only by the state through taxation, not by private individuals. We have seen that Rousseau not only permits but advocates the retention of private property and its transmission through inheritance, provided that steps are taken to prevent the development of large inequalities of wealth. His position is therefore compatible with a system in which private capitalistic enterprises on a small scale are permitted. But his position, if applied to an industrial society, would seem to require that such small-scale enterprises be supplemented with a system of large-scale industrial enterprises in which the capital is acquired by the state through taxation. This means that his position, if applied to an industrial society, would seem to permit, if not indeed to require, a mixed economy consisting of small-scale private enterprises on the one hand and large-scale public or socialistic industrial enterprises on the other.

It is important, however, to remember that Rousseau does not himself, in any of the three discourses or in *The Social Contract*, explicitly advocate even so modest a form of socialism as this. This may be because the industrial revolution was only in its infancy during his lifetime. Marx and Engels lived during a period when this revolution was an accomplished fact, and therefore were in a position, as Rousseau was not, to appreciate the tremendous capital required for the financing of large-scale industrial enterprises. Living prior to the full flowering of the industrial revolution, Rousseau cannot reasonably be expected to have foreseen fully what Marx and Engels were in a position to see from historical experience. And before Marxists in particular hasten to condemn Rousseau for a deficiency of foresight they would do well to remember that neither Marx nor Engels were themselves gifted with such infallible and complete prescience that they were able to predict accurately all the major social, economic, and political developments of the twentieth century, as they have occurred either in Communist or in non-Communist countries. As is well known, some of their predictions have been proved false by developments that they simply failed to foresee. Marxists would do well also to remember that Rousseau, unlike Marx and Engels, never pretended to be able to predict scientifically the course of future historical developments.

The truth of the matter is that Hegel's dictum, "The owl of Minerva spreads its wings only with the falling of the dusk," applies to Marx and Engels as well as to Rousseau. The philosopher depends not only upon what may be referred to as the common experience of mankind to supply him with data for philosophical reflection, but also upon what may be referred to as the cultural and historical experience of mankind. Since cultural developments vary from age to age, the experience they supply for philosophical reflection also varies, so that there can be no absolutely final and comprehensive system of philosophy. Insofar as the philosopher reflects upon and endeavors to understand such cultural and historical experience he is necessarily limited by the extent to which such developments have occurred down to his own age, and can never transcend absolutely the limitations of his own epoch. This applies to Rousseau on the one hand and to Marx and Engels on the other as much as it does to any other philosopher, and Marx and Engels no more succeeded in transcending the limitations and illusions of their epoch than Rousseau succeeded in transcending those of his time.

Thus far we have been concerned with certain similarities between the thought of Rousseau on the one hand and that of Marx and Engels on the other and with certain respects in which Rousseau did and did not anticipate the later thinkers. We turn now to discuss certain rather pronounced differences between them. One of the most important has to do with the economic determinism of Marx and Engels. For Marxists, economic modes of production and exchange constitute the substructure of a society, and as such determine, at least in broad outline, the superstructure of the society, which consists of such aspects of society as its law, politics, morality, religion, art, and philosophy. This means that for Marxists the most fundamental and important class divisions within society are those that are economic in character. We have seen abundantly that Rousseau does not by any means minimize the importance of such divisions. But he does not ascribe to them the importance that Marxists do. Instead, his account of partial associations and of the baneful effects they may have is such that non-economic associations may be as fundamental and exert as great an influence upon the society as do those that are economic. Some of the most important of such non-economic divisions within a society are those along national, racial, or religious lines. The history of the twentieth as well as of previous centuries seems to demonstrate clearly that such divisions may have effects as baneful for the body politic as those that are economic in character, and that such divisions and their effects cannot adequately be accounted for entirely in economic terms. Various examples from the middle third of the twentieth century that illustrate the truth of this contention are so obvious that it would be pointless to cite them.

A second pronounced difference between Rousseau and Marxism is connected with the first. Marxists sometimes tend to write as though the attainment of an economically classless society provides a final solution to the problem of corruption, in the sense that once such a society is attained it will be permanent and never degenerate into a corrupt society composed of classes, as the primitive stage of communism did. For Rousseau, on the other hand, the antithesis between nature and morality is permanent. We have seen that for Rousseau the fundamental natural principle of human nature is self-love, and that this principle cannot be eradicated from the nature of man even after he attains the level of self-consciousness and rationality at which he is metaphysically free to impose moral law upon himself. The claims of self-love constantly assert themselves and cannot be ignored if the claims of morality are also to be satisfied. All that morality can legitimately require of us, in view of the claims of our nature as natural beings, is that we seek our own good in ways compatible with the attainment of the non-egoistic good of everyone affected by our action. But not only is the principle of self-love ineradicable—in addition not even the best-constituted government can succeed in eliminating all traces of egoism. The result is that "the natural and inevitable tendency of the best constituted governments" is to degenerate. The following passage makes this clear.

The body politic, as well as the human body, begins to die as soon as it is born, and carries in itself the causes of its destruction. But both may have a constitution that is more or less robust and suited to preserve them a longer or a shorter time. The constitution of man is the work of nature; that of the State the work of art. It is not in men's power to prolong their own lives; but it is for them to prolong as much as possible the life of the State, by giving it the best possible constitution. The best constituted State will have an end; but it will end later than any other, unless some unforeseen accident brings about its untimely destruction.[2]

The difference between Rousseau and the Marxists with regard to the permanence of the classless society issues fundamentally from an essential difference in their view of the nature of man. Both agree that the ultimate source of the loss of the innocence of the pre-historic, classless, pre-civil society is the introduction of private property. Both also agree that the nature of man is plastic, and can be molded now one way, now another, depending upon how society is constituted. But they disagree as to the extent to which it is plastic. For Rousseau the fundamental principle of self-love cannot be eradicated from the nature of man regardless of how or to what extent changes are effected in the constitution of society. Moreover, once man attains the self-consciousness and metaphysical freedom that make him a moral agent and enable him to become morally free, the principle of self-love threatens constantly to develop into egoism, and does in fact do so to some extent in the case of every man, with the possible exception of a few saints. It is at least partly because of this that Rousseau says, at the very beginning of *The Social Contract*, that he proposes to inquire whether there can be any stable and legitimate form of political association, taking laws as they might be and men as they are, not as they might be. Given self-consciousness, metaphysical freedom, and moral agency, the threat of egoism as well as the presence of self-love is an ineradicable presence that cannot be eliminated regardless of how society happens to be re-constituted. The only way in which this threat could be eliminated would be through the elimination of self-consciousness, metaphysical freedom, and moral agency. But these are eliminable only through a return to the pure state of nature, and such a return is neither possible, for reasons already given, nor is it recommended by Rousseau. The only alternative is to attempt to establish a classless society in which the effects of egoism are minimized as much as possible, while keeping in mind the fact that every political association, regardless of how excellent its constitution may be, eventually dies a natural death from the operation of the virus of egoism, if indeed it does not first die an untimely death through the occurrence of some unforeseen accident. No political association, regardless of its excellence, endures forever. Even if a classless society were attained, the forces of egoism working within it would sooner or later lead to its destruction and to the re-emergence of classes. The problem of politics—the reconciliation of the claims of nature and the claims of morality through the satisfaction of the claims of each—is thus a never-ending problem to which there is and can be no final or permanent solution.

For Rousseau, then, once man attains the level of self-consciousness, metaphysical freedom, and moral agency, there is a certain constancy to his nature, as determined by his capacity for moral freedom and the presence within him of the ineradicable natural principle of self-love and its tendency to develop into egoism and thus to conflict with the claims of morality. His nature as thus constituted is constant throughout his history. Marxists, on the other hand, tend to regard human nature as more malleable. The moral purity of the pre-historic man of the primitive stage of communism will be regained in the future classless society. Once regained, it will presumably never again be lost, for the future classless society will apparently never degenerate into one composed of classes, as the primitive pre-historic classless society did. This permanent re-capture of the purity of the primitive stage of communism presupposes that the tendency of the principle of self-love to develop into egoism will be permanently arrested or eliminated. More specifically, it presupposes that the tendency toward egoism, rather than being inherent in the possession of self-consciousness, as it is for Rousseau, is a product of the possession of private property, and therefore will disappear when all systems of private ownership of property are eliminated. Thus for Marxists human nature is even more pliable than it is for Rousseau, and can be molded more thoroughly in different directions by changing the institutions of society. It is no accident that the young Marx, in his essay, "On the Jewish Question,"[3] quotes with approval from the following passage of Rousseau.

He who dares to undertake the making of a people's institutions ought to feel himself capable, so to speak, of changing human nature, of transforming each individual, who is by himself a complete and solitary whole, into part of a greater whole from which he in a manner receives his life and being; of altering man's constitution for the purpose of strengthening it; and of substituting a partial and moral existence for the physical and independent existence nature has conferred on us all. He must, in a word, take away from man his own resources and give him instead new ones alien to him, and incapable of being made use of without the help of other men. The more completely these natural resources are annihilated, the greater and the more lasting are those which he acquires, and the more stable and perfect the new institutions; so that if each citizen is nothing and can do nothing without the rest, and the resources acquired by the whole are equal or superior to the aggregate of the resources of all the individuals, it may be said that legislation is at the highest possible point of perfection.[4]

This passage certainly has an ominous sound to it, and, when taken in abstraction from the total context of Rousseau's social and political philosophy, might easily lead the reader to suppose that Rousseau believes the nature of man to be more malleable than in fact he does. But, as we have seen, he ascribes a constancy to human nature that makes the attainment of an interminable classless society impossible. It is only if one ascribes a degree of plasticity to human nature greater than that ascribed to it by Rousseau, despite the passage just quoted, that one can consistently suppose the attainment of such an interminable classless society to be possible. It is precisely because Marx does not hesitate to ascribe to it such a high degree of plasticity that he can postulate the possibility of the attainment of such a society. Given the ascription of such a high degree of plasticity to human nature and the assumption of the attainability of an interminable classless society, the passage in question becomes subject to an interpretation that opens the way for the use that Marx, Engels, Lenin and their disciples have made of their view of human nature and of the classless society. For Marxists it is the contradictions between classes that constitute the continuing source of the corruption of man. These contradictions, however, contain the seeds of the eventual destruction of class society, for they will eventually work themselves out and issue in a classless society in which they are permanently transcended or overcome. When this society is attained the state, as an instrument of oppression used by the dominant economic class to oppress other classes, will disappear, for where there are no classes there is no possibility of the oppression of one class by another.

For Rousseau, on the other hand, the fundamental contradiction is that between egoism on the one hand and the claims of morality on the other. What may be referred to as "economic egoism" is only one of the many forms egoism may take. Though the faces of egoism may shift and change with changes of time and circumstance, the inclination of man toward egoism, and particularly toward economic egoism, is constant as long as men remain in society and retain the capacity to compare themselves with one another. It is because of the ever-present virus of egoism in its various forms that every political association "begins to die as soon as it is born, and carries in itself the causes of its destruction." A classless society, like any other, is infected with this virus, and thus, like a society composed of classes, eventually dies. Given the constant presence of this virus even in a classless society, all that can be done is to postpone for a time the death of a society from its virulent operation. For this purpose a sovereign to enact law and a government to administer the laws are constant necessities that can never be abandoned. Indeed, even if all men were to receive such irresistible grace that egoism disappeared permanently, the enactment and administration of law would still be necessary if men were to live together in society, since chaos would ensue in the absence of law. This is the rather obvious answer of St. Thomas to the suggestion of St. Augustine that the state is necessary only because of man's sinfulness. Marxists incline toward the Augustinian view, although, of course, they do not talk in terms of sin, and believe that the acts that Augustine labels "sinful" are eliminable on earth in time, whereas Augustine does not. Rousseau, on the other hand, takes the Thomistic position. The state is necessary and politics an interminable art not only because of the presence of egoism, but also because of the possibility of conflicts between the non-egoistic interests and acts of men.[5]

We therefore see once more that Rousseau is essentially within the Christian tradition. Egoism is analogous to original sin when the latter is conceived as an innate propensity on the part of each man to seek his own good in preference to and even at the expense of the non-egoistic good of others. Like original sin, egoism persists as long as man exists as a self-conscious, rational, metaphysically free moral agent capable of imposing moral law upon himself. Thus as far as the possibility of the elimination of egoism and its effects are concerned Rousseau is pessimistic as compared to the Marxists. This pessimism, however, seems at the same time to be a more realistic assessment of the condition and prospects of man on earth than the optimistic Marxist assumption of the earthly moral perfectibility of man. This optimistic Marxist assumption is the consequence of their economic determinism. For if the ultimate source of man's moral corruption is the existence of distinct economic classes within society, then man can be morally perfected simply through the elimination of such classes and the establishment of a classless society.

This leads to a third pronounced difference between Rousseau and Marxism, having to do with their attitude toward religion. For Marxists religion is an essentially corruptive influence, since it leads men to hope for the existence of a life after death in which justice is attained and the evils and injustices of this life are rectified, and thereby to neglect the rectification on earth of these evils and injustices, through working toward the attainment of a classless society in which they are finally and permanently rectified. But since the attainment of the classless society is the inevitable outcome of the working out of the contradictions implicit in class societies, the injustices arising from the existence of classes will eventually and inevitably be eliminated. This Marxist optimism is a species of Hegelian historicist optimism. Hegel states explicitly that his method in developing his philosophy of history is that of a theodicy. For Hegel the philosophy of history is thus explicitly an attempt to justify the ways of God through showing how in history the problem of evil is solved.[6] This is done through showing how the evils and injustices of history have been and are necessary for the realization of Spirit in time, through showing that their occurrence is a means necessary for the actualization of greater human freedom and potentialities than could be realized in the absence of their occurrence. It is especially noteworthy in this connection that neither Hegel nor the Marxists assert the immortality of the individual person. The latter explicitly deny personal immortality, and Hegel, at least in his *Phenomenology of Mind*, *Philosophy of Right*, and *Philosophy of History*, the works in which he presents most explicitly and fully his social and political philosophy and philosophy of history, evinces little interest in the question, neither asserting nor denying the immortality of the individual person. The failure of Hegel in these works explicitly to assert or to deny the immortality of the individual person and the Marxist denial of personal immortality are intimately connected with the Hegelian treatment of the philosophy of history as a theodicy and the Marxist contention that the inevitable outcome of history is the attainment of a just society. For if there is no life after death the problem of evil can be solved and justice attained only in this life in time on earth.

This Hegelian-Marxist position contrasts sharply with the traditional orthodox Christian position. The latter position is fundamentally individualistic in a sense in which the former is not. For the orthodox Christian perfect justice is attainable only if each and every person, regardless of whether he lives in the past, the present, or the future, receives his just deserts. Such perfect justice is attainable only if there is a personal life after death, for it is not attainable on earth. Although this fact is sometimes neglected or even denied, it ought nonetheless to be obvious to anyone who accepts an individualistic ethic. For someone who accepts such an ethic each human being has ultimate moral worth and is to be treated as an ultimate end in himself. We have seen that this is the position of both Rousseau and Kant, so that to this extent at least they are both within the Christian tradition. For Rousseau the common good of humanity is nothing other than the non-egoistic good of each and every human being. And the second formulation of Kant's categorical imperative is such as to require us to treat humanity, whether in ourselves or others, always as an end, never merely as a means. For Rousseau moral goodness consists in willing the common good and in acting accordingly, and for Kant it consists in acting in accordance with the categorical imperative out of respect for it. A man has a good will only if and insofar as he does so. But the possession of a good will, according to Kant, is a necessary condition of being worthy of happiness. This is clear from the following passage: "the sight of a being adorned with no feature of a pure and good will, yet enjoying uninterrupted prosperity, can never give pleasure to a rational impartial observer. Thus the good will seems to constitute the indispensable condition even of worthiness to be happy."[7] This is to say that a man deserves happiness if and only if and only insofar as he is morally good. This is the essential truth at the core of retributivist theories of reward and punishment.

But even though, as Kant claims, a good will or moral goodness be the only good that can possibly be conceived to be unqualifiedly or unconditionally good, either in this world or in any other world—such as heaven—it is still not the complete good. This is blessedness, which consists of the union of a good will and happiness, or, to revert to the language used earlier, of a union of the moral and non-natural good, which consists in willing the common good of humanity, with the natural and non-moral good, which consists in the satisfaction of the non-egoistic claims of natural self-love. Yet the history of mankind has certainly been such that there has been no perfect correlation between the moral goodness and the happiness of individuals. This would be admitted by Hegel and the Marxists as well as by Rousseau and Kant. Indeed, it is precisely because there is no such correlation in history that it presents a problem of evil, which Hegel endeavors to solve in his philosophy of history and which the

Marxists attempt to solve by asserting the inevitability of the attainment of the classless society and by working toward its attainment. Yet the problem presented throughout history by the absence of a perfect correlation between or union of individual moral goodness and happiness is one that cannot possibly be solved through using the methods of either Hegel or the Marxists. For their solutions are essentially secular and temporal, whereas the only possible solution requires personal immortality. This is the case for the following reasons.

First, it is extremely doubtful, to say the least, that Hegel in his philosophy of history succeeds in presenting an acceptable theodicy. This is so for two reasons. The first is that it is extremely doubtful that he does in fact succeed in showing that all the suffering to which men have historically been subjected has in fact been necessary for the actualization of greater human freedom and potentialities than could have been achieved had this suffering been somewhat less severe. Second, even if this first point were waived it does not follow that the actualization of human freedom and potentialities that has been or will be achieved at the cost of this suffering would in fact justify it completely or satisfactorily. To suppose that it does amounts to a repudiation of the kind of Christian individualism espoused by Rousseau and Kant. For if there is no individual life after death in which those individuals of the past and the present, and doubtlessly also of the future, receive the happiness their moral goodness merits but which they do not receive in this life, then they are treated, not as ultimate ends in themselves, as the Christian individualism of Rousseau and Kant requires, but, instead, merely as means whose sacrifice on Hegel's "slaughterbench of history" is necessary for the attainment of a good greater than any that could be achieved were they not sacrificed. This being the case, Hegel's theodicy can consistently be accepted only if one also rejects the Christian individualism of Rousseau and Kant. For if there is no personal immortality then none of those men of good will who never receive in this life the happiness their moral goodness merits will ever receive it, regardless of the extent to which human freedom is enlarged and of the heights to which human culture is raised as a consequence of their sacrifice.

Somewhat similar, although also different, considerations apply to the Marxist assertion of the inevitability of the attainment of the classless society. It is true that Marxists do not present their philosophy of history as a theodicy in the way that Hegel does. For an explicit atheist there is no theological problem of evil to be solved, and thus neither a necessity for nor a possibility of a theodicy. Although Hegel, as we have just seen, unlike Rousseau and Kant, is not within the orthodox Christian tradition of individualism, he nevertheless continues to use theistic and Christian categories and language, at least in a philosophically demythologized way, and thus feels a need to attempt a theodicy. But Marxists do not even so much as pretend to be theists, much less Christian theists, and therefore have no need to and logically could not even attempt to present a theodicy. Nonetheless, their assertion of the inevitability of the attainment of the classless society, even if it were true, does not constitute even a theoretical solution to the problem of evil that confronts anyone who, like Rousseau and Kant, is in the Christian individualistic tradition. It is doubtful, for reasons already given, that an interminable classless society is attainable, and therefore even more doubtful that its attainment is inevitable. And it is doubtful in the extreme that in such a society there would be an absolutely perfect union of moral goodness and happiness in the case of each and every individual within the society. But even if all these doubts were one day removed through the actual attainment of such an absolutely just and interminable society, the problem confronting the individualist would still remain. For even though the individual members of such a society receive the happiness their moral goodness merits, this would not mean that the individuals living prior to the attainment of such a morally perfect society would also all receive the happiness their goodness merits. All too many men of good will have already died, and doubtlessly countless others will die in the future, without receiving the happiness their goodness merits. And if there is no individual life after death they will never receive it, regardless of whether or not in the distant future a morally perfect society is attained. But if they never receive the happiness they merit the problem of evil will never be adequately solved to the satisfaction of the individualist.

If anything at all is obvious from the preceding considerations, it is that for the Christian individualist this problem can never be solved satisfactorily on earth, regardless of whether or not the optimistic assumptions or predictions of Hegel and the Marxists are borne out in time. For the Christian individualist heaven is for the dead as well as the quick, and for those who live in the present as well as for those who will come in the future. This being the case, the actual course of history for him is such that the attainment of heaven on earth, which would be the existence of a situation in which each individual who has ever lived receives the happiness his moral goodness merits, is an absolute impossibility, regardless of how greatly human freedom is extended in the future, regardless of how great the heights human culture attains in the future, and regardless of how completely in some future classless society each individual receives the happiness his goodness merits. From this it follows that if there is no personal life after death the course of human history, regardless of its earthly outcome, can be for the Christian individualist only a tragedy in which individual goodness is not adequately rewarded. In the absence of personal survival of death the course of human history can be regarded as other than tragic only if one rejects such individualism. You cannot have it both ways. If you accept such individualism and there is no personal survival of death, then human history is ultimately tragic; but if you regard human history as other than finally tragic even if there is no personal survival of death, then you cannot consistently accept such individualism.

This, however, does not mean that from the standpoint of Christian individualism human history, in the absence of personal survival of death, loses all its value and significance and becomes merely "a tale told by an idiot, full of sound and fury, signifying nothing." There are various reasons why this does not follow. One is that there are non-moral values that have in varying degrees been realized throughout the course of human history, even though sometimes, as Rousseau points out in the first discourse, at the cost of the realization of moral values. Another is that moral goodness has been exhibited by various individuals throughout the course of history, and the exhibition of such goodness is intrinsically good regardless of whether or not it is rewarded with the non-moral and natural good of happiness. The fact that perfect justice is not and—because of the actual course of history—cannot be perfectly realized on earth does not mean that human history in its entirety is merely something to be lamented. Life still remains essentially good, and is regarded as such by each person who clings to it, as is proved by his clinging to it, even though he may not be aware that in practice he regards it as good and even though he may deny with his lips that it is. It is the recognition and admission of the goodness of life, coupled with the recognition that life is given us independently of our meriting it, that is at least part of the source of the religious attitude at its highest or best. But even though all this is true, the fact remains that the course of human history can only be ultimately tragic for the Christian individualist unless there is a personal survival of death in which those men of good will who never on earth receive the happiness their moral goodness merits do finally receive it.

This is seen as clearly by Kant as by anyone. The complete good, blessedness, cannot possibly be perfectly attained on earth. But practical reason and justice require its attainment. Given that it cannot be perfectly attained on earth, it can be attained only in a life after death. Practical reason and justice therefore require the existence of such a life, regardless of whether theoretical reason can establish its existence. They also require the existence of God, or a being possessing sufficient wisdom, power, and

goodness to insure that the complete good is attained. Given these considerations, practical reason is justified in postulating the existence of God
and the immortality of the individual person, even though reason may be
incapable of establishing theoretically the truth of either of these postulates. These postulates of practical reason are also among the dogmas of
the civil religion Rousseau proposes in the penultimate chapter of *The
Social Contract*. To an examination of this chapter we now turn.

XXX. Politically Pernicious Forms of Religion

In this chapter Rousseau distinguishes among four kinds of religion—the
religion of man, the religion of the citizen, the religion of the priest, and
the civil religion just mentioned. In this section we shall discuss only
Rousseau's treatment of the first three of these forms of religion, and
postpone until the next section our examination of his civil religion.

The religion of man "is the religion of the Gospel pure and simple, the
true theism, what may be called natural divine right or law." It "has
neither temples, nor altars, nor rites, and is confined to the purely internal
cult of the supreme God and the eternal obligations of morality." This
Christianity of the Gospel, according to Rousseau, is entirely different
from the Christianity of today. "By means of this holy, sublime, and real
religion all men, being children of one God, recognize one another as
brothers, and the society that unites them is not dissolved even at death."
The religion of the citizen, on the other hand, comprehends "all the
religions of early peoples," and may be defined as "civil or positive divine
right or law." A religion of this kind "is codified in a single country," to
which it gives its gods, and "has its dogmas, its rites, and its external cult
prescribed by law." In the eyes of its adherents all the world outside their
nation is "infidel, foreign, and barbarous," and "the duties and rights of
man extend . . . only as far as its own altars." This kind of religion "is a
form of theocracy, in which there can be no pontiff save the prince, and no
priests save the magistrates." Finally, the religion of the priest "gives men
two codes of legislation, two rulers, and two countries, renders them
subject to contradictory duties, and makes it impossible for them to be
faithful both to religion and to citizenship." An example of a religion of
this type is Roman Catholicism, for Roman Catholics are subject to the
canon law of the Church as well as to the civil law of the state, to ecclesiastical authorities as well as to civil authorities, and presumably Rousseau
intends also to say that they are subjects of the Vatican as well as their
own state.[1]

Rousseau has nothing good to say about the religion of the priest, which he regards as being "so clearly bad, that it is a waste of time to stop to prove it such. All that destroys social unity is worthless; all institutions that set man in contradiction to himself are worthless." The religion of the citizen "is good in that it unites the divine cult with love of the laws, and, making country the object of the citizens' adoration, teaches them that service done to the State is service done to its tutelary god." But it is also bad, since, "being founded on lies and error, it deceives men, makes them credulous and superstitious, and drowns the true cult of the Divinity in empty ceremonial." It is also bad "when it becomes tyrannous and exclusive, and makes a people bloodthirsty and intolerant, so that it . . . regards as a sacred act the killing of everyone who does not believe in its gods." Rousseau's approval of the religion of man is evident from his laudatory description of it as "the true theism," as "natural divine right or law," and as "this holy, sublime, and real religion" by means of which men "recognize one another as brothers." But his approval is by no means unqualified. His criticism of it is essentially a repetition of the criticisms discussed by Machiavelli, and it adds nothing of importance to the discussion of the earlier thinker. This criticism consists essentially in contending that the Christianity of the Gospel, because of its otherworldliness, distracts the attention of its true adherents too much away from the public affairs of earthly life. The result is that the genuine adherents of this religion are thereby prevented from being good citizens and good soldiers, and become instead easy prey for unscrupulous individuals who know how to use the otherworldly devotion of pious Christians to promote their own private purposes at the expense of the promotion of the public common good.[2]

Rousseau's distinction between what he refers to as "the religion of man" and "the religion of the priest" and his criticism of both are subject to certain rather obvious replies. First, the distinction he draws between these two kinds of religion is subject to criticism on theological grounds. The fact that he draws this distinction in the first place is evidence of his generally Protestant and specifically Calvinistic bias. For this distinction can be accepted by a Christian only if he happens to be a Protestant. Although a Roman Catholic would be quite unlikely to accept the pejorative adjectives that Rousseau applies to what he refers to as the religion of the priest, he, along perhaps with eastern Orthodox and Anglican Christians within the Catholic tradition, would doubtlessly insist that what Rousseau refers to as the religion of the priest, when stripped of the pejorative predicates Rousseau applies to it, is contained at least implicitly within the so-called religion of man or Christianity of the Gospel, and is therefore a legitimate development of the latter. Such Catholic Christians, whether Roman, eastern Orthodox, or Anglican, would argue, that is, that the accounts in the Gospels of Jesus' conferring upon Peter and the other apostles the power to bind and loose constitute the scriptural basis for regarding the priesthood as divinely instituted and holy orders as a divinely instituted sacrament. Whether this Catholic interpretation of scripture can be adequately defended against opposing Protestant interpretations is a theological question, which we cannot examine here. But in *The Social Contract* Rousseau does not even so much as attempt a justification of his Protestant distinction between the religion of man and the religion of the priest.

Second, although there is some truth to Rousseau's characterization of what he refers to as the religion of the priest, he nonetheless also oversimplifies, exaggerates, and presents only part of the truth. It is true that Roman Catholics are subject to the canon law of the Church as well as to the civil law of the state in which they live and that they are subject to ecclesiastical as well as to civil authorities. Insofar as this is what Rousseau means when he says that the religion of the priest "gives men two codes of legislation, two rulers, and two countries," then we may agree with him. It is true also that conflicts may and in fact sometimes do occur between either the canon law of the Church or the requirements imposed by ecclesiastical authorities on the one hand and the civil law of the state or the requirements imposed by civil authorities on the other. But from this it does not follow that the so-called religion of the priest renders its adherents "subject to contradictory duties, and makes it impossible for them to be faithful both to religion and to citizenship," nor does it follow that such a religion "destroys social unity" and sets "man in contradiction to himself." For the obligation of a Roman Catholic to obey human law is conditional upon its compatibility with divine law, as interpreted and developed by the canon law of the Church. On this view a Roman Catholic does not have two distinct duties that are equally obligatory or unconditional, one an unconditional duty to obey divine or canon law and the other an equally unconditional duty to obey human or civil law. On the contrary, he has only one unconditional duty, which is to obey divine law as interpreted by the canon law of the Church. His duty to obey human or civil law is conditional upon its compatibility with divine or canon law, so that if the former conflicts with the latter his obligation is to disobey the former in order to obey the latter.

The Roman Catholic might also reply to Rousseau by arguing that his attack upon the so-called religion of the priest, if developed consistently, applies also to all those Protestant versions of the religion of man that deny that the subject of the state has an unconditional obligation to obey its civil law. For many Protestant thinkers also maintain that the Christian's obligation to obey the civil law of the state and the commands of civil authorities is conditional upon the compatibility of such obedience with obedience to the requirements of divine law, as the latter are determined by the individual conscience through prayerful reflection upon holy scripture. If such reflection leads the individual Protestant conscientiously to believe that obedience to certain civil laws or to certain commands of civil authorities is incompatible with obedience to divine law, then his obligation is to disobey the former in order to obey the latter. Such a position is in fact anticipated by Thomas Aquinas, since he maintains that what may be referred to as a man's subjective duty, as distinct from his objective duty, is always to do what he conscientiously believes to be right, even though his belief may be mistaken.[3] Given these considerations, the Roman Catholic may reasonably reply to Rousseau that if the so-called religion of the priest renders its adherents "subject to contradictory duties, and makes it impossible for them to be faithful both to religion and to citizenship," and thus "destroys social unity" and sets "man in contradiction to himself," then so also do those Protestant versions of the religion of man which maintain that the individual's obligation to obey civil law and the commands of civil authorities is conditional upon the compatibility of such obedience with obedience to the requirements of divine law, as these are determined by the individual conscience.

Similar considerations apply also to those who, independent of an acceptance or rejection of the Christian religion in either its Roman Catholic or Protestant forms, maintain that the individual's obligation to obey civil law and the commands of civil authorities is conditional upon the compatibility of such obedience with the requirements of natural law and the protection of natural rights. For those within the natural right/natural law tradition the obligation to obey civil law is a conditional rather than an unconditional obligation. If civil law conflicts seriously with the requirements of natural law and the protection of natural rights, and if there is no reasonable hope of eliminating these conflicts by working within the limits of civil law, then the individual's natural obligation is to disobey rather than obey. This position is taken by Rousseau himself. For, as we have seen, the terms of the social contract are such that no individual is obligated to obey as a subject the laws of the body politic unless he is granted membership in the sovereign and a voice as a citizen equal to that of everyone else in the body politic in determining these laws. Thus Roman Catholic and Protestant thinkers could reasonably argue that Rousseau's uncompromising advocacy of republicanism subjects him, along with others within the natural right/natural law tradition, to precisely the same kind of criticism as that to which he subjects his so-called religion of the priest. For neither he nor others within this tradition maintain that the individual has an unconditional obligation to obey civil law, regardless of who enacts it and of what its content is.

Indeed, one could reasonably argue that Rousseau, because of his uncompromising insistence that the only possible legitimate form of political association is a republic, is even more fully subject to the sort of criticism he levels against the so-called religion of the priest than are thinkers within the natural right/natural law tradition such as Hobbes and Locke. Whereas Rousseau insists that a republic is the only possible legitimate form of political association, Hobbes and Locke do not. For Hobbes any form of political association is legitimate, regardless of whether it is monarchic, aristocratic, or democratic, and regardless of whether it is hereditary or elective, provided that those possessing sovereignty have both the power and the will to maintain public order and peace and to protect their subjects. And Locke admits the legitimacy of forms of government containing a hereditary component, provided that they also contain a democratic component. Thus whereas Rousseau is uncompromising in his insistence that a republic is the only possible legitimate form of political association, both Hobbes and Locke admit the legitimacy of various non-republican forms of political association. As we pass from Hobbes to Locke to Rousseau we find that the number of possible regimes that each would accept as legitimate grows progressively smaller. For Hobbes any regime is legitimate, provided that the conditions specified above are satisfied, and for Locke, unlike Rousseau, a political association need not be purely republican to be legitimate.

This being the case, the inflexibility of Rousseau's position as compared to those of Hobbes and Locke renders him even more subject than they are to the criticism he levels against Roman Catholicism. For since the number of possible regimes that Hobbes would accept as legitimate is greater than the number that Locke would accept, and the number that Locke would accept is greater than the number Rousseau would accept, the acceptance and application of Rousseau's position by persons who are not citizen-subjects within the kind of republic of which Rousseau would approve would more likely lead to the destruction of social order and to the setting of man in contradiction to himself, which Rousseau condemns as following from Roman Catholicism, than would an acceptance and application of the positions of either Hobbes or Locke. Given, that is, the narrowness of Rousseau's position as compared with those of Hobbes and Locke, and given the fact that most men were not in the past and are not in the present members of the kind of republic of which Rousseau would approve, an acceptance and application of his position would make it impossible for one to be faithful both to the obligations imposed upon him by Rousseau's principles and to the conflicting obligations imposed upon him by the civil laws and authorities of the non-republican body politic in which he happens to live.

Indeed, given the non-republican character of most societies, both past and present, it is by no means an exaggeration to say that an acceptance of Rousseau's position by a minority of the members of these societies, and perhaps even by a majority, would have an even greater divisive effect than would an acceptance of Roman Catholicism itself. Here Rousseau's criticism of the so-called religion of the priest comes full circle and applies more fully to his own position than to the position it is directed against. For Roman Catholicism, although it is perhaps not so accommodating as, and would not accept as legitimate, so wide a variety of regimes as proposed by Hobbes, is nonetheless more accommodating to a greater variety than is Locke's position, and certainly would accept as legitimate a greater variety than Rousseau does. For although the position of the Church, as presented by St. Thomas, is that civil ordinances and authorities are never to be obeyed when what they require is incompatible with obedience to divine law as interpreted by the ecclesiastical authorities of the Church, this still leaves room for great variety, within the limits of divine and natural law, both as to the content of the requirements of civil laws and authorities and as to the form of the constitution of the body politic. In particular, it does not uncompromisingly maintain, as does Rousseau, that the only possible legitimate form of political association is a republic in which every subject is also a citizen, but, instead, admits the legitimacy of monarchic, aristocratic, and democratic constitutions, whether simple or mixed and whether hereditary or elective, provided only that they operate within the limits imposed by divine and natural law. This being the case, the position of the Church is such as to require submission to the requirements of civil laws and authorities, on the ground that such submission is morally obligatory, in cases in which Rousseau would deny its moral obligatoriness and permit such submission only from prudential considerations issuing from one's recognition of one's lack of power to disobey with impunity. Given these considerations, it seems clear that, given the non-republican constitution of most actual societies, both past and present, an acceptance of Rousseau's position would lead to a greater divisiveness and contradiction within man and society than does the so-called religion of the priest.

One might, however, attempt to come to Rousseau's defense by arguing that Roman Catholicism, though perhaps not as hospitable to as great a variety of social and political situations as Hobbes, is nonetheless too accommodating to too great a variety, and accommodates itself to and even gives its approval to certain regimes which it ought rather to condemn. There is undoubtedly some truth to this contention. Priests, bishops, and popes have doubtlessly at times, perhaps rather frequently, been properly subject to this criticism. Although at times they have opposed unjust civil ordinances and acts of civil authorities, sometimes even at the risk of their lives, at other times they have acquiesced to and even approved regimes that they ought instead to have condemned. This objection, however, essentially misses the point, and amounts to an *ignoratio elenchi*. For even if it be true that Roman Catholic ecclesiastical authorities have sometimes accommodated themselves to and even approved regimes that they ought rather to have condemned, their accommodation to and approval of these regimes do not necessarily constitute a source of divisiveness within society. It is because of the alleged socially divisive effects of Roman Catholicism that Rousseau condemns this religion in *The Social Contract*, whereas his uncompromising republican principles, if applied by individuals living within non-republican societies, would have an even greater divisive effect. The only kind of society in which an acceptance of his republican principles would have no greater divisive effect than would an acceptance of those of Roman Catholicism would be one exemplifying the principles he espouses. This, however, applies to the political principles espoused by Locke and by most Protestant thinkers as well as to those advocated by Roman Catholic thinkers.

Another point has to do with the question of whether the fact that an acceptance of the political principles implicitly or explicitly contained in some religion or system of philosophy would have a divisive effect upon society means that these principles are necessarily to be condemned. The answer implicit throughout most of Rousseau's political philosophy is that it does not mean this. On the contrary, the dominant theme running through most of his political thought is that the answer to the question of whether a set of political principles is to be condemned must be determined primarily by considering the question of whether they are compatible with republicanism and with the attainment of the common good, not by considering the question of whether an acceptance of them would have a divisive effect upon society. The important question, that is, is the question of whether a set of principles is compatible with the attainment of a just society, not the question of whether an acceptance of them would have a divisive effect. Although social unity is important, it is not as important as justice. Although Rousseau believes that there is a correlation between social unity and justice, he does not believe that this correlation is perfect. Although there would be considerable social unity in a just society, an unjust society may also have considerable unity. Thus although the espousal of certain political principles, such as those of Rousseau or Locke or of certain Roman Catholic or Protestant thinkers, may disrupt the unity of an unjust society, such disruption, rather than being undesirable, may in fact be just the reverse. Whether it is desirable or not would depend upon its consequences. If it contributes to the establishment of a more just society, then it is desirable; if not, then it is to be condemned. If, then, Rousseau is legitimately to condemn Roman Catholicism or certain forms of Protestantism, the essential logic of his position requires that he do so not merely on the ground that they have a divisive effect upon society, but rather because they would have such an effect upon a just society or upon the sort of society he espouses.

It is interesting in this connection to observe that Rousseau, in the chapter on civil religion, commends Hobbes, despite the fact that various parts of the second discourse and of Book One of *The Social Contract* are either explicitly or implicitly directed against him. It is true that he lauds him only for recommending that the church as well as the state be subject to the direction of the sovereign, so that a union of church and state is effected, and still maintains that there are "false and terrible" things in his political philosophy. But the interesting point in connection with the present discussion is that Rousseau's condemnation of Roman Catholicism in the chapter on civil religion is essentially Hobbesian in spirit, and therefore inconsistent with the fundamental principles of Rousseau's own position. This is the case because, as we have seen, he attacks this religion not because it is false, unjust, or incompatible with the attainment of a just society, but simply on the ground that it "destroys social unity" and sets "man in contradiction to himself" by refusing to accept the sovereign or the head of the state as the sovereign or the head of the Church. To condemn a religion or a philosophical position simply on the ground that an acceptance of it would tend to destroy social unity, rather than being consistent with Rousseau's fundamental principles, is to come quite close to adopting the Hobbesian position that any political system in which peace, the safety of the subjects, and social unity are preserved is preferable to permitting the dissemination and practice of doctrines that have a tendency to disrupt this unity. If Rousseau is to justify his condemnation of Roman Catholicism in terms consistent with his own fundamental principles, he cannot rely simply on the Hobbesian contention that such a religion has a divisive effect upon society. Instead, what he must do is to show that its practice is incompatible with the existence of the kind of republican society he proposes.

But not only does Rousseau condemn the so-called religion of the priest. He also subjects the religion of man or the Christianity of the Gospels to criticism on the ground that it, like the religion of the priest, has socially pernicious consequences. This, in effect, means that he regards Christianity itself as being essentially pernicious in its social and political effects, regardless of whether it be the pure and simple Christianity of the Gospels or the Christianity practiced by Roman Catholics or by various Protestant groups. That he regards Christianity itself as essentially involving pernicious political consequences is evident from the following passages from the chapter on civil religion. "Jesus came to set up on earth a spiritual kingdom, which, by separating the theological from the political system, made the State no longer one, and brought about the internal divisions which have never ceased to trouble Christian peoples." These divisions "have made all good polity impossible in Christian states," so that "the law of Christianity at bottom does more harm by weakening than good by strengthening the constitution of the State." The expression "Christian republic" is a contradiction in terms, for "Christianity as a religion is entirely spiritual, occupied solely with heavenly things; the country of the Christian is not of this world." These passages make it clear that Rousseau condemns the Christianity of the Gospels and Protestant Christianity as well as Roman Catholicism as having a divisive and therefore pernicious effect upon society. All these forms of Christianity are pernicious insofar as they refuse to recognize the sovereign or the head of the state as being also the sovereign or the head of the church within his realm. It is therefore no accident that Rousseau evinces admiration for thinkers such as Calvin and Hobbes—the latter for advocating such a union "of the two heads of the eagle" and the former for accomplishing it in his theocracy in Geneva.

In addition to condemning all these forms of Christianity for having a pernicious, divisive effect upon society, Rousseau also, as we have seen, condemns the Christianity of the Gospels on the ground that its essentially otherworldly orientation prevents its true adherents from being good citizens and soldiers and renders them easy prey for unscrupulous individuals with decidedly worldly interests. To this extent Rousseau's criticism of Christianity simply repeats certain aspects of Machiavelli's treatment of the Christian religion. In doing so, however, it is a repetition of only one aspect of the earlier thinker's treatment, and ignores completely another aspect which is of at least equal importance. For Machiavelli, immediately after presenting the kind of criticism Rousseau repeats, goes on to point out that such criticism applies only to an excessively otherworldly interpretation of the Christian religion and to suggest that another, less otherworldly, interpretation of it can reasonably be given to which the criticism in question would not apply. This is clear from the following passage.

And although it would seem that the world has become effeminate and Heaven disarmed, yet this arises unquestionably from the baseness of men, who have interpreted our religion [Christianity] according to the promptings of indolence rather than those of virtue. For if we were to reflect that our religion permits us to exalt and defend our country, we should see that according to it we ought also to love and honor our country, and prepare ourselves so as to be capable of defending her. It is . . . this false interpretation of our religion, that is the cause of there not being so many republics nowadays as there were anciently; and that there is no longer the same love of liberty amongst the people now as there was then. I believe, however, that another reason for this will be found in the fact that the Roman Empire, by force of arms, destroyed all the republics and free cities; and although that empire was afterwards itself dissolved, yet these cities could not reunite themselves nor reorganize their civil institutions, except in a very few instances. [4]

Elsewhere Machiavelli writes that "if the Christian religion had from the beginning been maintained according to the principles of its founder, the Christian states and republics would have been much more united and happy than what they are."[5]

These passages make it clear that in Machiavelli's view the kind of criticism that Rousseau levels against the Christianity of the Gospels, which Machiavelli himself anticipates in the paragraph immediately preceding that from which the first quotation is extracted, rests upon a "false interpretation" of the Christian religion. Whether it does or not is a theological question that we cannot examine here. We can, however, make two comments. One is that the majority of Christian theologians would undoubtedly agree with Machiavelli's interpretation of the social and political implications issuing from a sound interpretation of the Christian religion and reject that of Rousseau. The other is that the course of world history since the Renaissance and the Reformation conflicts with Rousseau's assessment of the social and political effects of an acceptance of the Christian religion. His criticism of the Christianity of the Gospels is that it leads to such excessive otherworldliness that its true adherents are prevented from being good citizens and soldiers and become easy prey for those individuals who have decidedly worldly interests. Yet since the Renaissance and the Reformation it has been precisely within the nations of western Christendom, more than among non-western and non-Christian peoples, that most progress has been made in approaching a realization of Rousseau's republican ideals. And, with certain exceptions such as the Ottoman Empire and the emergence of the Soviet Union as a military and imperial power, it has been certain nations of western Christendom, such as Spain, France, Britain, and the United States, which, among the peoples of the world, have succeeded since the Renaissance and the Reformation in becoming, at one time or another, the greatest military and imperial powers. It has been these nations, along with such smaller nations of western Christendom as Portugal, Holland, and Belgium, that have succeeded in modern times in establishing the greatest empires and in subjugating entire continents by means of military conquest.

It is doubtlessly true that these conquests and empires have frequently violated both the political principles of Rousseau and the teachings of the Christian religion, so that in at least some instances these nations could not have undertaken these conquests or formed their empires as they did had they been wholly animated by the principles of Rousseau or by the teachings of the Christian religion. But the point to be made against Rousseau is not that these nations have always acted compatibly with the requirements of the Christian religion in achieving their conquests and establishing their empires. Nor is it that they have succeeded during the period in question in making greater conquests, in establishing greater empires, and in realizing more fully Rousseau's republican ideals than most non-western and non-Christian peoples *because* they have been nations that at least have professed some form of the Christian religion. The point is rather that, contrary to Rousseau's claim, the profession of Christianity by these nations historically has not had such a pernicious otherworldly effect upon them that their individual members were thereby transformed into such bad citizens and soldiers that they became incapable of the accomplishments cited.

The preceding considerations are sufficient, I believe, to show that Rousseau's condemnation in *The Social Contract* of the Christian religion, whether it be the so-called Christianity of the Gospels, Roman Catholic, or Protestant Christianity in its various forms, is throughout mistaken and misdirected. Yet his condemnation of the various forms of Christianity and of the so-called religion of the citizen does not amount to a wholesale rejection of religion. On the contrary, he goes to the extreme of claiming that "no State has ever been founded without a religious basis." This being the case, the question is not whether the state is to have such a foundation, but rather what kind of religious basis is best. This brings us to his civil religion.

XXXI. Civil Religion and Religious Tolerance

Rousseau admits that "the right which the social compact gives the Sovereign over the subjects does not . . . exceed the limits of public expediency," and maintains that the invariable limitation of this right cannot be defined more exactly than in these words from the Marquis d'Argenson: "In the republic each man is perfectly free in what does not harm others." This being the case, "The subjects . . . owe the Sovereign an account of their opinions only to such an extent as they matter to the community." But, Rousseau continues,

> it matters very much to the community that each citizen should have a religion. That will make his love his duty: but the dogmas of that religion concern the State and its members only so far as they have reference to morality and to the duties which he who professes them is bound to do to others. Each man may have, over and above, what opinions he pleases, without its being the Sovereign's business to take cognizance of them; for, as the Sovereign has no authority in the other world, whatever the lot of its subjects may be in the life to come, that is not its business, provided they are good citizens in this life.[1]

This means that the dogmas of a religion are of concern to the sovereign only insofar as an acceptance of them has moral, social, and political consequences. But the terms of the social contract are such that it is the sovereign, not the individual, who has the right to determine whether they have such consequences and whether these consequences are beneficial or pernicious. Moreover, since "it matters very much to the community that each citizen should have a religion," the sovereign has the right to require each of its subjects to act compatibly with certain religious articles, which it also has the right to fix. Not only does it have the right to do so— Rousseau also writes as though it has an obligation to do so, on the ground that its subjects will more fully and more readily fulfill their moral, social, and political obligations if it does so. "There is therefore a purely civil profession of faith of which the Sovereign should fix the articles, not exactly as religious dogmas, but as social sentiments without which a man cannot be a good citizen or a faithful subject."[2]

The dogmas or articles of faith of this civil religion "ought to be few, simple, and exactly worded, without explanation or commentary." Its positive dogmas are these: "The existence of a mighty, intelligent, and beneficent Divinity, possessed of foresight and providence, the life to come, the happiness of the just, the punishment of the wicked, the sanctity of the social contract and the laws." Its single negative dogma will consist simply of a condemnation of intolerance.[3] The justification of the issuance by the sovereign of these dogmas is practical, not theoretical. Regardless of whether they happen to be theoretically true or demonstrable, the sovereign ought to pronounce them and require conformity to them for the practical reason that if it does so the subjects of the state will more readily and completely fulfill their moral, social, and political obligations. Their justification is therefore similar to Kant's justification of the postulates of practical reason. As we have seen, for Kant the justification of these postulates is practical, not theoretical. This, indeed, is why they are postulates of practical rather than theoretical reason. Regardless of whether or not we can establish theoretically that God exists, that the soul is immortal, and that in a future life men of good will receive the happiness their moral goodness merits, we are justified practically in postulating the truth of each of these propositions on the ground that the complete good (blessedness) and justice cannot be perfectly attained unless they are true. Similarly, for Rousseau the sovereign is justified practically in pronouncing and compelling compliance with the dogmas of the civil religion, even though they may not be theoretically true or demonstrable, on the ground that a closer approximation to perfect justice within the body politic is possible if it does so.

Rousseau admits that no one can be compelled to believe these dogmas. But men can be compelled to profess belief in and to act as if they believe them. It is easy to understand what is involved in compelling someone to profess belief in them, since one professes such belief simply by saying that one believes them. Whether Rousseau is proposing that the sovereign require an explicit verbal profession of such belief by its subjects is not clear from what he says in *The Social Contract*. But it is clear that he is proposing that the sovereign require its subjects to act as if they believe them. For he says that if anyone acts as if he does not believe them the sovereign can banish him from the state, "not for impiety, but as an anti-social being, incapable of truly loving the laws and justice, and of sacrificing, at need, his life to his duty." Moreover, he proposes that anyone be "punished by death" who, "after publicly recognizing these dogmas, behaves as if he does not believe them," for "he has committed the worst of all crimes, that of lying before the law."[4] Yet, with the exception of the dogma pronouncing the sanctity of the social contract and the laws, it is not clear what acting as if one does not believe these dogmas

amounts to. Presumably one acts as if one does not believe in the sanctity
of the social contract and the laws if one culpably violates either the terms
of the former or any of the latter. But it is not clear what kind of action
would constitute acting as if one did not believe in either the existence of
God, the existence of a future life, or the happiness of the just and the
punishment of the wicked in such a life.

It is easy, as we said above, to understand what is involved in professing
belief in these articles. It is also easy to understand what is involved in
expressing disbelief in them. But such professions of belief or disbelief are
not equivalent to acting as if one does or does not believe them. Or, if it is
maintained that they are equivalent, then acting as if one believes them
consists simply in professing such belief, and acting as if one does not
believe them consists simply in professing disbelief. It might, however, be
suggested that acting as if one believes them consists simply in acting as if
one believes in the sanctity of the social contract and the laws. If so, then,
since it is relatively easy to determine whether one is acting in the latter
way, it would also be easy to determine whether one is acting as if one
believes in the other dogmas. This suggestion, however, will not do. For
one can believe in, profess belief in, and act as if one believes in the
sanctity of the social contract and the laws without believing in, professing
belief in, and perhaps also without acting as if one believes in the other
articles. Moreover, if believing in, professing belief in, or acting as if one
believes in the other dogmas is equivalent to adopting such stances toward
the sanctity of the social contract and the laws, then the pronouncement of
the other dogmas would seem to be otiose. The pronouncement of these
other articles would therefore seem to have some point only if the subjects
of the sovereign are either required to profess belief in them or else at least
forbidden to deny or question them. For although it is difficult, if not
impossible, to determine whether or not another person believes them or
is acting as if he believes them, it is not at all difficult to determine whether
he professes belief in, questions, or denies them.

But, the question arises, if one can believe in and act as if one believes in
the sanctity of the social contract and the laws regardless of whether or not
one believes in or professes belief in the other dogmas, then what is the
point either of requiring the subjects to profess belief in the latter or else of
forbidding them to deny or question their truth? So long as one does not
violate either the terms of the social contract or any of the laws, what
difference does it make whether one professes belief in the other articles or
questions or denies them? This question is particularly appropriate to ask
Rousseau, for, as we have seen, he maintains that the dogmas of the
religion professed by any of the subjects of the sovereign "concern the

State and its members only so far as they have reference to morality and to the duties which he who professes them is bound to do to others," and that "each man may have, over and above, what opinions he pleases, without its being the Sovereign's business to take cognizance of them." Rousseau therefore seems to be contradicting himself. On the one hand he seems to be saying that so far as the sovereign is concerned its subjects ought to be free to believe what they please concerning the lot of men in the life to come so long as they believe nothing that would prevent them from fulfilling their moral, social, and political obligations. Yet on the other hand he maintains that anyone who acts as if he does not believe in the existence of God, in a future life, and in the reward of the just and the punishment of the wicked in this future life ought either to be banished from the state or "punished by death." This apparent contradiction can be removed, if indeed it can be removed at all, only if it can be shown that the subjects of the sovereign can or will more readily and fully fulfill their moral, social, and political obligations by believing what may be referred to as these otherworldly dogmas. It is precisely because Rousseau believes that this can be shown that he believes that "it matters very much to the community that each citizen should have a religion" and should be either banished from the state or punished by death if he acts as if he does not believe the otherworldly dogmas of the civil religion.

It is important to remember that Rousseau does not maintain in *The Social Contract* that any of these otherworldly articles are true. As far as the sovereign is concerned the important question is not the theoretical question of whether they are true, but rather the practical question of what the moral, social, and political consequences are of believing or disbelieving them. Regardless of whether they happen to be true, false, or doubtful, the sovereign ought to forbid any of its subjects to question or deny them if belief in them has better moral, social, and political consequences than does disbelieving or doubting them. Here again we see that Rousseau is essentially a moralist and is asserting the primacy of the practical over the theoretical. The mere fact that certain propositions happen to be false or doubtful does not always justify those who believe them to be so in either asserting, arguing for, or acting on their belief. Whether they are justified in doing any of the latter depends upon the practical consequences of their doing so. If these consequences are compatible with the common good of the body politic, then those who hold the beliefs in question may rightly assert, argue for, and act on them, and ought to be permitted to do so by the sovereign. But if they are incompatible with the common good, then those who hold the beliefs in question ought to keep them to themselves and may rightly be punished by the sovereign if they do not.

This consequence of the primacy of the practical or the moral over the theoretical or the speculative has particular importance for and application to intellectuals. For it is primarily intellectuals who are most likely to deny or to question the beliefs held by the mass of men, particularly if these beliefs happen to be religious or theological or otherworldly in character. Intellectuals have moral, social, and political obligations to the body politic as much as do non-intellectuals, and can be intellectually and morally irresponsible as fully as the latter can be. Just as non-intellectuals may exhibit their moral irresponsibility by substituting their own private or particular good for the common good of the body politic, so also may intellectuals exhibit their moral irresponsibility by pursuing certain intellectual interests at the expense of the common good. It is especially important to point this out in view of the fact that their intellectual attainments are sometimes a source of pernicious pride and hypocrisy. Their attainments sometimes lead them so to preen themselves on their intellectuality that they act as if they believe that these attainments accord them a special privilege to pronounce their views and even to impose them upon the less tutored masses regardless of the moral, social, and political consequences. And although intellectuals are often ever-ready to warn others of the incompatibility with the common good of the activities of certain non-intellectuals, particularly if these activities be economic in character, and to point out to others their obligations and the right of the sovereign to regulate their activities to assure their compatibility with the common good, they are not always so ready to recognize and to publicize their own failings and the right of the sovereign also so to regulate their own activities.

Rousseau, however, despite his exceptional and undoubted intellectual greatness, or rather perhaps because of it, has the great merit, at least in the discourses and *The Social Contract*, of never so preening himself upon his own intellectuality as to suggest that it exempts him from the obligation of subjecting his intellectual as well as his non-intellectual activities to the requirements of morality and to the direction and regulation of the general will as declared by the sovereign body of citizens, composed of non-intellectuals as well as intellectuals. He sees, as clearly as any man has ever seen, that the intellectual activities of intellectuals are as fully subject to regulation by the sovereign body of citizens to insure their compatibility with the common good as are the humblest non-intellectual activities of the most untutored non-intellectual. This is the humility that is essentially involved in genuine democracy or republicanism. The intellectual who refuses to concur with Rousseau on this point is guilty of the sin of intellectual arrogance or pride, a sin essentially incompatible with democracy or republicanism, regardless of how loudly or how insistently he may proclaim his allegiance to democratic or republican principles.

But even after these concessions are made to Rousseau, the question still remains as to whether the common good of the body politic would be more fully promoted or approximated if its subjects are forbidden on pain of punishment to deny or question the otherworldly dogmas of the civil religion. It is important that this question be specified somewhat more precisely, for there are two distinct questions that ought not to be confused with one another. One is the question of whether belief in these otherworldly dogmas is invariably either a necessary or a sufficient condition of an individual's voluntarily fulfilling his moral, social, and political obligations, as distinguished from his fulfilling them through fear of punishment for failing to do so. Rousseau's answer to this question in *The Social Contract* is not as clear as it could be. It is true that he argues that "it matters very much to the community that each citizen should have a religion" on the ground that his doing so "will make him love his duty," that the articles of the civil religion are "social sentiments without which a man cannot be a good citizen or a faithful subject," and that anyone who does not believe these articles can rightly be banished from the state "as an anti-social being, incapable of truly loving the laws and justice, and of sacrificing, at need, his life to his duty." Although one could possibly argue with some plausibility that these remarks indicate that Rousseau feels that belief in the otherwordly dogmas of the civil religion is either a necessary or a sufficient condition of an individual's voluntarily fulfilling his obligations, one could also argue with some plausibility that these remarks are inconclusive and constitute only a hyperbolic expression of Rousseau's conviction of the importance of his civil religion.

But regardless of what the proper interpretation of Rousseau's position concerning this question may be, the correct answer seems to be that belief in such otherwordly articles as those of Rousseau's civil religion is in fact neither an invariably necessary nor an invariably sufficient condition of an individual's voluntarily fulfilling his obligations. There may be some positive correlation between an individual's holding such otherworldly beliefs and his readiness to fulfill such obligations voluntarily, i.e., independent of any consideration of the infliction upon him or others of temporal punishments for failing to do so. Thus it may be the case that a larger percentage of those who hold such beliefs than of those who do not voluntarily fulfill such obligations. It is also undoubtedly the case that sometimes a belief in the existence of God as the ultimate ground or source of one's coming into being and of one's continued existence, life, and consciousness is the source of such gratitude to God that one is led readily to fulfill voluntarily what one believes to be one's moral, social, and political obligations. Indeed, one may even reasonably argue that if God does thus exist as the ultimate source or ground of one's coming into being and of one's continued existence, life, and consciousness, then, given the goodness of life, the theist alone, as distinguished from the atheist or religious sceptic, can completely fulfill all his moral obligations. For if God does thus exist, then human beings have an obligation of gratitude, adoration, and worship toward Him, which can be fulfilled only if one believes in His existence. Yet even after all these concessions or qualifications are made, the fact remains that atheists and religious sceptics sometimes more readily and fully fulfill their non-religious moral, social, and political obligations than theists do, and in this sense at least they sometimes manifest moral goodness more fully than some theists do. If so, then belief in such otherworldly articles as those of Rousseau's civil religion is neither an invariably necessary nor an invariably sufficient condition of one's fulfilling such obligations.

But even if this is true, it still does not follow that the common good would not more readily and fully be sought and approximated in a generally theistic than in a generally atheistic or religiously sceptical society. It is one thing to claim that an individual atheist or religious sceptic may more readily and completely fulfill his moral, social, and political obligations than some theist may, and thus that there is no invariable correlation in individual cases between one's religious beliefs and attitudes and one's readiness to fulfill such obligations. But it is quite another thing to claim that in a generally atheistic or religiously sceptical society such obligations would as readily and fully be fulfilled as in a generally theistic society. This is a second question, quite distinct from the first. Although Rousseau's answer to the first question is not quite as clear as it could be, his answer to the second, as we have seen, is clear and unequivocal. For it is precisely because he believes that a general readiness on the part of the members of a society voluntarily to fulfill the terms of the social contract depends upon a general belief on their part in such otherwordly articles as those of his civil religion that he suggests that the sovereign fix such articles as dogmas and require each of its subjects to act as if they were true. Although the sovereign cannot compel its subjects to believe these dogmas, it can take steps to prevent the growth of atheism and religious scepticism. This it can do either through requiring its subjects to profess belief in them or else through forbidding them on pain of punishment to deny or question them. We have seen that Rousseau does not explicitly recommend the first alternative, perhaps because an adoption of it would needlessly involve requiring those individuals who do not believe these dogmas to lie. Such a requirement would be needless because its purpose—the prevention of the growth of atheism and religious scepticism—could be achieved equally well through adopting the second alternative, which consists simply in forbidding any of its subjects to deny or question them.

Rousseau is dealing here with essentially the same problem as Locke deals with in his first *Letter Concerning Toleration*. Like Locke, he believes that the growth of atheism and religious scepticism has an essentially corruptive influence upon public morals. Just as Locke believes that the danger of such corruption justifies the state in forbidding the expression and dissemination of atheistic opinions, so also Rousseau believes it to be so great as to justify the sovereign in forbidding any of its subjects to deny or question any of the articles of his civil religion. Whether the danger to public morals is as great as they think it is may, of course, be questioned. But the general principle they appear to be applying in this particular case seems essentially sound. To use Rousseau's language, it is that the fundamental moral obligation of each person within the body politic is to act compatibly with the attainment of the common good. If an act of some kind, regardless of whether it involves overt bodily behavior or is merely an act of speech, is incompatible with the attainment of this good, then it may rightly be prohibited. This means that there is no more an unlimited or unconditional right to express verbally or in writing one's beliefs or attitudes regardless of the effect upon the body politic than there is to perform some bodily act regardless of its effects. Thus just as an individual may rightly be required on pain of punishment to refrain from performing those bodily acts, the performance of which is incompatible with the common good, so also may he rightly be required to keep to himself those of his opinions or attitudes whose expression would also be incompatible with the common good.

But although this principle seems essentially sound, one may nonetheless with some justification question the application of it by Locke and Rousseau to the question of the relationship of atheism and religious scepticism to public morals. If widespread atheism and religious scepticism do in fact have as pernicious an effect upon public morals as Locke and Rousseau think, then the state might well be morally justified in attempting to prevent their growth, regardless of whether theism be theoretically true or demonstrable. The burden of proof, however, is on Locke and Rousseau and those who side with them on this issue. For it is also one of their principles that acts of various kinds, regardless of whether they be bodily or speech acts, can rightly be either required or prohibited by the government or the sovereign only if its doing so is either necessary for or contributes to the attainment of a greater good than could otherwise be attained. That Locke and Rousseau succeed in shouldering this burden is doubtful, to say the least. Indeed, as we saw in the discussion of Marxism, one may take a position diametrically opposed to that of Locke and Rousseau on the effect of religion on public morals and argue, as Marxists do, that it has an essentially pernicious effect. And if one accepts, as Marxists do, the principle espoused by Locke and Rousseau that the state may rightly prohibit the expression of opinions that have a pernicious effect upon public morals, and if one also accepts the Marxist position that religious beliefs have such an effect, then one may conclude, as certain Marxists do, that the state may rightly suppress the dissemination of such beliefs.

This means that an application of the principle espoused in common by Locke, Rousseau, and Marxists has different effects, depending upon which opinions and attitudes are believed by those who apply it to be such that a widespread dissemination of them would have a pernicious effect upon public morals. Whereas Locke and Rousseau use this principle to justify the suppression of atheism and religious scepticism, Marxists have sometimes used it for precisely the opposite purpose of suppressing theism. This, however, does not mean that the principle itself is essentially unsound. Instead, it means only that Locke and Rousseau on the one hand and Marxists on the other disagree as to whether it is the widespread dissemination of theism or atheism that has pernicious effects upon society. Although Locke and Rousseau on the one side and Marxists on the other cannot both be correct in their estimate of the moral effects of atheism and theism, and may in fact both be mistaken, the principle they espouse in common is not thereby invalidated. But since this principle can be used to prohibit the dissemination of diametrically opposed opinions and attitudes, it ought to be applied sparingly, and then only after the most careful deliberation. It is important also to remember that when a question arises as to whether the prohibition of the expression of some opinion is justified the burden of proof is always upon those who recommend the prohibition. Marxists do no better job in shouldering this burden when they recommend the suppression of theism than Locke and Rousseau do when they advocate the suppression of atheism.

But although Rousseau, like Locke, does clearly advocate the prohibition of the expression of atheistic views, he also, again like Locke, recommends that all tolerant theistic religions be tolerated. "Now that there is and can be no longer an exclusive national religion, tolerance should be given to all religions that tolerate others, so long as their dogmas contain nothing contrary to the duties of citizenship."[5] This is an expression of the one negative dogma of the civil religion, which forbids intolerance. "But whoever dares to say: 'Outside the Church is no salvation,' ought to be driven from the State, unless the State is the Church and the prince the pontiff. Such a dogma is good only in a theocratic government; in any other, it is fatal."[6] Rousseau goes on to make it clear that in his view Roman Catholicism is intolerant of other religions, and therefore ought not itself to be tolerated. In this his position coincides again with that of Locke, for the historical context of Locke's first *Letter Concerning Toleration* makes it clear that in Locke's view Roman Catholicism is one of the intolerant religions that ought not to be tolerated. That the Roman Catholic religion has throughout much of its history been intolerant of other religions cannot reasonably be denied. But it has by no means had an exclusive monopoly on intolerance among Christian groups, and at various times has at least been rivalled in intolerance by various Protestant groups. Indeed, the very fact that Locke and Rousseau single it out, from among all the Christian groups which have at various times in their history been guilty of intolerance, as the one Christian church that ought not to be tolerated seems to manifest a certain Protestant bias on their part and to convict them of the very intolerance for which they condemn it.

Given their recommendation that Roman Catholicism not be tolerated, Locke and Rousseau could not very well expect their position on religious liberty to be accepted by Roman Catholics. They undoubtedly did not expect that it would be. Yet they also present the fundamental principles of their political philosophy as specifying the universally necessary conditions that must be accepted and applied in practice if morally legitimate and just political constitutions are to be established. If their principles do in fact do this, then there is little if any likelihood that Roman Catholics will accept them if a necessary condition of their doing so is that they commit the absurdity of adopting an intolerant attitude toward their own religion. If, then, Roman Catholics are reasonably to be expected to accept these principles, the proscription of their religion must not be taken to be an essential or indispensable component of them. Hence, if intolerance of Roman Catholicism is an indispensable component of the fundamental principles of Locke and Rousseau, these principles cannot in fact have the universal respect which Locke and Rousseau believe they ought to have. Similar considerations apply also to their proscription of atheism and religious scepticism. Although they believe that their fundamental principles ought to be universally accepted, it is quite unlikely that they would be accepted by atheists and sceptics if the proscription of expressions of atheism and scepticism is an inseparable component of these principles.

The question therefore arises of whether the proscription of Roman

Catholicism, atheism, and religious scepticism is in fact an inseparable component of these principles. The answer seems clearly to be that it is not—that one can consistently accept these principles and reject this proscription. Indeed, if an acceptance of these principles is universally obligatory, then, as we have seen, it is impossible, or at least unlikely in the extreme, that this obligation could or would be universally fulfilled if, in order to fulfill it, one had to accept the proscription in question. For Roman Catholics would be quite unlikely to accept it insofar as it forbids them to practice their religion, and atheists and religious sceptics would be quite unlikely to accept it insofar as it prohibits an expression of their opinions. This being the case, the proscription in question, rather than being an inseparable component of the fundamental principles of Locke and Rousseau, is in fact incompatible with their universal acceptance. There is already a sufficiently large number of persons who would be unwilling to accept them, and there is no point in needlessly adding to their number. These principles, then, rather than containing the proscription in question as an inseparable component, are in fact incompatible with it, in the sense that an inclusion of it among them would serve only to diminish the number of persons who would be willing to accept them. What these principles require is rather precisely the reverse of the proscription in question. Rather than requiring the proscription of the expression of certain opinions concerning religious questions and the practice of certain religions, they require instead the toleration of the expression of all forms of opinion concerning religious matters and the practice of all forms of religion unless and until it can be clearly shown that certain opinions and practices are incompatible with the attainment of the common good. They require, in short, only that each person within the body politic act compatibly with the terms of the social contract, regardless of what his religion or beliefs about religion may happen to be.

This completes our examination of Rousseau's treatment of religion in *The Social Contract*. Perhaps the most charitable thing that can be said about it is that it leaves something to be desired.

XXXII. Sovereignty, Government, and Law

Thus far we have discussed Rousseau's conception of the terms of the social contract, of the various impediments inhibiting their fulfillment, and of what must be done to eliminate or at least to lessen these impediments. It is time now to discuss more fully his notion of two of the instruments or institutions required for the satisfaction of its terms. These are the legislator and the government.

Although Rousseau speaks of the legislator as a single individual, it would seem that it may also consist of a group of individuals. This is the case because the task of the legislator is to propose law and a constitution to a people, and this is a task that can be accomplished by a group as well as by an individual. The task of the legislator requires great wisdom, since it is to propose laws and a constitution that will be both just and enduring, and this requires great knowledge of the character of the people to whom the proposition is directed. Their details must vary as the character of the people varies if they are to be both just and enduring. Although the terms of the social contract are invariable, the character of various peoples is not, and the details of laws and constitutions must be molded to fit the character of the people to whom they are proposed. Yet regardless of how great the wisdom of the legislator may be, he has a right only to propose laws and a constitution to a people, never to attempt to impose it upon them. Although he may legitimately resort to deceit and present his wisdom as divine wisdom revealed to him by God or the gods in order to induce the people to accept it, he still has no right to attempt to impose it upon them should they still reject it. The possession of great wisdom therefore does not constitute a legitimate claim to sovereignty, regardless of how great this wisdom may be. Sovereignty is possessed only by the people themselves, who alone as citizens have sovereign authority to impose laws upon themselves as subjects.[1]

Once a constitution is accepted by a people, a government, which Rousseau refers to also as the prince, must be instituted in order to execute the laws enacted by the sovereign. The sovereign may institute any form of government it pleases and may also alter the form of government and change the officers of the government whenever it sees fit to do so. It may institute a simple monarchy, either elective or hereditary, a simple aristocracy, again either elective or hereditary, a simple democracy, or a mixed form of government, consisting of a combination of any two or more of these simple forms. The difference between monarchy, aristocracy, and democracy consists in the number of governmental officers who, subject to the will of the sovereign body of citizens, have ultimate governmental authority. In a monarchy, regardless of whether it is elective or hereditary, all governmental officials are subject to the authority and direction of one supreme officer, the monarch. In an aristocracy, whether it is elective or hereditary, all governmental officials are subject to the authority and direction of a number of supreme officers, none of whom are subordinate to any of the others. What distinguishes an aristocracy from a democracy is the number of supreme officers within the government. In an aristocracy they constitute less than half the total number of citizens within the body politic, whereas in a democracy they constitute at least half the total number of citizens.[2] This helps to explain why Rousseau claims that "there never has been a real democracy, and there never will be."[3] For a democracy would require an impossible situation in which at least half the total number of citizens would have ultimate governmental authority, none subject to the authority of the others.

In democracies and aristocracies governmental policy binding upon all the officers of the government would presumably be determined by taking votes among the supreme officers of the government. Unless this were done chaos would likely result. For if each of the supreme officers were free to set his own policy without co-ordinating it with that set by the others, conflicts between these independently determined policies would be quite likely to occur. Thus in saying that in an aristocracy the number of supreme officers is less than half the total number of citizens, whereas in a democracy it is at least half, what is intended is not that each has the right to set his own policies independently of those set by the others. Instead, what is meant is that the policy of the government is to be determined by taking a vote among the supreme officers, each of whom has one and only one vote. It is in this sense that each is supreme. Whereas subordinate officers are subject to the direction of their superior officers, there are no officers to whom the supreme officers are subordinate. Instead, they are subject only to the policy determined by a vote taken among them, not to any other officer. The relationships of the supreme officers in aristocracies and democracies to one another and to government policy are therefore analogous to the relationships of the citizens of the body politic to one another and to the laws of the body politic. For, as we have seen, no citizen is subordinate as a citizen to any other citizen, and each is to have only one vote in determining the general will of the body politic as expressed in its laws and to which each as a subject is equally subject. In a monarchy, on the other hand, government policy is determined solely by the monarch. Although he might, and undoubtedly would, consult with others as to which policies ought to be adopted, he alone would have the right to decide whether in fact to adopt them. Once his decision is made, all other officials of the government are subject to it.

Not only are subordinate government officials subject to the policies determined by the supreme officers of the government—all the subjects of the body politic are too, regardless of whether or not they are officials of the government. This, however, does not mean that the supreme officers of the government are empowered to enact law. On the contrary, the right to enact law can be possessed only by the sovereign body of citizens, for law is an expression of the general will of the body politic, and this will can be expressed only by the body politic itself, as consisting of the sovereign body of citizens. The object of this will, as we have seen, is the common good of the body politic, and it may happen that some individual, such as the legislator, the monarch, or some lesser official of the government, knows in some detail what this common good is and what must be done to attain it. Or it may happen that this knowledge may be possessed by some small group within the body politic, perhaps some group of intellectuals. Not only may some individual or group possess such knowledge—they may also in fact will the common good, so that the object of their will is general. It is true that the source of their will is particular. But Rousseau never maintains that the fact that the source of a will is particular means that its object cannot be absolutely general. Instead, he clearly maintains that some individual or small group may see in some detail both what the object of the general will is and what must be done to attain it when the people themselves fail to do so, and also that this individual or group may in fact will the attainment of this object.

Of itself the people wills always the good, but of itself it by no means always sees it. The general will is always in the right, but the judgment which guides it is not always enlightened. It must be got to see objects as they are, and sometimes as they ought to appear to it; it must be shown the good road it is in search of, secured from the seductive influences of individual wills, taught to see times and spaces as a series, and made to weigh the attractions of present and sensible advantages against the danger of distant and hidden evils. The individuals see the good they reject; the public wills the good it does not see. All stand equally in need of guidance. The former must be compelled to bring their wills into conformity with their reason; the latter must be taught to know what it wills. If that is done, public enlightenment leads to the union of understanding and will in the social body: the parts are made to work exactly together, and the whole is raised to its highest power.[4]

By nature each person, whether it be natural or corporate, wills its own good. A natural person, in willing its own good, also wills the good of each of its members. So also a corporate person, in willing its own good, wills the non-egoistic good of each of its members, which, as we have seen, is the general or common good of the corporate person. But although each person, whether natural or corporate, by nature wills its own good, it may fail to see either what its good consists of or what must be done in order to attain the good it wills. This means that it may have to be enlightened by some person or group who sees clearly what it fails to see. This task Rousseau assigns to the legislator. From *The Social Contract*, however, it is

unclear whether the task of the legislator is completed once he has proposed laws and a constitution to a people or whether, instead, it continues
even after the people to whom he proposes them have accepted them.
Regardless of the answer to this question, the people would seem to stand
constantly in need of enlightenment. Such enlightenment could be provided in various ways. One way would be through proposals made in
various public media such as newspapers by various intellectuals who hold
no governmental office. Another would be through proposals made by
various governmental officials, in much the same way as the executive
branch of the American government makes recommendations to the Congress. These alternatives are not, of course, exclusive—both could simultaneously be employed. Those who make such proposals, regardless of
whether they are private citizens, presumably intellectuals, or government
officials, might be said to constitute a continuing legislator seeking to
enlighten the people. The term "legislator" is being used here in the sense
in which Rousseau uses it: to refer to a group of persons who merely seek
to enlighten the people by recommending legislation, not to a group who
have authority to enact legislation. This right, as we have seen, belongs
only to the sovereign body of citizens. Although some group of intellectuals may see precisely what the common good is and what must be
done to attain it, and although they may also will the attainment of this
good, which is the object of the general will, this does not mean that their
will is identical with the general will, nor that it can legitimately be taken
as or substituted for the general will. For, as we have seen, the general will
is general both in its source and in its object, whereas the will of some
group of intellectuals or government officials within the body politic is
merely particular in its source in relation to the will of the entire body
politic.

The preceding points may be summarized in the following way. The
will of the body politic is necessarily general both in its source and in its
object. It is necessarily general in its source simply because it is the will of
the body politic, which is a more comprehensive association than any
association within itself. Its object is also necessarily general, since it
always by nature wills its own good. But it is not necessarily enlightened,
and may fail to see clearly either precisely what the common good it wills
consists in or else precisely what must be done to attain this good. The
source of the will of any individual or partial association within the body
politic, on the other hand, is necessarily particular in relation to the source
of the will of the entire body politic. But the object of the will of an
individual or partial association may be identical with the object of the will
of the body politic, since an individual or partial association may also will
the common good of the entire body politic. Indeed, as we have seen, a

necessary condition of the attainment of the common good is that the people act as moral agents, both in their capacity as citizens and in their capacity as subjects. This is to say that a necessary condition of the attainment of the common good is that each citizen, in voting, will the attainment of the common good, which includes his own non-egoistic good, rather than the attainment of some particular good, either his own, that of someone else, or that of some partial association, at the expense of the attainment of the common good. It is to say also that a necessary condition of the attainment of the common good is that each person, as a subject, willingly subject himself to those laws which he as a citizen participates in enacting on terms of equality with every other citizen-subject. To the extent, and only to the extent, that each person within the body politic thus acts as a moral agent both in his capacity as a citizen and in his capacity as a subject is the common good of the entire body politic in fact attained.

But moral agency on the part of the citizen-subjects is only a necessary condition of the attainment of the common good. It is not a sufficient condition. Instead, it is also necessary that they be enlightened, so that they see clearly both precisely what the common good consists in and what must be done to attain it. Yet the mass of men are by no means always sufficiently enlightened. Moral goodness is one thing, enlightenment another. Neither is either a necessary or sufficient condition of the other. A man can be morally good without being enlightened, and enlightened without being morally good. A man can will the common good without seeing either what it precisely consists in or what must be done to attain it, and a man who does see both clearly may still not will the common good. From time to time exceptional individuals may appear who are graced both with such constant clear vision and with a constant will to subordinate all particular goods, their own as well as those of others, to the requirements of the common good. But such perfectly wise and wholly moral agents are rare. All men are natural beings even if they are also moral agents. As such they have an innate natural inclination to seek their own particular good, and almost all from time to time evince an egoistic tendency to prefer their own good at the expense of the common good. This being the case, it is rarely if ever the case that there is a perfect constant coincidence between the object of the will of even the most enlightened person and the object of the will of the body politic. This point is made by Rousseau in the following passage.

In reality, if it is not impossible for a particular will to agree on some point with the general will, it is at least impossible for the agreement to be lasting and constant; for the particular will tends, by its very nature, to partiality, while the general will tends to equality. It is even more impossible to have any guarantee of this agreement; for even if it should always exist, it would be the effect not of art, but of chance. The Sovereign may indeed say: "I now will actually what this man wills, or at least what he says he wills"; but it cannot say: "What he wills tomorrow, I too shall will" because it is absurd for the will to bind itself for the future, nor is it incumbent on any will to consent to anything that is not for the good of the being who wills. If then the people promises simply to obey, by that very act it dissolves itself and loses what makes it a people; the moment a master exists, there is no longer a Sovereign, and from that moment the body politic has ceased to exist.[5]

Rousseau's object in this passage is to show that "Sovereignty, being nothing less than the exercise of the general will, can never be alienated, and that the Sovereign, who is no less than a collective being, cannot be represented except by himself."[6] His argument for the inalienability of sovereignty is essentially a development of his position, discussed earlier, that liberty is inalienable. In our earlier discussion we were concerned with the argument he designs to establish the inalienability of the will of the individual. Here we are concerned with the argument designed to establish the inalienability of the general or corporate will of the body politic. In both cases his position is essentially the same. It is that the will of a person, whether that person be individual or corporate, cannot be alienated.

A corporate person, like an individual, may at one time will that some other person, either individual or corporate, will for it. It may even will that the other person will for it permanently, and may authorize it to do so. But whether at some later time it does in fact will as the other person wills cannot be determined by any act of will it performs at some earlier time. Indeed, it may not even continue in the future to will that the other person will for it. Thus although one person may in the present confer upon another permanent authority to declare its will in the future, it cannot determine in the present that what at some future time the other person declares its will to be shall in fact be its will. Whether what in the future the other person declares its will to be is in fact its will depends upon what it does in fact will in the future, and this can be determined only if it has some means of declaring its will in the future independently of the declaration expressed by the other person.

The preceding considerations can also be put in the following way. A person, either natural or corporate, may in the present promise another person, also either natural or corporate, that in the future it will do whatever the other wills that it do, and may also in the present will, intend, or resolve to keep the promise. But whether the promise is in fact kept depends upon whether the promisor does in fact continue to will, intend, or resolve to do whatever it is that the promisee wills that he do. If, when the promisee declares it to be his will that the promisor perform a certain act, the promisor wills or decides not to do so, then he fails to keep his promise, even though when he made it he did then will, intend, or resolve to do whatever the promisee might in the future will that he do. But even if the promisor does in fact do whatever it is that the promisee declares, he can do so only if he wills to do so. This is to say that a promisor can intentionally do whatever it is that he has promised to do only if he wills to do so when the time comes to do it. To will to do it at the time the promise is made is not sufficient to guarantee that the promisor will continue to will to do it when the time arrives for the fulfillment of the promise by the performance of an act. Instead, it is also necessary that the promisor will the performance of the act when the time for its performance arrives.

These considerations, I think, are sufficient to show that Rousseau is essentially right in insisting upon the inalienability of the will and of liberty, regardless of whether this be the will and the liberty of a natural or of a corporate person. As was said earlier, it is impossible for a person completely to puppetize himself. The only way in which one could attempt to do so would be through agreeing to subject oneself to a complete and permanent hypnosis, if there is such a thing, in which one simply does whatever one is commanded to do by the hypnotist, without being able to will either to comply with the command or to refuse to do so. It is only in such cases of complete and permanent hypnosis, if indeed there could be such cases, that one person could be so completely subject to the will of another that the will of the latter could reasonably be said to be the will of the former. Even this, however, would be a misleading way of stating what would be involved in such a situation. For to say that in such cases the will of the hypnotist would be the will of the hypnotized person is to suggest that the latter still has a will, whereas in fact there would be only one will—that of the hypnotist. The hypnotized person, rather than willing to do whatever the hypnotist commands him to do, would no longer have a will. For the possession of will involves the possibility of either complying with or refusing to comply with the commands of another. Although one person may always in fact will to comply with the commands of another each time the other commands him to do something, he could rightly be said to will to comply, as distinct from merely complying without willing to do so, only if he could also rightly be said to be able also to will not to comply. This is to say that a necessary condition of the occurrence of an act of will is the possibility of choosing between two or more alternatives. Where there is no possibility of choice there is no possibility of an act of will.

Just as the will of an individual is essentially inalienable, so also the will of a corporate person, and therefore the general will of the body politic, is essentially inalienable. And since sovereignty is "nothing less than the exercise of the general will," it too is inalienable. We have seen that some individual or group may know in some detail what the common good of the body politic is and what must be done if it is to be attained, and that the object of their will may also be the attainment of this common good. But we have seen also that although the object of their will may be identical with the object of the will of the body politic, its source is not. For the source of the will of any individual or group within the body politic is particular, whereas the source of the will of the body politic is general. Given this difference in the source of the will of an individual or group as contrasted with the source of the will of the body politic, a difference in the object of their wills may also appear. This being the case, it can be known whether such a difference does in fact exist only if both the body politic and the individuals or groups in question have some means of expressing or declaring precisely what the object of their respective wills is. Thus although the object of the will of some individual or group within the body politic may agree or be identical in detail with the object of the will of the body politic, it can be known whether it does in fact agree only if the body politic as well as these individuals or groups expresses or declares its will. The expression of the will of the body politic can be accomplished only through taking a vote in which each person who is to be subject to this will is eligible to participate. Only when such a vote is taken can the determinate object of the general will be known. Should some individual or group who claims to know what this object is happen to be contradicted by the majority of the citizens when they vote to determine what it is, their claim is thereby shown to be mistaken.

When in the popular assembly a law is proposed, what the people is asked is not exactly whether it approves or rejects the proposal, but whether it is in conformity with the general will, which is their will. Each man, in giving his vote, states his opinion on that point; and the general will is found by counting votes. When therefore the opinion that is contrary to my own prevails, this proves neither more nor less than that I was mistaken, and that what I thought to be the general will was not so.[7]

Given the possibility of a disagreement between the opinion of some individual or group and that of the majority of the citizens as to what the determinate object of the general will on any given occasion is, there can be no way of knowing, outside of taking a vote in which all who are to be subject to this will are eligible to participate, whether the declaration of some individual or group regarding this object is correct or not. Thus if the people promise simply to obey some individual or group and to accept its declaration of what its will is as a genuine determination of it without taking a vote as to whether in fact it is or not, then "by that very act it dissolves itself and loses what makes it a people; the moment a master exists, there is no longer a Sovereign, and from that moment the body politic has ceased to exist." Rousseau is here supposing that the promise is kept. If it is, then there is no longer a sovereign and therefore no longer a people and a body politic. There is no longer a sovereign because "Sovereignty, being nothing less than the exercise of the general will, can never be alienated." There is no longer a people and a body politic because a people and a body politic constitute a corporate person, and a corporate person, like a natural person, can exist only if it possesses a will and some means of expressing or declaring its will. Thus should a corporate person in the present will that in the future the will of some individual or group be taken as its will it ceases to exist as a corporate person unless it retains some means whereby in the future it is able to declare that the will of this individual or group either is or is not in fact its will. But if it does the latter then it does not in fact will that the will of the individual or group be taken simply as its will.

Rousseau's argument here has two aspects, both of which were approached earlier in the discussion of his position concerning the inalienability of liberty. One of these aspects may be said to be metaphysical, whereas the other is moral. The metaphysical aspect is that since the will, whether it be the will of a natural or of a corporate person, is necessarily inalienable, sovereignty is also necessarily inalienable, since it is "nothing less than the exercise of the general will." The moral aspect is that even if sovereignty were alienable, the sovereign association of citizens could never have a right to alienate their sovereignty. For in doing so they would thereby be subjecting their descendants to the will of the person or group to whom they transfer their sovereignty. They would thus be depriving them of their citizenship, their sovereignty, and their freedom, and this they have no right to do. Given that there is a natural right to freedom, no man or group has a right to deprive any other man or group of their freedom. But this is precisely what would be done should a sovereign association of citizens transfer their sovereignty to some individual or group. If, then, there is a natural right to freedom, sovereignty is morally inalienable, regardless of whether or not it is metaphysically possible to alienate it.

If sovereignty can be possessed only by the collective body of citizens, then it is necessarily indivisible as well as essentially inalienable. Its indivisibility follows from its inalienability. "Sovereignty, for the same reason as makes it inalienable, is indivisible; for will either is, or is not, general; it is the will either of the body of the people, or only of a part of it. In the first case, the will, when declared, is an act of Sovereignty and constitutes law: in the second, it is merely a particular will, or act of magistracy—at the most a decree."[8] Since sovereignty is inalienably possessed by the collective body of citizens, acts of sovereignty can consist only in acts of voting by means of which the citizens declare the general will of the body politic.

This, of course, does not mean that the vote of the citizens as to what the general will is must be unanimous if it is to be a declaration of the general will. If unanimity were required then the general will would rarely if ever get expressed. "To be general, a will need not always be unanimous; but every vote must be counted: any exclusion is a breach of generality."[9] The only law that requires unanimous consent is the social contract itself. "Every man being born free and his own master, no one, under any pretext whatsoever, can make any man subject without his consent."[10] But in consenting to the terms of the contract each person consents to accept the will of the majority of the citizens, as expressed in a vote in which he is granted the right to participate on terms of equality with everyone else, as a declaration of the general will. Given the impossibility of attaining unanimity each time a vote is taken, the only alternative to accepting the will of the majority as expressive of the general will would be to accept the will of the minority or of some still smaller designated minority or of some designated individual as expressing it. This, however, would amount to a violation of the principle of the inalienability of sovereignty. Since, then, it would be absurd to expect unanimity to be attained each time a vote is taken, each person, in consenting to the terms of the social contract and thus in accepting the status of citizen and the right to vote on what the laws of the body politic are to be, thereby consents to accept the will of the majority as expressing the general will. Thus "the vote of the majority always binds all the rest. This follows from the contract itself."[11] Although unanimity is unattainable each time a vote is taken, all who consent to the terms of the contract and accept the status of citizen thereby agree unanimously to accept the will of the majority as expressing the general will each time a vote is taken. "The citizen gives his consent to all the laws, including those which are passed in spite of his opposition, and even those which punish him when he dares to break any of them."[12]

Rousseau is here touching upon an important point. This is that unanimity is morally presupposed by or implicit in every act of voting, in the sense that every person who participates in a vote thereby incurs an obligation to abide by the outcome of the vote. Thus the man who participates in a vote on terms of equality with others, yet refuses to accept the outcome of the vote, is guilty of voting in bad faith. A necessary moral condition of one's possessing the right to vote is that one consent to abide by the outcome of every vote in which he is granted the right to participate, and his participation in a vote may be said to constitute his implicit or tacit consent to accept its outcome. Thus the person who refuses to subject himself on terms of equality with others to the laws which he participates in enacting, also on terms of equality with others, may rightly be punished. And if these laws provide for the punishment of those who refuse to subject themselves to them, then the person who is granted the right to participate on terms of equality with others in their enactment, yet refuses to subject himself to them, may be said without metaphor to consent to his punishment.

But although each person who consents to the terms of the social contract and accepts the status of citizen thereby consents to abide by the will of the majority when a vote is taken, this does not mean that the will of the majority is absolute or unlimited. On the contrary, there are certain limits upon its will that it can never legitimately exceed or violate. These may be referred to as the formal limits of republicanism or democracy, and are implicit in what has already been said. First, as we have seen, the majority can never alienate the sovereignty of the citizens by transferring it to some individual or group, for this would constitute a violation of the natural right to freedom not only of the minority of the citizens but also of all the descendants of those who participate in the vote. Second, the majority can never deprive any individual or group of their citizenship and membership in the sovereign, for this too would constitute a violation of the natural right to freedom of those thus deprived of their citizenship. A man can legitimately be separated from his citizenship in only two ways. One way is through his renouncing it, and perhaps emigrating to another body politic. The other is through forfeiting it through refusing to subject himself on terms of equality with others to the laws in the enactment of which he has been granted the right to participate on terms of equality with other citizens. Third, the majority, whose will expresses the will of the sovereign, must restrict itself solely to the enactment of laws. The first two limits follow from this third limit, as can be seen by considering what Rousseau means by the term "law."

Laws are expressions of the general will of the body politic. As such they must be general both in their source and in their object. They can be general in their source only if each person who is to be subject to them has an equal voice in determining them. From this it follows that laws can be enacted only by the sovereign body of citizens, the will of the majority of which is to be taken as expressing the will of the sovereign. The declaration of an individual or of a partial association within the body politic therefore cannot constitute a law, since its source is particular, not general. It is necessary that such declarations be issued from time to time by officers of the government, since the laws enacted by the sovereign cannot be executed and applied to particular individuals and situations unless they are so issued. But such declarations are decrees, not laws. Although laws require the issuance of decrees if they are to be administered, decrees are not laws. But not only are laws general in their source—they are also general in their object. This means that they must apply equally to each person within the body politic. The sovereign by means of the laws may establish different "classes of citizens, and even lay down the qualifications for membership of these classes, but it cannot nominate such and such persons as belonging to them; it may establish a monarchical government and hereditary succession, but it cannot choose a king, or nominate a royal family."[13] Since the laws must apply equally to every person within the body politic, they cannot specify that some particular individual or group shall have some right or privilege that others shall not have. They may specify that persons having certain characteristics or qualifications may or shall have certain special rights or privileges conferred upon them, but they cannot designate who these persons are, for if they did so the generality of their object would be lost. It is true that laws must be applied to particular persons and situations if they are to be administered. But this is the task of the government, not of the sovereign.

The preceding may also be expressed in the following way. The concern of the sovereign is and can only be with the general. Since its acts are laws, or at least the source of laws, laws too can only be concerned with the general. But since laws apply to nothing whatever unless they apply to particular persons and situations, and since they are useless and pointless unless they are so applied, it is necessary that an instrument be established whose task is thus to apply the general to the particular. This instrument is the government or the prince. Although it cannot itself enact law, it can issue decrees applying to particular persons and situations in order to execute the laws enacted by the sovereign. But the decrees it issues can be valid only if they do not exceed the limits of the laws and only if they are necessary for or contribute to the just and efficient administration of the laws. Thus within the general framework of the laws, the source of decrees is particular, since their source is the will of the government, which is particular in relation to the general will of the body politic, and their object may also be particular, since they may apply only to certain particular persons and not to others. But although decrees are particular in their source and may also be particular in their object and application, laws must be general both in their source and in their object and application. They can therefore be enacted only by the body politic itself. Their enactment is a moral act in which the body politic imposes law upon itself. The ultimate object of this self-imposition of law is the attainment of the common good of the entire body politic, which is nothing other than the non-egoistic good of each and every one of its members.

But not only is the imposition of law upon itself a moral act on the part of the body politic—it also requires a moral act on the part of each and every citizen. The body politic is a corporate person, and as such it can do nothing unless the natural persons comprising it do something. A corporate person cannot act unless the natural persons comprising it also act, and the character of their action determines the character of its action. This being the case, a corporate person cannot act morally unless the natural persons comprising it also act morally. Indeed, to say that the body politic performs a moral act by imposing law upon itself is only a condensed way of saying that the collective body of natural persons who comprise it, in their capacity as the sovereign body of citizens, perform a moral act in imposing laws upon themselves. That a moral act is required on their part is evident from the fact that the laws they impose upon themselves will in fact contribute to the attainment of the common good only insofar as each citizen, in voting, concerns himself primarily with the attainment of this good. This no citizen does by nature. By nature each tends to will his own good first, that of the partial associations of which he happens to be a member next, and that of the entire body politic last of all. This means that the more restricted or particular the object of the will of a person, the more fervently he persists by nature in striving to attain it, and, conversely, that as the object of his will grows more unrestricted or general, he naturally becomes less persistent in endeavoring to attain it. In this sense the natural order is precisely the reverse of the moral order, so that the natural inclinations of an individual can be reversed only by means of moral effort.

From this it is evident that a necessary condition of the attainment of the common good is that each person, both in his capacity as a citizen and in his capacity as a subject, act as a moral agent. The common good is attainable only insofar as its attainment is the primary object of each citizen in voting and only to the extent that each person subjects himself to the laws which he participates in enacting. But, as we have seen, although moral action by the citizen-subjects is necessary if the common good is to be attained or approached, it is not sufficient. Instead, enlightenment is also necessary, and, as we have seen, there is no necessary connection between moral goodness and enlightenment. An individual or a group may be morally good without being enlightened, and, conversely, may be enlightened without being morally good. It is still nonetheless the case that there is sometimes a union of a high degree of enlightenment and a high degree of moral goodness in the same individual. Such individuals both will the attainment of the common good and also know in some detail in what it consists and what must be done if it is to be attained. This being the case, why not establish an intellectual aristocracy, transfer sovereignty to intellectual aristocrats, and entrust them not merely with the task of executing the laws but also with the task of enacting them, as Plato may be read as suggesting in his *Republic?* Rousseau's answer is, of course, implicit in the exposition and development of his position which has already been presented. There are, however, three further arguments for republicanism which, though contained implicitly in what has already been said, merit some further consideration.

XXXIII. Intellectual Aristocracy and Republicanism

1. The first argument rests upon Rousseau's conception of the common good. We have seen that this is nothing other than the non-egoistic good of each and every person within the body politic. We have also seen that this non-egoistic good consists in part of the satisfaction of the individual's natural non-egoistic desires. But it does not consist entirely in this; it consists also in the attainment of moral freedom. This is to say that the non-egoistic good of an individual has two components—one a natural component consisting of the satisfaction of natural desires, the other a moral component consisting of the attainment of moral freedom. We have seen, finally, that moral freedom consists in the imposition of moral law upon oneself, and that this involves one's seeking one's natural good in ways compatible with the attainment of the good of everyone affected by one's action, which is to say that it involves seeking one's natural good in ways compatible with the attainment of the common good.

Given these considerations, it is only in a republic, not an intellectual aristocracy, that what may be referred to as the complete good can be most closely approached. The complete good consists in the attainment, on the part of each and every individual, of a union of the natural good—the satisfaction of natural non-egoistic desires—and the moral good—moral freedom. To use Kant's language, it consists in blessedness, or a union within the individual person of the natural good of happiness and the moral good of moral goodness or good will. Kant, as we have seen, denies the perfect attainability of blessedness on earth, but maintains that its attainability is of such great practical importance that we are practically justified in postulating the conditions necessary for its attainment, namely, the existence of God and the immortality of the individual person, even though the existence of neither of these conditions can be established by means of theoretical reason. Rousseau also has no illusions about the perfect attainability of the complete good on earth, and, as we have seen, maintains that the sovereign ought to proclaim as dogmas of the civil religion the existence of God, the immortality of the individual person, and the happiness of the just and the punishment of the wicked regardless of whether or not these articles can be established as theoretically true. But although Rousseau has no more illusions than Kant about the perfect attainability of the complete good on earth, the fact remains that a closer approximation to its attainment can be made in a republican political association than in an intellectual aristocracy.

The central reason for this is that the proponent of intellectual aristocracy places such great emphasis upon the attainment of the natural good that for its sake he is willing to sacrifice the attainment of the moral good. He finds the tension between the natural good and the moral good to be so great that he is willing to sacrifice the moral good, and therefore the complete good, which is a union of the natural and the moral good, for the sake of the natural good. He believes that the happiness of the individual members of the body politic will be more fully promoted if all but the intellectual aristocrats are absolved of the moral responsibility of imposing law upon the body politic than if each person within it shares this responsibility equally. This belief is accompanied by the assumption that the attainment of happiness by the members of the body politic is of greater importance than is their attainment of full moral freedom through having the responsibility of imposing moral law upon themselves. Such moral freedom presupposes such responsibility and is impossible without it. Such responsibility the proponent of intellectual aristocracy reserves for the intellectual aristocrats alone, with the result that they alone are granted the possibility of attaining full moral freedom. This means in effect that the advocate of intellectual aristocracy is proposing that the possibility of fully attaining the complete good be reserved for the intellectual aristocrats alone. The great mass of men, who fail to qualify for membership in this elite group, must content themselves with the possession of merely the natural component of the complete good.

This argument for intellectual aristocracy can be used in various ways, depending upon the form advocated by those who use it. It can be used to justify the authority of parents over their children, of masters over their slaves, and of imperial rulers over their subjects as well as to justify the kind of intellectual aristocracy advocated by Plato. Rousseau, as we have seen, admits, at least implicitly, the legitimacy of the argument when it is used to justify parental authority, for he admits that parents have a natural right to govern their children until the latter reach the age at which they can assume the moral responsibility involved in freedom from parental subjection. But from the fact that the argument can legitimately be used to justify parental authority it does not follow that it can also be used to justify either slavery, imperialism, or Platonic aristocracy. There are two related reasons why this is so. The first is that parental rule is rule over children, whereas slavery, imperialism, and Platonic aristocracy all involve rule over adults. The second is that part of the object of parental authority is to prepare the child for the assumption of adulthood and the concomitant moral responsibility of freedom from parental authority that the attainment of adulthood merits. This can be put by saying that part of the purpose of parental authority is its eventual termination through preparing the child to assume the moral responsibility involved in his freedom from such authority. And for a republican or democrat such as Rousseau part of its purpose may also be said to be to prepare the child for the assumption of the moral responsibility of citizenship.

As contrasted with Rousseau, the proponent of either slavery, imperialism, or Platonic aristocracy may, in effect, be said to regard the slave or the subject of imperial rule or Platonic aristocracy as a kind of perpetual child. He is regarded as being perpetually incapable of assuming the moral responsibility of citizenship. The object of such forms of rule, when they are not employed as merely temporary measures, is therefore not the preparation of those subject to them for the assumption of such responsibility. Such forms of rule do not aim ultimately at their own termination, but rather at their indefinite or interminable continuation. The advocates of these forms of rule may therefore be said to look upon those they regard as fit subjects of them as constituting a kind of brute animal rather than as constituting a class of children. For children do eventually reach the stage at which they can assume the moral responsibility the assumption of which terminates their subjection to parental authority, whereas brute animals never attain the stage at which they can assume the moral responsibility of citizenship. Just as a brute animal is capable of attaining only a natural good that consists in the satisfaction of its various wants, and not the moral good of moral freedom, so also, according to the advocate of the forms of rule in question, those who are fit subjects of them are capable of attaining only the natural good of happiness or the satisfaction of their natural desires, not the full moral freedom that citizenship involves.

The fact of the matter, however, is that neither slaves nor the subjects of imperial rule or Platonic aristocracy are either perpetual children or brute animals. They are adult human beings, and the complete good of *every* man, not merely of some, consists in a union of the natural good and the moral good. If this be so, then arguments for slavery, imperialism, and Platonic aristocracy cannot be sustained. The only way they could consistently be sustained would be through eliminating the moral good from the complete good and thereby reducing the latter to its natural component. For if the common good of the body politic consists in the attainment of the good of each and every person within it, and if this good contains an ineliminable moral component, which consists in the attainment of the full moral freedom which requires the civil freedom of citizenship, i.e., the freedom to impose moral law upon oneself on equal terms with everyone else, then the common good is simply unatttainable so long as such citizenship is denied any man who is willing to subject himself to self-imposed laws on equal terms with others. But if the moral component of the complete good is eliminated and only the natural component retained, the way is then opened for a justification of slavery, imperialism, and/or Platonic aristocracy. For then the complete good would consist simply of happiness or the satisfaction of natural non-moral desires, and the common good of the body politic simply of the satisfaction of the non-egoistic natural desires of each person within it, and it might then well be the case that this common good or general happiness could more effectively be promoted through enslaving some men or through subjecting them to imperial rule or to the rule of Platonic aristocrats than through establishing a republic in which each subject is also a citizen.

The preceding considerations can also be expressed in the following way. The complete good of an individual may be conceived either naturalistically or non-naturalistically. It is conceived naturalistically if it is held to consist simply in the attainment of a purely naturalistic good, such as happiness or the satisfaction of natural or non-moral desires. But it is conceived non-naturalistically if it is viewed as containing a non-naturalistic or moral component such as moral freedom or moral goodness as well as a naturalistic component. Such a conception of the complete good may be characterized as moderate non-naturalism, since it views the complete good as containing a natural or non-moral as well as a moral or non-natural component. Moderate non-naturalism contrasts with extreme non-naturalism, or the view that the complete good is reducible entirely to what for the moderate non-naturalist is only its moral component. Thus for the extreme non-naturalist the complete good consists simply of some moral non-natural good such as moral freedom or moral goodness, and does not contain a natural non-moral component. In this sense extreme non-naturalism may be said to be the polar opposite of naturalism. It reduces the complete good to what for the moderate non-naturalist is only its moral component, whereas naturalism reduces it to its natural component.

Both Rousseau and Kant are moderate non-naturalists, for, as we have seen, they advocate neither kind of reductionism, and insist that the complete good contains both a natural and a moral component. Although the moral component is not reducible to the natural component, it nonetheless presupposes it, in the sense that what may be referred to as the content or the object of moral freedom or goodness would be either empty or else purely arbitrary unless there were something, such as the satisfaction of natural non-egoistic desires, which is naturally good. This can be put by saying that moral freedom or goodness could not consist in freely making the ultimate object of one's action the attainment of the complete good, containing both a moral and a natural component, of each individual affected by one's action unless this natural component were naturally good.

In addition to the distinction between extreme and moderate non-naturalism, a distinction between two kinds of moderate non-naturalism may also be made. These two forms of moderate non-naturalism may be referred to as the universal and the particular form. Both forms, in being forms of non-naturalism, deny that the complete good can be simply and universally reduced to some natural good. But whereas the universal form of moderate non-naturalism maintains that the complete good of *every* individual contains a moral component consisting of moral freedom, the particular form maintains only that the complete good of *some* individuals contains such a component. In this sense universal non-naturalism, like extreme non-naturalism, may be said to be a polar opposite of naturalism. For it maintains that the complete good of *every* individual contains an irreducible moral component, whereas the naturalist, in denying that there is such a component of the complete good, is thereby also denying that it is a constituent of the complete good of *any* individual. In this respect naturalism, like universal non-naturalism, may be said to be egalitarian. Particular non-naturalism, on the other hand, is non-egalitarian. For in maintaining that the complete good of some but not all individuals contains a moral component, it is thereby also holding that the complete good of some individuals does not contain such a constituent.

Rousseau and Kant advocate the universal form of non-naturalism.

Among others who embrace this form of non-naturalism we may mention Locke, in virtue of his contention that each man has a natural right to liberty (and thus despite his naturalistic and hedonistic definition of "good" and "evil" in his *Essay Concerning Human Understanding*[1]), Hegel, and perhaps Marx. Among those who embrace the particular form we may mention here Plato and Aristotle. Neither Plato nor Aristotle holds a naturalistic view of the complete good, for they deny that the complete good of *every* individual is reducible to its natural component. But neither do they hold the universal form of non-naturalism, for they do maintain that the complete good of *some* individuals is so reducible. This is manifest in the case of Aristotle, for he explicitly maintains that some men are born to be slaves, and thus consistently approves of slavery. It is also manifest, though perhaps less explicitly so, in the case of Plato, for his argument for intellectual aristocracy rests upon his implicit denial that justice and the common good can be attained if each person within the body politic is granted citizenship on terms of equality with everyone else. As we re-marked earlier, Hegel distinguishes between three great epochs of world history, which he classifies as the Oriental, the Greco-Roman, and the Germanic. The Idea of the first is that only one man is and is recognized to be free, of the second that some but not all men are and are recognized to be free, of the third that all men are and are recognized to be free. If, then, these epochs are classified in terms of the idea of freedom, the Oriental epoch may be said to be the singular epoch, the Greco-Roman the particu-lar, and the Germanic the universal. And since, according to Hegel, the social and political philosophies of Plato and Aristotle are essentially philosophic representations of the social and political life and ideals of the Greeks, we find in them only a non-egalitarian development of the Greek Idea that only some men, not all, are free.

But the fact that a philosopher embraces the universal form of non-naturalism is no guarantee that he will develop its implications consis-tently or fully. Neither Locke before Rousseau nor Kant and Hegel after him did so. Of these thinkers it is Rousseau alone who does so. For these implications are such as to rule out the legitimacy of all forms of monarchy and aristocracy and to require republicanism as the only legitimate form of political association. For if an indispensable constituent of the complete good of each and every individual is the moral good of moral freedom, then the common good can be most adequately attained only in an associa-tion in which each person subject to its laws has, equally with every other, full moral responsibility as a citizen for imposing moral law upon himself. If this responsibility is placed only upon one individual, as in a monarchy, or only upon some, as in an aristocracy, then the conditions necessary for the attainment of full moral freedom by everyone are not satisfied. It is in this sense that the attainment of the complete good of everyone, including the attainment of full moral freedom on the part of all, presupposes republicanism or democracy and the possession of the civil freedom of citizenship by all. Rousseau is the first great thinker in the history of political philosophy to see this clearly and to develop consistently and in detail its republican implications.

Locke, in maintaining that each man has a natural right to liberty, falls within the class of universal non-naturalists. But in admitting the legitimacy of forms of government containing a hereditary component as long as they also contain a democratic component, he falls short of fully and consistently developing the implications of his universal non-naturalism. Although he may perhaps be excused on the ground that he recognized that within his own time and country the only practically attainable form of government consistent with his universal non-naturalism was one containing a hereditary component, the fact nonetheless remains that he never expresses even philosophically or theoretically an adequate conception of the republicanism implicit in such non-naturalism. He may also perhaps be excused on the ground that since he antedates Rousseau he had no access to Rousseau's republican development of the implications of universal non-naturalism as a basis on which to construct his own position. This excuse, however, is unavailable as an exculpatory plea in the case of Rousseau's successors Kant and Hegel, for both had access to his work, yet fail to accept fully his republicanism.

That both Kant and Hegel accept the principle of universal non-naturalism is evident from Kant's conception of the nature of the complete good and from Hegel's use of the principle of universal freedom as a criterion for assessing the value of historical epochs, both in themselves and as contributing toward the realization of such freedom. Yet parts of Hegel's *Philosophy of Right* may reasonably be read as an explicit repudiation of Rousseau's republicanism. And although Kant's moral philosophy, as distinct from his legal and political philosophy, perhaps represents as consistent a development of the principle of universal non-naturalism as is to be found in Rousseau's three discourses and *Social Contract*, he nonetheless recoils from a full acceptance of Rousseau's republicanism in his legal and political philosophy. This is evident throughout much of Part I of *The Metaphysics of Morals*, on the metaphysical elements of justice, much of which consists of a farrago of contradictions, but especially in his distinction between an active and a passive citizen. Active citizens are those citizens who are fit to vote, passive citizens those who are not. To use Rousseau's terminology, active citizens alone are citizens as well as subjects; passive citizens are subjects but not citizens. A necessary condition of active citizenship and thus of fitness to vote is self-dependency. This means that all persons falling within the following classes are not fit to vote.

an apprentice of a merchant or artisan; a servant (not in the service of the state); a minor (*naturaliter vel civiliter*); all women; and generally anyone who must depend for his support (subsistence and protection), not on his own industry, but on arrangements by others (with the exception of the state)—all such people lack civil personality. . . . The woodcutter whom I employ on my estate; the smith in India who goes with his hammer, anvil, and bellows into houses to work on iron, in contrast to the European carpenter or smith, who can offer the products of his labor for public sale; the private tutor, in contrast to the schoolteacher; the share-cropper, in contrast to the farmer; and the like—all are mere underlings of the commonwealth, because they must be under the orders or protection of other individuals. Consequently, they do not possess any civil independence.[2]

The examples of Locke, Kant, and Hegel are sufficient to illustrate the claim that a philosopher's acceptance of the principle of universal non-naturalism is not by itself sufficient to guarantee that he will also go on to develop the implications of this principle in such a way as to lead him to an acceptance of the sort of pure republicanism espoused by Rousseau. Such thinkers, however, may perhaps be said to be inconsistent in their rejection of republicanism in a way in which the naturalist who rejects republicanism is not. This is the case for the following reasons. The naturalist simply reduces the complete good to what for the non-naturalist is only its natural component. For the naturalist the only intrinsic good is a natural good such as happiness or the satisfaction of natural desires. Moral freedom or moral goodness is at best only an extrinsic good, not an intrinsic good, and therefore is not an intrinsic component of the complete good. It is extrinsically good only if and insofar as it contributes to the attainment of some natural good. If and insofar as some natural good such as happiness is attainable independently of the existence of moral freedom or goodness, such freedom or goodness is superfluous, dispensable, and therefore valueless relative to the attainment of the natural good in question.

This, of course, is not to say that the existence or possession of such freedom or goodness is never a necessary condition of the attainment of some natural good. Indeed, one might plausibly argue that the possession of such freedom or goodness by or its embodiment in a given individual or group who govern a given community is a necessary condition of the attainment of the common natural good of happiness by the individual members of that community who are subject to their rule. One might, in

fact, go even further and argue that happiness is unattainable in the case of
at least certain individuals who are subject to the rule of others. This is to
say that although some persons may be content to be ruled by others so
long as their rulers possess sufficient enlightenment and moral goodness to
enable them to satisfy their natural desires, there are others who
cannot—or at least do not—content themselves with their subjection to
others, regardless of the extent to which under such subjection they are
able to satisfy their natural desires. Such persons are not content merely to
enjoy the various creature comforts afforded them by benevolent masters,
comforts that enable them to satisfy their various natural desires. Instead,
they desire to be free from their subjection to others, whether this subjection take the form of enslavement to a master or subjection to the rule of
some foreign imperial power or some native monarch or aristocratic class.
In their case happiness does not consist merely in the possession of an
abundance of creature comforts sufficient to enable them to satisfy their
various natural desires. Instead, it depends upon their possession of the
freedom to govern themselves, and until such freedom is attained the
comforts their masters supply them, rather than constituting for them a
source of happiness, serve only as objects of their contempt. For such
persons the freedom to govern themselves is not merely a means to the
attainment of a happiness that consists in the satisfaction of natural desires, but is rather an ultimate end sought for its own sake. It is for them
an intrinsic good, regardless of its relation to the natural happiness that
comes in the course of satisfying natural desires, and for the sake of its
attainment they are willing not only to forgo the comforts afforded by a
benevolent master, but also to risk life itself. They are, in short, sometimes willing to risk death in the fight to obtain their freedom, regardless
of how happy an animal existence they might thereby forgo by refusing to
submit to their masters.

For the naturalist and the particular non-naturalist their aspirations and
behavior may be only so much unintelligible nonsense or madness. And it
is indeed understandable that from these perspectives they should be so
regarded. For if, as the naturalist claims, the complete good for everyone
consists merely in the satisfaction of natural desires, or if, as the particular
non-naturalist claims, it consists merely in this for a class of childlike or
brutelike beings into which these unhappy rebels fall, then their rebellion
against the benevolent rule that provides them the creature comforts
sufficient to satisfy such desires is insane folly indeed. But whether their
rebellion be insanity or not, the fact of its existence is proof that at least
some of these rebels are men who by their actions show their rejection of
naturalism and who by their willingness to risk death manifest their desire

for a non-natural good. This, however, does not mean that naturalism and particular non-naturalism are thereby proved false. Instead, it means only that such rebels manifest by their behavior their rejection of and even contempt for these positions. Nor does it mean that all such rebels reject these positions. History is replete with betrayed revolutions in which members of successful revolutionary groups, upon overthrowing their old native or foreign masters or rulers, proceed almost immediately to ape them and to impose upon their former fellow subjects a despotism frequently more intolerable than that from which they have succeeded in freeing themselves. But such betrayals still do not show that there are no men who manifest by their actions their rejection of and contempt for naturalism and particular non-naturalism and their contempt for the creature comforts afforded them by their masters or rulers when these must be bought through sacrificing their freedom to assume the moral responsibility of imposing laws of their own legislative action upon themselves.

I have maintained that Plato and Aristotle are particular non-naturalists and that Locke, Rousseau, Kant, and Hegel are universal non-naturalists, even though Rousseau alone among the latter develops consistently and fully the republican implications of such non-naturalism. Examples of naturalists are Hobbes, Hume, Bentham, and hedonistic utilitarians in general. All these thinkers reduce the complete good to what for the non-naturalist is only its natural component. Although the details of their positions differ, they all nonetheless fundamentally reduce the complete good in some way to the satisfaction of natural desires, and they all deny that moral freedom or goodness has any intrinsic value. Any value it may have is purely extrinsic, and consists in its contributing to the attainment of some natural non-moral good such as the satisfaction of natural desires. It is ultimately because of the naturalism that Hobbes, Hume, and Bentham share that Hobbes admits the legitimacy of any form of government, whether monarchic, aristocratic, or democratic, which has both the power and the will to protect its subjects from one another and from foreign powers, regardless of how it may have acquired its power, that Hume attacks social contract theories of political obligation and authority and attempts to derive such obligation and authority from utilitarian considerations, and that Bentham claims that "*Natural rights* is simple nonsense: natural and imprescriptible rights, rhetorical nonsense,—nonsense upon stilts."[3]

It must, I think, be admitted that if moral freedom or goodness has no intrinsic value, then one cannot reasonably argue that republicanism is the only possible legitimate form of political association on the ground that it alone is consistent with the attainment of a common good an indispensable constituent of which is the assumption of moral responsibility by each person subject to the laws of the association for the character of these laws. If moral freedom and goodness are indispensable components of the complete good of each and every person, then republicanism is the only possible legitimate form of political association, since it is only in a republic that each person subject to the laws has a responsibility equal to that of every other for imposing law upon the body politic and thus upon himself. But if naturalism be true, then republicanism is only one possible form of political association among others. Whether it is the best or not would depend upon whether it is more conducive than any other possible form to the attainment of whatever it is that one supposes the natural good to consist in. Under certain conditions it may be more conducive to the attainment of the natural good than is any other form, and under certain other conditions certain other forms, such as monarchy or aristocracy, may be preferable. Thus given that the complete good is reducible to a purely natural good of some sort, the question of what form of government is best or legitimate becomes simply an empirical question. But if the complete good contains an irreducible and indispensable moral component consisting of moral freedom or goodness, then the question of what form of political association is best ceases to be simply an empirical question. For if the complete good does contain such a component, then the only possible legitimate form of association is republican, since it is only in a republic that the necessary conditions for the attainment of complete and universal moral freedom and goodness can possibly be satisfied.

2. Rousseau, however, does not rest his argument for republicanism solely upon the *a priori* consideration that, given that universal moral freedom and goodness is an irreducible component of the common good, it is the only possible legitimate form of political association, since it is the only possible form of association in which such a common good is attainable. Given the soundness of this argument, no further argument for republicanism is required. Rousseau nevertheless buttresses it with an empirical or utilitarian argument to the effect that since a government is itself one partial association among others within the body politic, it, like other partial associations, has a will that, though general in relation to its members, is nonetheless only particular in relation to the general will of the body politic.

In a perfect act of legislation, the individual or particular will should be at zero; the corporate will belonging to the government should occupy a very subordinate position; and, consequently, the general or sovereign will should always predominate and should be the sole guide of all the rest.

According to the natural order, on the other hand, these different wills become more active in proportion as they are concentrated. Thus, the general will is always the weakest, the corporate will second, and the individual will strongest of all: so that, in the government, each member is first of all himself, then a magistrate, and then a citizen—in an order exactly the reverse of what the social system requires.[4]

The natural order is the reverse of the moral order, in the sense that whereas individuals and partial associations ought to seek their good in ways compatible with the attainment of the common good of the body politic, in fact they naturally tend to seek first their own good. Individuals tend naturally to seek first their own good even at the expense of the good of the partial associations of which they are members and of the common good of the body politic, and partial associations similarly tend naturally to seek their good at the expense of the common good. This applies to governments and their officers as well as to other partial associations and individuals. Thus although a government and its officers may be sufficiently enlightened to see in detail what the common good consists in and what must be done to attain it, they may nevertheless still not possess a will sufficiently good to lead them to subordinate their particular wills to the general will. Regardless, then, of how enlightened a monarch or an intellectual aristocracy may be, their natural tendency is to seek first their own particular good and thus to subordinate to its attainment the attainment of the common good. The only remedy for this situation is the establishment of a republican sovereign with the authority to change either the form or the officers of the government whenever in its judgment the common good requires such a change.

In this connection it might be mentioned that even so uncompromising an advocate of intellectual aristocracy as Plato admits that even the best form of government has a tendency to degenerate into inferior forms. Thus aristocracy tends to degenerate into timocracy. This happens when soldiers who are not also philosophers and who therefore have no right to rule replace those soldiers who are philosophers and therefore do have a right to rule. Timocracy in turn tends to degenerate into oligarchy, oligarchy into democracy, and democracy into tyranny. One of Plato's recommendations for preventing the degeneration of the best form of rule into inferior forms is to make the position of intellectual aristocrat so unattractive to men of inferior quality, through depriving the soldier-philosopher-kings of such things as private property and a family, that inferior men will have no wish to rule. This recommendation, however, is confronted by the fact that men of inferior quality who lust after fame or power or riches have sufficient insight to recognize that the possession of political power is a ready means of satisfying such lusts and consequently

to endeavor to acquire such power, and, once having acquired it, to use it
to satisfy their lusts. At the same time, however, Plato does not suggest
that the implementation of his recomendation would suffice to prevent
permanently the degeneration of aristocracy into inferior forms of rule.
He, like, Rousseau, recognizes the natural mutability and tendency to
decay and die of even the best-constituted forms of state.

3. A third argument which may be presented in opposition to intellectual aristocracy and in defense of republicanism has to do with the
absence of unanimity among intellectuals as to which laws and policies
among various possible alternatives are most conducive to the promotion
of the common good. Often, of course, such disagreements are due to the
intrusion of particular interests into deliberations about what ought to be
done to attain this good and to the substitution by various of the deliberat-
ing parties of their particular good for the general good. Such intrusions of
particular interests are quite possibly, as Rousseau suggests, the prime
impediment to an emergence of the general will when a vote is taken. But
even when such interests do not intrude there may be honest disagreements among intellectuals as well as among non-intellectuals, all of
whom will the attainment of the common good, as to precisely which laws
and policies would be most conducive to its attainment. This is to say that
there is rarely if ever unanimity on the part of intellectuals for the adoption of one law or policy and unanimity on the part of non-intellectuals for
the adoption of some alternative law or policy. On the contrary, almost
invariably certain intellectuals and non-intellectuals will opt for the adoption of one law or policy, whereas other intellectuals and non-intellectuals
will opt for the adoption of some alternative law or policy. Rather than a
situation in which 100 percent of the intellectuals opt for policy A and 100
percent of the non-intellectuals opt for policy B, a much more likely
situation is one in which, say, 60 percent of the intellectuals and 30
percent of the non-intellectuals opt for policy A, and 40 percent of the
intellectuals and 70 percent of the non-intellectuals opt for policy B. This
may be put by saying that both intellectuals and non-intellectuals split
along conservative and liberal lines. Some intellectuals are conservative
and some are liberal, and some non-intellectuals are also conservative and
others liberal.

When such disagreements occur the disagreeing parties cannot both be
correct. In a given situation it cannot be the case both that policy A is more
conducive to the attainment of the common good than is policy B and also
that policy B is more conducive to its attainment than is policy A. And
since intellectuals as well as non-intellectuals disagree as to which policy is
preferable, the policy that is in fact preferable cannot be said to be simply

the one preferred by intellectuals. Nor is the policy preferred by the majority of intellectuals necessarily preferable. For just as a group of intellectuals that is less numerous than a group of non-intellectuals may be correct in their estimate as to which policy is preferable and the group of non-intellectuals mistaken, so also may a minority of intellectuals on some given occasion be correct in their estimate of which policy is preferable and the majority of intellectuals mistaken. Thus the 40 percent of the intellectuals and the 70 percent of the non-intellectuals may in fact be correct in thinking policy B to be preferable to policy A, and the 60 percent of the intellectuals and 30 percent of the non-intellectuals who think A preferable to B may therefore be mistaken.

Given these considerations, and given also (1) the truth of the universal non-naturalist contention that universal moral freedom or goodness is an intrinsic component of the complete common good and (2) the natural tendency of intellectuals as well as non-intellectuals to prefer the attainment of their own particular good or that of the partial associations of which they are members to the attainment of the common good of the entire body politic, we have an additional argument in support of republicanism.

XXXIV. The Practicability of Republicanism

This completes our exposition, development, and defense of Rousseau's philosophical or theoretical argument that the only possible legitimate form of political association is a republic. But, it may be argued, even if his argument be philosophically sound, his case for republicanism is nonetheless confronted with an insuperable objection. This is that the sort of republicanism he espouses is in practice unattainable. This being the case, the objection continues, there is a sense in which his argument is philosophically or theoretically sound only in appearance, and not in reality. For the ultimate test of the philosophical soundness of a political philosophy is the applicability of its fundamental principles to practice. If these principles cannot be applied in practice, then they lose whatever theoretical soundness they may at first appear to have. Since Rousseau's principles cannot meet this pragmatic test, they must therefore be rejected as philosophically unsound. The republicanism of Rousseau thus meets the same fate as that which the intellectual aristocracy of Plato is sometimes alleged to have met—they both founder on the shoals of practicality. It must be admitted at once that this objection, if it can be sustained, is fatal to Rousseau's republicanism. If a political philosophy cannot meet successfully the pragmatic test in question it must be rejected as philosophically unacceptable. Can, then, Rousseau's republicanism meet this test?

Many will doubtlessly be inclined, merely from a consideration of those aspects of his position that have already been discussed, to reply that it cannot. This inclination may be strengthened rather than weakened when one considers a further aspect of his position which has not heretofore been discussed. This is his repudiation of what is usually referred to as representative democracy or republicanism and his insistence upon direct democracy or republicanism. His repudiation of the former and insistence upon the latter is manifest in the following passages.

Sovereignty, for the same reason as makes it inalienable, cannot be represented; it lies essentially in the general will, and will does not admit of representation: it is either the same, or other; there is no intermediate possibility. The deputies of the people, therefore, are not and cannot be its representatives: they are merely its stewards, and can carry through no definitive acts. Every law the people has not ratified in person is null and void—is, in fact, not a law.

. . . Law being purely the declaration of the general will, it is clear that, in the exercise of the legislative power, the people cannot be represented; but in that of the executive power, which is only the force that is applied to give the law effect, it both can and should be represented. We thus see that if we looked closely into the matter we should find that very few nations have any laws.

. . . the moment a people allows itself to be represented, it is no longer free: it no longer exists.[1]

But not only is Rousseau's repudiation of representative democracy likely to strengthen the inclination of many to reject his republicanism as impractical—in addition, he draws from this repudiation a conclusion that is likely to strengthen this inclination even further. This is the conclusion that, given that sovereignty cannot be represented, it is not possible "for the Sovereign to preserve among us the exercise of its rights, unless the city is very small."[2] If Rousseau is correct in drawing this conclusion, then his republicanism is inapplicable to the large nation-states that had already come into existence when he wrote.

The preceding passages make it clear that Rousseau's repudiation of representative democracy is based essentially upon his argument that sovereignty and the general will are inalienable. It is thus merely an application to representative democracy of essentially the same argument he presents against the legitimacy of monarchic and aristocratic forms of sovereignty. Indeed, part of his point may perhaps be understood to be that if the authority to enact laws is transferred to a body of men elected by those who are to be subject to these laws, then in effect sovereignty is transferred to what may properly be referred to as an elective aristocracy. If so, then a representative democracy is in effect an elective aristocracy. But laws, as distinct from decrees, are expressions of the general will, and as such must be imposed by the entire body politic, as active and as consisting of the sovereign body of citizens, upon itself as passive and as consisting of the same persons as subjects who as active are citizens. The representatives in a representative democracy, like the aristocrats in an aristocracy, constitute a partial association or corporate person within the body politic with a will of its own, the source of which is particular in relation to the general will of the body politic. If they were to impose laws upon the body politic we should have a situation precisely analogous to that in which an elective aristocracy or elective monarch imposes such laws. This is a situation in which one person, either corporate as in a representative democracy or an aristocracy or else natural as in a monarchy, imposes law upon another larger and more comprehensive corporate person consisting of the entire body politic. In this event the law of the body politic would not be self-imposed, and the moral component of the common good, which consists in the imposition of moral law upon itself by the entire body politic, would be unattainable.

Given, then, that representative democracy is indistinguishable from and reducible to a situation in which sovereignty is transferred to an elective aristocracy, Rousseau's repudiation of representative democracy cannot reasonably strengthen any inclination a critic might have to condemn his republicanism as impractical. If his republicanism is impractical it is because he maintains that sovereignty, the general will, and the authority to enact law are inalienable and thus non-transferable, and not because he repudiates representative democracy. For this repudiation, as we have seen, is a consequence of his contention that sovereignty is inalienable. This being the case, his republicanism can reasonably be condemned as impractical only by attacking it at its source, through attacking his argument for the inalienability of sovereignty. This would ultimately involve a repudiation of his particular version of universal non-naturalism, and thus a repudiation of his view that universal moral freedom or goodness is an irreducible and indispensable component of the common good of the body politic.

Since, however, one of the prime motives that might prompt someone to repudiate Rousseau's version of universal non-naturalism is the conviction that his republicanism is impractical, it might be helpful, both for those who find his version of universal non-naturalism appealing and also for those who do not, to show that this conviction is essentially mistaken and rests upon a failure to read Rousseau carefully. That this conviction is mistaken can be shown quite simply by reflecting briefly on distinctions which Rousseau carefully and clearly makes and which have already been discussed.

We have seen that he distinguishes sharply between sovereignty and government and between laws and decrees. The sovereign is composed of the collective body of citizens who impose laws upon themselves as subjects. The sovereign is limited solely to the imposition of law upon the state, and the laws the citizens collectively impose upon themselves as subjects must be general both in their source and in their object. This is to say that each person as a citizen must have one and only one vote in determining the laws and that each person as a subject must be subject to the laws on equal terms with every other person. The task of the government is to execute and enforce the laws enacted by the citizens. In order to do so it may issue decrees of various sorts dealing with various particular situations that cannot be dealt with appropriately by the sovereign. Within the limits of the laws the government has the prerogative of operating in various ways. This is to say that it is the prerogative of the government to make detailed decisions concerning how in particular the laws may best be executed and the common good promoted. Rousseau never suggests that it is the task of the sovereign to make such decisions, nor does he ever suppose that it is within its competence to do so. On the contrary, as the body politic grows larger and more complex the amount of expertise required of the members of the government increases and the competence of the sovereign to handle the affairs of government correspondingly diminishes, so that the government must be granted an increasingly greater prerogative to handle such affairs. This is the source or ground both of Rousseau's contention that democracy as a form of government is suitable only for small and simple states and of his view that as the body politic increases in size and complexity the danger of the government's usurping the right of the sovereign to enact law also increases.

Not only does Rousseau permit the government considerable liberty in determining how best to implement the laws enacted by the sovereign—he also, as we have seen, admits the legitimacy of any form of government the sovereign wills to institute, whether it be monarchic, aristocratic, or democratic and, if it be monarchic or aristocratic, whether it be hereditary or elective. But although the sovereign may legitimately institute any form of government it pleases, it cannot, for reasons already given, transfer to any government its inalienable sovereignty to declare the general will through the enactment of laws. Within these limits, the frequency with which it enacts laws may vary widely, extending from a definable lower limit to an unspecifiable upper limit.

The lower limit would be reached if the citizens enact no laws at all after they have established a form of government, appointed officials of the government, and specified the times at which they are regularly to assemble to consider the enactment of legislation. Each assembly of citizens is to be opened by asking and answering two questions. The first question is: "Does it please the Sovereign to preserve the present form of government?" If the sovereign answers negatively, then it establishes a new form of government. Having done this, it transforms itself into a temporary democracy for the purpose of electing the officers of the government. The reason the sovereign must transform itself into such a temporary democracy is that the sovereign is limited solely to the enactment of law. Laws, as we have seen, are general not only in their source but also in their object. They must be enacted through taking a vote in which everyone who is to be subject to them is granted one and only one vote, and they must apply equally to every subject. Thus whereas the establishment of a form of government is a legislative act, the appointment of its officers is not, since it involves singling out certain individuals from among others. The election of the officers of the government is therefore a governmental act, not a legislative act of sovereignty, and it is for this reason that the sovereign must transform itself into a temporary democracy in order to elect the officers of the government.[3] But if the sovereign answers the first question affirmatively, then it raises the second question: "Does it please the people to leave its administration in the hands of those who are actually in charge of it?" This question, for the reasons just given, is answered by the people, not by the sovereign. This is to say that whereas the collective body of citizens answer the first question in their capacity as sovereign, they can answer the second only in their capacity as a temporary democracy into which they transform themselves for the purpose of answering it. Elections of representatives or of officers of the government are governmental rather than legislative acts, and therefore require the transformation of the sovereign body of citizens into a temporary democracy. If the second question is answered affirmatively, then the present officers of the government are retained; if it is answered negatively they are discharged and new officers are chosen to replace them.[4]

All that Rousseau's position requires is that the sovereign body of citizens assemble regularly to answer the two questions specified above. So long as they continue to answer the first question affirmatively it does not require that they enact any laws at all. Indeed, it does not even require that they periodically elect any representatives or officers of the government. For it permits the establishment of a hereditary monarchic or aristocratic form of government, and once the citizens establish such a form of government and a hereditary line of succession they may continue each time they assemble to answer affirmatively each of the two questions specified above. In such an eventuality the body politic would be governed legitimately, even though no laws are enacted and no representatives or government officers are elected once the citizens establish a hereditary form of government and a hereditary line of succession. Should, however, the citizens establish a non-hereditary form of government it would be necessary that they elect from time to time various representatives or officers of the government. But this would not mean that they would also be required, once they establish a form of government, to enact any further laws. If, however, they do not enact any further laws, then the body politic would be governed independently of the enactment of any further laws. For the citizens alone, for reasons already given, can enact law. In the absence of the enactment of any further laws the body politic would be governed by the issuance of decrees by the officers of the government. Such decrees would not be laws, even though some of them might be general in the sense that they apply equally to all the subjects, since their source would be particular rather than general, i.e., they would be issued by an individual or group within the body politic rather than enacted by the entire body of citizens.

The preceding considerations are intended to show that Rousseau's position is compatible with a situation in which the citizens enact no laws at all once they establish a form of government—a form which may be either monarchic, aristocratic, or democratic, and, if either monarchic or aristocratic, either hereditary or elective. Such a situation would exemplify the lower limit mentioned above. This limit can be departed from indefinitely, depending upon the frequency with which the citizens enact laws. The more frequently they do so, the more they depart from this lower limit. It is obvious that no definite upper limit can be precisely specified. As was suggested earlier, as the body politic grows larger and more complex the knowledge and expertise required of the officers of the government correspondingly increases. This means that as the body politic grows larger and more complex the lower limit must be increasingly approached and the task of the citizens comes increasingly to be solely elective in character rather than both elective and legislative. This is at least part of the reason why Rousseau maintains that democracy as a form of government is suitable only for very small and simple states. It is also at least part of the reason why he claims that although the government of a people of gods would be democratic, such "a government is not for men."[5]

The preceding considerations, however, do not mean that Rousseau advocates that the citizens restrict themselves solely to the election of officers of the government or, if the government be hereditary, that they restrict themselves to assembling periodically to vote on whether to continue or to alter the existing line of hereditary succession. Nor do they mean that he recommends that the citizens transfer to the representatives or officers they elect their sovereign authority to enact law. Such a transfer would be illicit, for reasons already given. It would also be illegitimate for the reason that if such a transfer were made the representatives or officers to whom such authority is transferred would thereby in effect be empowered, at least implicitly, to establish by law a form of government in which the citizens are deprived of their right even to assemble periodically to raise and to answer the two questions mentioned above. This is to say that if sovereignty were transferred, those to whom it is transferred would thereby acquire the right to deprive the citizens of their citizenship, if, indeed, the citizens themselves would not immediately deprive themselves of it simply by virtue of their transferring their sovereignty to representatives or officers of the government. Rousseau's animadversions on representative democracy can be understood adequately only when one understands that by "representative democracy" he intends to designate situations in which the authority to enact law, and thus sovereignty, is possessed by the representatives of the citizens rather than by the citizens themselves. In such situations the citizens are no longer citizens, but are rather merely the subjects of their ostensible representatives. Once this is understood his position on representative democracy can be seen to be by no means a wholly unreasonable one.

Once the preceding considerations are understood it can also be seen that neither is Rousseau's advocacy of the retention by the citizens of their citizenship, i.e., of their sovereignty and thus of their right to enact law, either wholly unreasonable or wholly impractical. The legislative task of the citizens is to enact laws that are essentially general in nature. These laws constitute a broad general framework within which the government has the liberty to adopt various courses of action and to issue various decrees dealing with particular contingencies and situations that cannot, because of their particularity and contingency, be adequately dealt with simply by appealing to this broad general framework of law. Nor does the enactment of such laws require, as even Rousseau himself thought, that the state be very small. Even in states as large as those of the twentieth century referenda are frequently held in which such laws are enacted by the citizenry. Nor is it necessary that the citizens all assemble in one place in order that they may enact laws, any more than it is necessary that they assemble in one place in order to elect representatives. It is true that in the absence of the assembly in one place of all the citizenry laws could not be voted on through such means as having them moved and seconded by two of the assembled citizens. But such moving and seconding by individuals is not necessary. Instead, the laws to be voted on could be proposed either by the government, by petitions bearing the signatures of a certain percentage of the citizens, or by both these means. Nor is it any longer necessary, if indeed it ever was, that all the citizens assemble in one place in order to hear arguments supporting or opposing various legislative proposals. For with the development of media of communication such as radio and television it is possible for millions of citizens to listen simultaneously to the same speaker. Given these technical developments, Rousseau's pessimism concerning the applicability of his republican principles to large and complex societies loses at least some of the justification it may have had in his day.

XXXV. Summary

It is time now to summarize the course of our exposition and argument. In the first discourse Rousseau distinguishes sharply between civilization on the one hand and justice on the other. A society is civilized to the extent that in it the various arts and sciences are developed, just to the extent that each of its members can promote his good by acting in accordance with its laws and institutions. Civilization is therefore one thing, justice something else, and the two do not develop concomitantly. Instead, one society may be more civilized but less just than another. Indeed, the course of history has been such that in general civilization has advanced only at the cost of the sacrifice of the satisfaction of the claims of justice. But although historically civilization and justice have been incompatible, this does not mean that there is an essential or necessary incompatibility between the two. If the two were essentially incompatible, so that it were impossible that any society should be both civilized and just, then morality would require the sacrifice of civilization for the sake of justice. Before everything else, Rousseau is a moralist, and thus for him justice has greater value than civilization.

In the first discourse Rousseau does little more than announce the historical incompatibility between civilization and justice. It is not until the second discourse that he attempts to justify in detail the claim of the first by presenting a conjectural or philosophical history of the development of civilization and injustice. In order, however, to understand adequately this development, it is necessary to distinguish between the natural man and the social man. Natural man is man as he would be if he lived in complete isolation from all forms of settled society; social man is man as formed through living in society. A distinction may therefore be drawn between natural and social characteristics. Natural characteristics are those characteristics human beings would possess even if they lived isolated lives; social characteristics are those characteristics they can acquire only as a consequence of living in society. Unless a distinction is made between natural man and social man and between natural and social characteristics it will be impossible to determine the extent to which the advance of civilization has been achieved only at the cost of sacrificing the claims of justice.

Rousseau, accordingly, discusses the pure state of nature, or the condition in which men would find themselves if they lived in total isolation from all forms of society. He does not unequivocally assert the historicity of this state, but rather leaves open the question of its historicity. This question, however, is of little or no philosophical interest as contrasted with the question of what the nature and condition of man in such a state would be. Given the impossibility of an empirical examination of man in this state, the latter question can be answered only conjecturally or philosophically, by prescinding from all those characteristics which can be acquired only through living in society. The characteristics remaining after this process of abstraction has been completed will be the natural characteristics of the natural man of the pure state of nature. The justification of the ascription of these characteristics to the natural man is provided immediately simply through the development of the notion of the pure state of nature.

Given that the state of nature is the absence of all forms of society, the natural man would be independent or self-dependent. Each would be compelled to depend upon himself alone for his preservation, and each would therefore be self-sufficient and free from dependence on others. Each would also be free from subjection to an alien will, since no person would possess singly sufficient power to compel the permanent submission of another. Each would be animated by two fundamental practical principles—self-love and natural compassion. The first of these principles is more fundamental than the second, but the second is neither reducible to nor explicable in terms of the first. Self-love would lead each to seek his own good, and natural compassion would lead each to seek to avoid injuring another, so that each would seek his own good while endeavoring to do as little harm as possible to others.

Although men in the state of nature would be the most intelligent of the animals, none would be rational, since the development of rationality is dependent upon the development of language, which in turn depends upon life in society. This means that since language is a social product, so too is rationality, conceived as the capacity to apprehend, operate with, and apply abstract or general principles. Each generation in the state of nature would therefore live much the same as any other, and no development of, much less advance in, any of the arts or sciences would be possible. Thus although the natural man would have a natural history, he would have no cultural or spiritual history. And since the natural man would not be rational, neither would he be a moral agent, since moral agency presupposes rationality, or the capacity to apprehend moral rules or principles, which are abstract or general in nature. The natural man would therefore be free from the bonds of moral obligation. He would be a purely natural creature, subject to various laws of nature imposed upon him from without by God or nature independently of his consciousness of them, not a rational and moral agent capable of conceiving and operating in accordance with laws of reason and morality. He would possess the potentiality for rationality and moral agency, but this potentiality can be actualized only in society.

The earliest form of society was a pre-political society in which there was no private ownership of land. Its members subsisted by hunting, fishing, and gathering fruits, nuts, and berries. A division of labor between males and females may have existed, but no such division existed among males; instead, each led the same kind of life as the others. In the absence of the private ownership of land and a division of labor, no significant inequalities of wealth could appear. Life in such a society leads to the development of language and to the development of at least a rudimentary level of rationality and morality. But it leads also to the development of egoism, or a concern on the part of an individual, not merely with his own good, but to possess more of a good of some sort than others possess, even though he needs no more than others in order to attain his own non-egoistic good (which is his good taken in isolation from the good of others). Life in society therefore breeds not only rationality and moral agency, but also egoism. Yet prior to the introduction of the private ownership of land egoism cannot have the profoundly pernicious effects it begins to have once a society permits such ownership.

Prior to the development of agriculture there is no need that land be owned privately, and as long as a society remains at the pre-agricultural stage there is no private ownership of land. Once, however, the agricultural stage is reached such ownership comes to be permitted. This stage is reached only as metallurgy begins to develop, since iron implements are required if land is to be farmed effectively. The concomitant development of metallurgy and agriculture leads to a division of labor between workers and farmers. An inequality of wealth soon appears, partly because some occupations are more lucrative than others, partly because of the inheritance of land and wealth. Society is soon divided into two classes, the rich and the poor, and warfare between the two breaks out. Thus the second stage of pre-political society, in which private property in land is recognized, ends in class war.

This war is terminated only through the institution of civil or political society. Rousseau admits that he does not know how such a society first came to be instituted, but supposes that it was first proposed by the rich, since they had more to gain from it than the poor. In any event, laws protecting property came to be instituted. The institution of one political society led to the institution of others, with the result that men everywhere came to be subject to such societies. With the institution of political societies civilizations develop and the arts and sciences begin to flourish. But with this development there comes increasing inequality. The benefits of the development of the arts and sciences are enjoyed by only a few, rather than all the members of civilized societies; inequalities of wealth become increasingly great; and the laws governing political societies are imposed by a few men upon the rest and express the will only of those who impose them, so that the mass of men are increasingly subjected to an alien will. Civilization flourishes, but only at the cost of the sacrifice of justice. This, Rousseau contends, is the condition of mankind in his age.

Given this condition, only two solutions are possible. One is a return to the state of nature. This, however, is not a real solution. Only those who have not succumbed to the allures of civilization could attempt to return, and even they could make the attempt only if they have not heard "the voice of heaven," which requires each person who has heard it to seek, not merely his own good, but also the good of every person affected by his action. The only real solution is the institution of a political association of such a nature that each of its members can promote his own good, which by nature he seeks, by acting in accordance with its laws and institutions. Such an association is one structured in terms of the social contract. This contract is not historical, and Rousseau never asserts its historicity. It is instead a contract whose terms must be adhered to if justice is to be possible and the common good attained; it is therefore a contract the terms of which we are morally required to fulfill, regardless of whether any group at any time has ever explicitly contracted to fulfill them.

The terms of this contract are these. Each person party to it agrees to subject himself to the laws of the political association formed as a consequence of the contract on the condition that he be granted the status of citizen and a voice equal to that of every other person in the association in determining its laws. Each person party to the contract therefore acquires dual roles—active and passive. As active he is a citizen and a member of the sovereign, with a voice equal to that of every other person in the association in determining what its laws are to be. As passive he is a subject and a member of the state, subject equally with other members of the association to the laws he and they participate on terms of equality in enacting as citizens and members of the sovereign. The preceding means that the political association that arises as a consequence of the contract also has an active and a passive side. As active, i.e., as imposing law upon itself, it is sovereign; as passive, i.e., as subject to the laws it imposes upon itself, it is the state. The sovereign is composed of the collectivity of citizens, the state of the collectivity of subjects, and the same individuals who as active are citizens and members of the sovereign are the ones who as passive are subjects and members of the state. Thus a rule, to be a law, must be imposed by those subject to it. A political association with this constitution is a republic, and a republic is the only possible legitimate form of political association.

Rousseau's specification of the terms of the contract in this way can be understood only if one understands his conception of the complete good. This good consists of two components: (1) a natural non-moral good consisting of happiness or the satisfaction of natural non-moral desires and (2) a moral non-natural good consisting of moral freedom or goodness, which consists in willing the complete good of everyone affected by one's action. It is conceivable, though unlikely, that the naturalistic good of the members of a society should be attained through their subjecting themselves to the rule of an intelligent and benevolent individual or group who knows what their naturalistic good consists in and what must be done to attain it and who accordingly wills its attainment. But the moral component of the complete good, and thus the complete good itself, can be most fully approximated only if each individual subject to the laws of an association bears a responsibility as great as that of any other for the character of these laws. This is to say that moral freedom or goodness can be fully attained only by those who have the responsibility of imposing law upon themselves, and thus only in a situation in which each person subject to law is a citizen and a member of the sovereign who imposes this law.

It is therefore no accident that Rousseau speaks of the general will rather than simply of the general or common good. If the general or common good of a society is construed naturalistically, then it is conceived as consisting simply of the attainment of the naturalistic good, i.e., of the happiness, of each member of that society. If so, then it is conceivable, though again unlikely, that it should be attained by becoming the object of the will of some enlightened individual or group endowed with sufficient power to attain this object. Although the source of such a will would be particular rather than general, since it would be the will of an individual or group within the larger association rather than the will of the association itself, its object would still be general. But the complete good of a society does not consist simply in the attainment of the naturalistic component of this good; instead, it is attainable only to the extent that its attainment is willed by the entire society. This can be put by saying that the object of the general will, i.e., the complete general or common good of the body politic, including the moral as well as the naturalistic component, is attainable only to the extent that it is in fact the object of the general will. This means that it is attainable only to the extent that each citizen, in voting on what the laws of the association are to be, wills its attainment. The act of voting is therefore a moral act.

But men are not by nature moral agents. Instead, the fundamental practical principle animating them, in society as well as in the state of nature, is the principle of self-love, and in society self-love frequently degenerates into egoism. By nature each person, rather than seeking first the common good, seeks first his own good, and in society men frequently concern themselves, not simply with the attainment of their non-egoistic good, but with the acquisition of a greater share of a good of some kind than others possess, even though they need no greater share in order to attain their non-egoistic good. The natural condition of men in society is therefore one in which their wills conflict. Each, animated either by self-love or by egoism, seeks his good in ways incompatible with the attainment of the good of others. This conflict of wills is exacerbated by the existence of powerful partial associations, especially those either economic or religious in character, who seek to impose their particular wills on others and even upon the body politic itself.

The problem of politics may therefore be characterized as the elimination of conflicts between particular wills. If such conflicts did not occur politics would cease to be an art. But, given that self-love is natural to man and that it constantly tends in society to develop into egoism, a final and complete elimination of such conflicts will never occur. Politics is therefore an endless art, the object of which can never be finally and fully attained. And since the attainment of the common good, which is the non-egoistic good of each member of the body politic, is possible only to the extent that conflicts between particular wills are eliminated, it too can never be finally and fully achieved. Rousseau is therefore fundamentally pessimistic. Given, however, the power of self-love and egoism, his pessimism is the result of a realistic assessment of the condition of man. But regardless of whether the common good can ever be permanently attained, one thing that is certain is that, given again the power of self-love and egoism, it is attainable only to the extent that its attainment is willed by all. This is to say that the object of the general will is attainable only to the extent that the general will becomes the will of all. The fact that there is little or no chance that the general will will ever perfectly and permanently become the will of all frees no man from the obligation of making the object of the general will the object of his will. For regardless of whether the common good is perfectly and permanently attainable, the attainment of the moral component of his own complete good is still within the power of every moral agent. Each has only constantly to will it in order to attain it.

If my interpretation and development of Rousseau's thought is sound, then his conception of the constitution which the body politic must be given if a solution is to be found to the problem the social contract is designed to solve will be seen to be, not an impractical concoction of a visionary and utopian romantic, but, on the contrary, an eminently practical (even more so than perhaps he himself thought) and carefully conceived plan developed by one who saw deeply into the nature of man, history, and society. It is, I think, no exaggeration to say that the political philosophy of Rousseau is a greater achievement than that of any other thinker within the natural right, natural law, social contract tradition. Certainly no philosopher within this tradition has succeeded since Rousseau in making a contribution as fundamental and as comprehensive as his.

SELECTED BIBLIOGRAPHY

I. EDITIONS OF ROUSSEAU'S WORKS ON POLITICAL PHILOSOPHY

The Political Writings of Jean Jacques Rousseau. Edited, with introduction and notes by C. E. Vaughan. Two volumes. Cambridge: Cambridge University Press, 1915. Reprinted, Oxford: Basil Blackwell, 1962.

The Social Contract and Discourses. Translated with introduction by G. D. H. Cole. London: J. M. Dent & Sons, 1913.

Political Writings. Translated and edited by Frederick Watkins. Edinburgh: Nelson, 1953.

The First and Second Discourses. Edited, with introduction and notes by Roger D. Masters. Translated by Roger D. and Judith R. Masters. New York: St. Martin's Press, 1964.

The Social Contract. An eighteenth century translation completely revised, edited, with an introduction by Charles Frankel. New York: Hafner, 1951.

The Social Contract. Translated, with an introduction by Willmoore Kendall. Chicago: Henry Regnery, 1954.

The Social Contract. Translated and introduced by Maurice Cranston. Baltimore: Penguin Books, 1968.

Social Contract: Essays by Locke, Hume, and Rousseau. Introduction by Ernest Barker. London: Oxford University Press, 1947.

II. COMMENTARIES ON ROUSSEAU'S POLITICAL PHILOSOPHY

Bosanquet, Bernard. *The Philosophical Theory of the State.* London: Macmillan, 1923. See especially chaps. 4 and 5.

Carritt, E. F. *Morals and Politics.* Oxford: Clarendon Press, 1935. Chap. 6.

Cassirer, Ernst. *The Question of Jean-Jacques Rousseau.* Translated and edited with an introduction and additional notes by Peter Gay. Bloomington: Indiana University Press, 1963.

Cassirer, Ernst. *Rousseau, Kant and Goethe.* Translated by James Gutmann, Paul Oskar Kristeller, and John Herman Randall, Jr. Introduction by Peter Gay. New York: Harper & Row, 1963.

Cobban, Alfred. *Rousseau and the Modern State.* London: George Allen & Unwin, 1934.

Cranston, Maurice, and Richard S. Peters, editors. *Hobbes and Rousseau: A Collection of Critical Essays.* New York: Doubleday, 1972. This collection contains the following essays on Rousseau: Peter Winch, "Man and Society in Hobbes and Rousseau"; Leo Strauss, "On the Intention of Rousseau"; John McManners, "The Social Contract and Rousseau's Revolt Against Society"; John Plamenatz, "On le Forcera d'Etre Libre"; Judith N. Shklar, "Rousseau's Images of Authority"; William Pickles, "The Notion of Time in Rousseau's Political Thought"; Roger D. Masters, "The Structure of Rousseau's Political Thought"; Ronald Grimsley, "Rousseau and the Problem of Happiness"; John Charvet, "Individual Identity and Social Consciousness in Rousseau's Philosophy"; Bertrand de Jouvenel, "Rousseau's Theory of the Forms of Government."

Crocker, Lester G. *Rousseau's "Social Contract."* Cleveland: Press of Case Western Reserve University, 1968.

Durkheim, Emile. *Montesquieu and Rousseau: Forerunners of Sociology.* Ann Arbor: University of Michigan Press, 1960.

Green, F. C. *Rousseau and the Idea of Progress.* Oxford: Clarendon Press, 1950.

Green, Thomas Hill. *Lectures on the Principles of Political Obligation.* London: Longmans, 1941. Lecture E.

Hendel, Charles William. *Jean-Jacques Rousseau: Moralist.* Two volumes. London: Oxford University Press, 1934.

Maritain, Jacques. *Three Reformers: Luther-Descartes-Rousseau.* London: Sheed & Ward, 1928.

Masters, Roger D. *The Political Philosophy of Rousseau.* Princeton: Princeton University Press, 1968.

McAdam, James I. "What Rousseau Meant by the General Will," *Dialogue,* V (1967), 498–515.

McAdam, James I. "The Discourse on Inequality and The Social Contract," *Philosophy,* XLVII (1972), 308–21.

Plamenatz, John. *Man and Society.* Two volumes. New York: McGraw-Hill, 1963. See especially vol. I. chap. 10.

Sabine, George H. *A History of Political Theory.* Revised edition. New York: Henry Holt, 1950. Chap. 28.

Strauss, Leo. *Natural Right and History.* Chicago: University of Chicago Press, 1953. Chap. 6.

NOTES

I. **1.** I Cor. 13:1. **2.** Immanuel Kant, *Foundations of the Metaphysics of Morals,* translated, with an introduction, by Lewis White Beck (Indianapolis: Library of Liberal Arts, 1959), p. 9.

II. **1.** Jean-Jacques Rousseau, *Discourse on the Origin and Foundations of Inequality among Men,* in *The Social Contract and Discourses,* translated with an introduction by G. D. H. Cole (London: J. M. Dent & Sons, 1913), p. 161. Hereafter the second discourse will be cited simply as *The Origin of Inequality.* All quotations from the discourses and *The Social Contract* will be taken from this edition of Cole's translation. This is not because Cole's translation is the best, but rather because this edition of his translation, which contains the three discourses and *The Social Contract,* is probably more accessible than any other edition containing all four of these works. Whether it is the best or not I do not wish to argue. But even though it may not be the best, it is sufficiently accurate for our purposes, as the reader can determine for himself by comparing it either with Rousseau's French or with other translations. **2.** *Hobbes's Leviathan,* reprinted from the edition of 1651 with an essay by the late W. G. Pogson Smith (Oxford: Clarendon Press, 1909), p. 97. **3.** *Two Treatises of Government,* Book II, Sections 100–3. **4.** *The Origin of Inequality,* pp. 161–62. **5.** *The Social Contract,* I, ii. **6.** Ibid., I, vi. **7.** Ibid., I, viii. **8.** Cf. *De Cive,* IX, 6; *Leviathan,* pp. 97, 154. **9.** *Two Treatises of Government,* II, 77. **10.** *The Origin of Inequality,* p. 175. **11.** Cf. ibid., pp. 161, 175. **12.** Cf. *De Cive,* IX, 6; *Leviathan,* pp. 97, 154. **13.** *The Social Contract,* I, vi. **14.** Ibid., I, viii.

III. **1.** *Two Treatises of Government,* II, 101. **2.** *The Origin of Inequality,* p. 156. **3.** Ibid., p. 157. **4.** Ibid., p. 185. **5.** Ibid., p. 175. **6.** Ibid., p. 177. **7.** Ibid., p. 178. **8.** Ibid., p. 170. **9.** Ibid., p. 163. **10.** Ibid., p. 171. **11.** *Foundations of the Metaphysics of Morals,* p. 29. **12.** *The Origin of Inequality,* p. 156. **13.** Ibid. **14.** Ibid., p. 158. **15.** Ibid. **16.** Ibid., p. 169. **17.** Ibid., pp. 169–70. **18.** Ibid., p. 169. **19.** Ibid. **20.** Ibid., p. 170. **21.** Ibid. **22.** Ibid. **23.** Ibid. **24.** Ibid., p. 171. **25.** Ibid., p. 188.

IV. **1.** *The Origin of Inequality,* p. 157. **2.** Ibid., p. 182, note. **3.** Ibid. **4.** Ibid., note. **5.** *Leviathan,* p. 96. **6.** *The Origin of Inequality,* p. 185. **7.** Ibid., p. 182. **8.** Ibid., p. 183. **9.** Ibid., p. 182. **10.** Ibid., p. 184. **11.** Ibid. **12.** Ibid. **13.** Ibid., pp. 184–85.

V. **1.** *Leviathan,* p. 97. **2.** *The Social Contract,* III, ii. **3.** Ibid., III, xi. **4.** Ibid. **5.** *The Origin of Inequality,* pp. 161–162.

VI. **1.** *The Origin of Inequality,* p. 190. **2.** Ibid. **3.** Ibid. **4.** Ibid., p. 188. **5.** Ibid., p. 189. **6.** Ibid., pp. 189–90. **7.** *The Social Contract,* I, ii. **8.** *The Origin of Inequality,*

p. 190. **9.** *The Social Contract*, I, ii. **10.** Ibid., I, vi. **11.** *The Origin of Inequality*, p. 194. **12.** Ibid., p. 195. **13.** Ibid., pp. 195–96. **14.** Ibid., p. 196. **15.** Ibid. **16.** Ibid., p. 197. **17.** Ibid., pp. 197–98. **18.** Ibid., p. 198. **19.** Ibid., pp. 198–99. **20.** Ibid., p. 199.

VII. **1.** *The Origin of Inequality*, p. 192. **2.** Ibid., pp. 200–201. **3.** Ibid., p. 199. **4.** Ibid., p. 200. **5.** Ibid., p. 201. **6.** Ibid., p. 192. **7.** Ibid., p. 201. **8.** *The Social Contract*, I, ix. **9.** Ibid. **10.** Ibid. **11.** Ibid. **12.** Ibid. **13.** Ibid. **14.** *The Origin of Inequality*, p. 192. **15.** Ibid. **16.** Ibid., p. 202. **17.** Ibid. **18.** Ibid., pp. 202–3. **19.** Ibid. p. 203. **20.** Ibid., pp. 203–4.

VIII. **1.** *The Origin of Inequality*, pp. 204–5. **2.** Ibid., p. 205. **3.** Ibid. **4.** Ibid., p. 207. **5.** Ibid. **6.** Ibid. **7.** Ibid., p. 205. **8.** Ibid. **9.** Ibid. **10.** Ibid. **11.** Ibid., p. 206. **12.** Ibid. **13.** Ibid., pp. 207–8. **14.** Ibid., p. 208. **15.** Ibid. **16.** Ibid. **17.** Ibid. **18.** Ibid., pp. 208–9. **19.** Ibid., p. 209.

IX. **1.** *The Origin of Inequality*, pp. 210–11. **2.** Ibid., p. 211. **3.** Ibid. **4.** *The Social Contract*, I, iv. **5.** Ibid. **6.** Ibid. **7.** Ibid. **8.** *The Origin of Inequality*, p. 211. **9.** *The Social Contract*, I, iv. **10.** *The Origin of Inequality*, pp. 211–12. **11.** *The Social Contract*, I, iv. **12.** *The Origin of Inequality*, p. 212.

X. **1.** *The Social Contract*, I, iv. **2.** *Two Treatises of Government*, II, 172. **3.** *The Social Contract*, I, v. **4.** Ibid., I, iii. **5.** *The Origin of Inequality*, p. 212. **6.** *Leviathan*, p. 99. **7.** *The Social Contract*, I, iii. **8.** Ibid., I, ii.

XI. **1.** *The Social Contract*, III, i. **2.** *The Origin of Inequality*, p. 212. **3.** Ibid. **4.** Ibid. **5.** Ibid., p. 207. **6.** *The Social Contract*, III, v. **7.** *The Origin of Inequality*, p. 213. **8.** Ibid., pp. 213–14. **9.** *The Social Contract*, III, iii. **10.** *The Origin of Inequality*, p. 214. **11.** Ibid. **12.** Ibid. **13.** Ibid., pp. 214–15. **14.** Ibid., pp. 218–19. **15.** Ibid., p. 219. **16.** Ibid., p. 215.

XII. **1.** *The Origin of Inequality*, p. 228. **2.** Ibid. **3.** Ibid., p. 229. **4.** Matt. 22:37–40. **5.** I John 4:20.

XV. **1.** *The Origin of Inequality*, p. 183.

XVI. **1.** *The Social Contract*, I, viii.

XVIII. **1.** *The Social Contract*, I, vi.

XIX. **1.** *The Social Contract*, I, vi.

XX. **1.** *Two Treatises of Government*, II, 6, 22. **2.** *The Social Contract*, I, vii.

XXI. **1.** *The Social Contract*, I, vi. **2.** Ibid. **3.** Ibid. **4.** Ibid., note. **5.** Ibid., I, vi. **6.** Ibid., IV, ii. **7.** Ibid., I, vi. **8.** Ibid., I, vii. **9.** Ibid. **10.** Ibid. **11.** Ibid.

XXII. 1. *The Social Contract*, I, vii. **2.** Ibid., III, xviii. **3.** Ibid., IV, ii. **4.** Ibid. **5.** Ibid., III, xviii. **6.** *Two Treatises of Government*, II, 121–22. **7.** *The Social Contract*, III, xviii, note.

XXIII. 1. *The Social Contract*, II, vii. **2.** Ibid., IV, viii. **3.** Ibid., II, vi.

XXIV. 1. *The Social Contract*, I, vi. **2.** *A Discourse on Political Economy*, p. 236. This work will be cited hereafter simply as *Political Economy*. **3.** Ibid. **4.** Ibid. **5.** Ibid. **6.** Ibid., pp. 236–37.

XXV. 1. *The Social Contract*, III, ii. **2.** *Political Economy*, p. 237. **3.** Ibid. **4.** Ibid.

XXVI. 1. *The Social Contract*, II, iii. **2.** Ibid. **3.** Ibid., note.

XXVII. 1. *The Social Contract*, II, iv. **2.** Ibid., II, iii. **3.** Ibid. **4.** Ibid., note.

XXVIII. 1. *Political Economy*, p. 254. **2.** Ibid. **3.** Ibid., p. 255. **4.** *The Social Contract*, I, vi. **5.** Ibid., I, ix. **6.** Ibid. **7.** Ibid. **8.** Ibid. **9.** *The Origin of Inequality*, p. 192. **10.** *Political Economy*, pp. 262–63. **11.** *The Social Contract*, I, ix, note. **12.** *Political Economy*, p. 262. **13.** Ibid., p. 268. **14.** Ibid. p. 250. **15.** Ibid. **16.** Ibid., p. 261.

XXIX. 1. Frederick Engels, *Herr Eugen Dühring's Revolution in Science*, translated by Emile Burns, edited by C. P. Dutt (New York: International Publishers, 1939), pp. 153–54. **2.** *The Social Contract*, III, xi. **3.** *Karl Marx: Early Writings*, translated and edited by T. B. Bottomore (New York: McGraw-Hill, 1964), p. 30. **4.** *The Social Contract*, II, vii. **5.** Cf. ibid., II, iii. **6.** G. W. F. Hegel, *The Philosophy of History*, translated by J. Sibree (New York: Dover Publications, 1956), p. 15. **7.** Immanuel Kant, *Foundations of the Metaphysics of Morals*, translated, with an introduction, by Lewis White Beck (Indianapolis: Library of Liberal Arts, 1959), p. 9.

XXX. 1. *The Social Contract*, IV, vii. **2.** Ibid. **3.** St. Thomas Aquinas, *Summa Theologica*, First Part of the Second Part, Question 19, Articles 5–6. **4.** Niccoló Machiavelli, *Discourses on the First Ten Books of Titus Livius*, translated by Christian E. Detmold (New York: Modern Library, 1940), Book II, chap. 2, pp. 285–86. **5.** Ibid., I, xii, 151.

XXXI. 1. *The Social Contract*, IV, viii. **2.** Ibid. **3.** Ibid. **4.** Ibid. **5.** Ibid. **6.** Ibid.

XXXII. 1. *The Social Contract*, II, vii. **2.** Ibid., III, iii. **3.** Ibid., III, iv. **4.** Ibid., II, vi. **5.** Ibid., II, i. **6.** Ibid. **7.** Ibid., IV, ii. **8.** Ibid., II, ii. **9.** Ibid., II, ii, note. **10.** Ibid., IV, ii. **11.** Ibid. **12.** Ibid. **13.** Ibid., II, vi.

XXXIII. 1. John Locke, *An Essay Concerning Human Understanding*, II, xx, 2. **2.** Immanuel Kant, *The Metaphysical Elements of Justice: Part I of The Metaphysics of Morals*, translated, with an introduction, by John Ladd (Indianapolis: Library of

Liberal Arts, 1965), p. 79; cf. also Kant's essay, *Concerning the Common Saying: This May Be True in Theory But Does Not Apply to Practice*. **3.** *The Works of Jeremy Bentham*, edited by Sir John Bowring (Edinburgh, 1838–43), II, 501. **4.** *The Social Contract*, III, ii.

XXXIV. **1.** *The Social Contract*, III, xv. **2.** Ibid. **3.** Ibid., III, xvii. **4.** Ibid., III, xviii. **5.** Ibid., III, iv.

INDEX

Marx, Karl, 75, 177, 180–81, 184, 231
Mechanism, 17–18
Metallurgy, 37–38, 45
Middle class, the, 176–77, 179
Monarchy, 54–55, 59–61, 71, 213–14
Moral, the, 83–84
Morality, the claims of, 83–85, 99–103, 106, 113–15, 140, 159, 172–73, 182–83, 185
Moralization, 131–32
Mother and child, 11–12
Multitudes, 62–63

Natural, the, 83–84, 100–102
Naturalism, 64, 230, 233–36
Nature: the claims of, 83–85, 99–103, 106, 113–15, 140, 172–73, 182–83; laws of, 17–18, 20, 27, 76, 96–97
Needs, 171–72, 174
Nobility, 21–22, 27
Non-naturalism, 229–35, 239, 241

Obligation: moral, 104–5, 108–9, 118–19, 130; natural, 17, 65
Occupant, the right of the first, 42–43
Optimism, 75, 186
Order, the moral and the natural, 28–30, 83–85, 140, 154, 163, 225, 237
Organisms, 134
Otherworldliness, 192, 199–201

Pain, 17, 101
Paul, Saint, 4–5, 25
People, a, 62, 64, 68, 118
Perfectibility, 19–21, 76, 81, 86
Persuasion, 50, 213
Pessimism, 75, 185
Peter, Saint, 193
Plato, 226, 228, 231, 235, 237–39
Politics, 144–45, 183, 185
Poor, the, 46, 48, 50–52, 72, 167–68, 172–77
Possession, 171–72
Potentialities, 29–30, 104
Powers, 118, 141, 151
Practical, the primacy of the, 205–6
Prince, the, 213, 224

Promises, 60, 69, 218–19
Protestantism, 131, 192–94, 197–201, 211
Prudence, 64–65, 196
Punishment, 150–51, 165, 167, 203–5, 207–8, 223, 227

Rationalism, ethical, 24, 26
Reason, 92, 95, 101–2, 105–6, 140, 190–91, 203, 227
Referenda, 245
Relativism, ethical, 24
Religion: of the citizen, 191–92, 201; of man, 191–94, 199, 201; of the priest, 191–96, 199
Representatives, 240–41, 243–45
Republicanism, 195–97, 199, 201, 206–7
Respectability, 176
Responsibility, 57–60, 80, 98, 131–32, 227–28, 231, 235–36
Retributivism, 187
Revolution, 64–65, 72, 75, 234–35
Rich, the, 46, 48, 50–52, 72, 163, 167–70, 172–77
Right: conventional, 40, 121; natural, 17, 38–44, 66–67, 121–22, 171–72, 194–95; of the strongest, 42, 62–65

Self-consciousness, 19, 25, 96–97, 108, 111, 182–83, 185
Self-determination, 97–99
Sentience, 17–18
Sin, 30–31, 185
Slavery, 33–34, 46, 54–55, 59–63, 72–74, 112, 115, 119, 123, 228–29, 231, 234
Social contract, the historicity of the, 102–3, 106
Socialism, 179–80
Society: classless, 177–79, 181–86, 188–89; natural, 10–13
Socrates, 26
Sovereign, the, 118–23, 129–32, 167, 172, 240–42, 245
Stability, 81–84, 101–2
State, the, 118–22, 129–32, 242